GRACE AND POWER

GRACE AND POWER

Base Communities and Nonviolence in Brazil

DOMINIQUE BARBÉ

Authorized and enlarged English version

Translated by John Pairman Brown

ORBIS BOOKS

Maryknoll, New York 10545

The Catholic Foreign Mission Society of America (Maryknoll) recruits and trains people for overseas missionary service. Through Orbis Books Maryknoll aims to foster the international dialogue that is essential to mission. The books published, however, reflect the opinions of their authors and are not meant to represent the official position of the society.

Originally published as *La grâce et le pouvoir*, © 1982 by Éditions du Cerf, 29, bd Latour-Maubourg, Paris and *A graça e o poder*, © 1983 by Edições Paulinas, São Paulo
English translation © 1987 by Orbis Books, Maryknoll, NY 10545
All rights reserved
Manufactured in the United States of America

Manuscript Editor: Lisa McGaw

Library of Congress Cataloging-in-Publication Data

Barbé, Dominique.
  Grace and power.

  Translation of: La grâce et le pouvoir.
  "Authorized and enlarged English version,
translated by John Pairman Brown"—T.p. verso.
  1. Christian communities—Catholic Church.
2. Christian communities—Brazil. 3. Catholic
Church—Brazil—History—20th century. 4. Liberation
theology. 5. Brazil—Church history. 6. Catholic
Church—Doctrines. I. Title.
BX2347.72.B6B3613 1987   262   86-23572
ISBN 0-88344-418-6 (pbk.)

Contents

Foreword

In recent years a number of Brazilian Christian thinkers have made an important contribution to the lives and thought of many of us in the First World. As we read the writings of Leonardo Boff, Rubem Alves, Dom Hélder Câmara, and Paulo Freire, we meet persons whose lives and faith have been transformed, and whose thought has been deepened, by their solidarity with the poor. And we are challenged by a type of theological reflection that speaks about the gospel in new and compelling ways.

Now, with the publication in English of *Grace and Power* we hear another voice that adds a new dimension to this witness from Brazil. Dominique Barbé, a French priest who has been living and working among the poor in São Paulo for a number of years, presents a powerful testimony to the movement of the Spirit taking place there; at the same time, his interpretation is enriched by the fact that he is an outsider, bringing his cultural heritage and knowledge to his analysis.

This book has much to offer to First World Christians. I consider it to be valuable especially for those whose growing concern for social justice is leading them to greater involvement in struggles for change. I think of many I know who realize that religion has played a major role in their personal development, but who are not at all clear about how this religious heritage can orient or sustain them in these struggles. Abstract theological language—including that used by theologians of liberation—has little meaning for them. What most fascinates me about Barbé's book is his ability to speak about the richness and meaning of Christian faith, and what it offers to the individual and to society, in language that can catch our interest, make sense to us, and communicate a spiritual reality many of us yearn for but have not found until now.

I would like to make this book required reading for North Americans and others in the First World who are inclined to believe those who are attempting to discredit the theology of liberation and the church of the poor in Latin America by saying that these movements are more Marxist than Christian, more political than religious. In these pages, Barbé presents a profoundly evangelical vision; he witnesses to *the power of God* in the lives of the poor and those who stand with them. In this way, he helps us to see what really disturbs the defenders of the status quo: the fact that these new movements are so deeply religious and thus capable of providing powerful motivation for social and political action.

A quick glance at the Contents gives the impression that we have here a number of chapters dealing with a rather wide range of apparently unrelated topics. Even the author speaks of his book as one "wherein are collected some texts born haphazardly from the urgencies of apostolic action in Brazil." I was thus quite surprised to discover here an unusually coherent statement on one theme, *the gospel as GRACE:* the presence of the Divine as Love in the midst of life and society opening us spontaneously to other persons and persuading us to give of ourselves; this is an experience of generosity and communion that leads people to work joyfully at building a new world, breaks down the human obsession with power, and can save a new social order committed to justice from falling into bureaucratic sterility and rigidity.

In the first chapter, Barbé presents excerpts from his diary, thus connecting the reader with the world of poverty, suffering, and violence that is the lot of the marginalized millions in São Paulo. He describes this "hell that is blazing in the basements of humanity," but he also depicts how "the prayer and suffering of the just can drive the flames back into the abyss," and he lays before us amazing examples of sharing and solidarity, of struggle and hope, which appear in the basic communities.

Throughout the book, his discourse is theological, as he deals with concrete human situations from the perspective of faith and, as he puts it, confronts our life with the life of Jesus so that, understanding how he lived his struggles, we will discover how we can live ours. Basing his theology on the Bible as it is now being read in Latin America, he restores the social and political to the place they should have in faith and portrays salvation as that divine action that, rather than drawing us out of the world, is drawing history and the world beyond present potentialities. "To believe that social evil can be overcome and that societies can rise above the death that lies in wait for them: that is to be a Christian."

Barbé's theological reflection, thus rooted in and nourished by the Bible and concrete involvement with the poor, is rich in insight. I value it for what it can contribute to us as we deal with a number of important issues. He sees the Christian responsibility as that of transforming "collectivity into community under the inspiration of grace," yet declares that this cannot be done without making full use of adequate instruments of social analysis. He recognizes the contribution Marxism has made to modern struggles for justice, and he provides a theological foundation for a critical engagement with it. Furthermore, his description of the basic communities—how they have developed, the central realities of their daily life and witness, and the new ecclesiology being created in them—is one of the best available in English. In it we can find much that will help us as we create new communities of faith in the First World.

Of all the issues he deals with, I found his reflections on "active nonviolence" especially helpful. His position is firmly grounded in his biblical faith and his identification with the poor. Out of this has come an ethical stance in which active nonviolence is affirmed as the direct outgrowth of the presence of the Spirit of Jesus in the world, which leads to the gracious giving of self and the experience of joy in the struggle to create a more just social order. *It is a way of life, at the heart of which is a total dedication to the poor, lived out daily; it should never be adopted as merely an ethical principle to be defended dogmatically by those who lack this passion and involvement.*

Barbé goes further; he claims that active nonviolence takes on special significance at the present time for the poor of the world. It not only provides an opportunity for them to confront the rich and powerful from a strong ethical position, deeply rooted in their religious faith; it is also strategically advantageous for the poor in their struggle, for it takes into account the emergence and grassroots strength of new popular movements, as well as the type of repression now being carried out by those in power. What Barbé has to say on this theme could, I believe, stimulate creative thought among those already committed to nonviolence; at the same time it could lead those not committed to it to reconsider it on theological, ethical, and strategic ground.

RICHARD SHAULL

Translator's Preface

The original French version, *La grâce et le pouvoir* (Paris: Editions du Cerf, 1982), lacked chapters 3 and 5 included in the subsequent Portuguese- and English-language editions. The author translated the book into Portuguese, in which language it was published entire as *A graça e o poder* (São Paulo: Edições Paulinas, 1983). My translation rests on the published French version plus the typescript of chapters 3 and 5; the author provided handwritten French retroversions of his longer additions in the Portuguese. Although I have not studied Portuguese, I could use it for help with the author's idiomatic French and for his smaller revisions. From the heart of the *favela* (shantytown) with infinite patience he has promptly responded to all my queries. Our correspondence has resulted in actual modifications of the text in chapters 2 and 9. All biblical quotations not otherwise attributed are my own translations from Hebrew or Greek in the light of the author's understanding. Verification of all other matter is due to the unchallenged competence of Orbis Books. This version restores the proper Portuguese names of specifically Brazilian institutions, while directing itself to the situation of North Americans, whether Catholic, Protestant, or simply lovers of justice.

JOHN PAIRMAN BROWN

1

Travel Diary

May 28–30, 1979

I arrive above the airport 80 kilometers out of São Paulo, in the middle of the countryside. Dazzling clarity, not a cloud, no smoke from a factory chimney. The plane clears the cypresses and comes to rest. At arrivals I find Joel, Joãozinho, José Pedro, Marinete, Ione, Miranda, Marcos, and Catatá who had come to pick me up with "our" communal van. *Abraços* (embraces) and two hours of briefing on the situation along the road to Osasco.

I am at home: in the morning Dona Maria, the widow with twelve children, comes to tell me that yesterday one of her little ones, not more than a baby, fell into the well. They lowered one of his little brothers in a bucket to look for the lost one (the wells are almost 10 meters deep). At that very instant Dona Maria, who was not there because she works, made this prayer: "O my Jesus, watch over my children." They pulled the baby out of the well, alive. Everybody said: "It's God's miracle; he was dead and was brought back to life; he fell into the earth and came out again; we'd given up hope."

I go to São Paulo, to the Secretariat of Non-Violence, then to the house of Mário C. of Jesus. I meet Pedro, twenty-six, two years and a half in prison in Paraguay (where he spoke only Guarani). Tortured, scars all over his body. *He did a total fast for fifty-seven days*; at the end of the thirty-sixth day he took a little salt and sugar water: he lost 19 kilos. He really believed that he was going to die and asked for extreme unction. The Marxists, his fellow prisoners, received it also out of solidarity. They never prayed together; and he doesn't pray either, except maybe to his patron saint (Saint Peter). He radiates gentleness and grace. He tells me he wants to dig more deeply into the gospel; he's never been able to do it properly before.

This morning José Ibrahim arrived after ten years of exile. I have this thought: nowadays psychiatrists have replaced ascetics. But the struggle against evil still requires ascetics, for neuroses at the root are spiritual sicknesses.

1

June 1, 1979

Last night I slept with all my clothes on, it was that cold. Sheets of icy dampness fell from the housetop and from the slabs of concrete that it's built out of. These houses don't have any kind of heating. This morning Chico, ten years old, came to see me, trembling from the cold. I discovered an old pair of shorts and an old shirt for him.

Dona Ana has never bought the six tiles that would fix up the roof of her *barraco* (hut). The community is not willing to help her any more and neither are the people of the *bairro* (the quarter), for they suspect that she used the money (500 cruzeiros) for something else. And so our embryonic solidarity in this corner of the *bairro* is stillborn. (The name of this community, all in the *favela* [shantytown], is Nossa Senhora do Desterro, "Our Lady of the Dispossessed.")

Yesterday evening, Mass with some members of the community of Mutinga (about fifteen of them). The gospel said that nobody can be the disciple of Jesus without giving up father and mother, wife and children, and without taking up one's cross. And in fact, the building of the kingdom requires that the interests considered as most sacred by human beings, family included, should be given second priority.

This past night I dreamed I was in a car that was going downhill at top speed in rolling country full of shadows. M. tried to make us give up this idea. But we forced her to be silent and she set herself to crying; she said that people always made her keep quiet. Suddenly the road was covered with a torrent of water, which threatened to drown the engine. The hood started to smoke, as if everything were going to catch fire when we stepped on the pedal hard enough to get out of this situation. Water and fire are in conspiracy to snuff out this car that is myself. Distress signals lit up on the fenders and started blinking. The dream didn't say that the car was destroyed.

June 6, 1979

Sebastião, my neighbor, black, father of three children, said during the Mass that we celebrated last Wednesday, in the building next to my room, "I thank God, for even though there are not many of us to celebrate because of the cold, *our* father Domingos is with us." That moved me.

Dona Maria, the widow with twelve children, works in a business that cleans buses. It's very hard work: she gets up at 4:30, not back home until 7:00 in the evening with a lot of the housework still to do. She makes $30 a month.

Last Saturday she came in the evening with a roast chicken, and told me that she had started to cry when she learned from her daughter (who had seen me) that for dinner I was having bread and garlic. I didn't want to eat this chicken all by myself, so instead I went and had dinner with them in their *barraco*. Dona Maria has all the simplicity of the countryside; she brought it to my mind that she wasn't embarrassed when she ate with her fingers in my presence (many people here eat rice and meat by handfuls with no implements).

Friday night I was sleeping at the Centro de Defesa dos Direitos Humanos (the Center for Defense of Human Rights) when I was waked up at 1:00 o'clock by Ana and Zé Cárlos. The brother of Sônia R., twenty-eight, automobile painter, had just been shot point-blank. The first inquiries made on the spot indicated that very likely it was the police who had fired. Two persons in civilian dress had come up to Silvino and killed him by putting eight bullets in his body. Afterward the two had been seen in police cars. A sixteen-year-old boy, O., had been a witness of the murder. We had to hide him in a community a long way off so that the police would leave him alone. When I went to look for him, his eyes filled with fear. He didn't know who I was. The Centro, in spite of its weakness in personnel and organization, is slowly starting to do its work: building cadres of the people with access to the means of putting pressure on the authorities—to the law, to the press, and so on—which generally aren't available to the poor.

That night I got back to bed again at 3:00 o'clock.

Saturday morning I went back to Munhoz, my *bairro*.

Sunday morning from 9:00 to 12:00 we had preparation for first communion: about fifteen children and twenty teenagers. I was surprised by the maturity and liveliness of the young people's answers. Ju, twenty-one, the young man in charge of the teenagers, and Nair, mother of a family, had done excellent work. Ju told me that when the children and young people are able to *speak* to somebody, they think they are turning into gods. Each in turn must say if they feel themselves ready for their first communion by three standards: (*a*) being in communion with God (by prayer, reading the gospel); (*b*) being in communion with the community (by participating in its activities); (*c*) being in communion with the people (serving them by taking up a concrete task).

We call those the three communions necessary to make a first communion. We are close relatives of God by grace!

Saturday, June 9, 1979

Wednesday night, at 4:30 on Thursday morning, the whole family that lives opposite the church was arrested by the police; on the scene there were six to eight cars from the Delegacia (precinct) of Rochedale. Four were put in jail: Jonas (the father), Elisa (the mother), Maria Odete (the aunt, Jonas's sister), and the grandmother Dona Nair (mother of Jonas and Maria). The grandfather was in the hospital. It was alleged that this house had sheltered a *quadrilha* (gang), which had operated as far as Rio. The vice-mayor of Sorocaba, a city near São Paulo, was supposed to have been attacked by them at São Roque. The police claimed to have found in the house, hidden in the well, stolen goods worth millions of cruzeiros: typewriters, camera equipment, and so on. It was alleged that the accused had most recently stolen a van full of cinema equipment. It was also claimed that there were a lot of weapons in the house. In fact, it seems that Jonas, Elisa, and the grandmother were innocent. At least that's what the police commissioner told me. Maria Odete apparently was part of the *quadrilha* along with "Big Robertão," the brother of Lourdes, who lives a few streets away. He and his eleven-year-old son had also been arrested. I knew from the neighbors that the boy had taken part in the armed assaults with his father (at least seven times, it was said). Once he had even been the one who drove the gang's car in a headlong getaway on the highway as far as kilometer 19. The other members of the gang are in flight: João Carlos the *rápido*, Jorge, Pedro, and Celso. "Big Robertão" had already had prison experience, but he had escaped from the São Paulo penitentiary (6,000 prisoners) after a month or two. In the house there were also three children: Jenaéna (five), Luciano (four), Julinha (three). These were the children of Elisa, who was released last night; the neighbors took care of them.

The prayer of a purified heart is like a hurricane that drives away evil spirits. From the house of the just there rises a column of fire, which purifies the atmosphere and makes the wolves flee. Jesus breathed on the apostles after the resurrection, to bestow on them the wind of Pentecost, which dissipates miasmas. We must breathe to the four corners of the horizon, with a burning prayer, on behalf of the world. This morning, I meditated on that word, "I am the Resurrection and the Life." To revive the *bairro* and give it life. How?

As I came back down from the church to my house, I saw a dog, mad or poisoned, as it was dying in the gutter, foam on its mouth, shaken by the convulsions of tetanus. Little children were playing nearby and called for me to show me the sight.

The Centro is in an unbelievable uproar. How to build a new society with people who talk so loud, make so much noise, and waste so much time—literally and figuratively?

This last night I dreamed that an enormous wave, or rather, several successive waves, were assaulting a big house. After the swells had subsided, in the house a woman seemed to be crying. The house was still standing. I dreamed also about Dom Fragoso (bishop of Crateús in the northeast, a nonviolent activist). He was doing a liturgy with me, in a room full of people who were in an uproar and praying in a loud voice in the style of the sects. It seems to me that the business on hand was an exorcism. I wasn't doing anything. Dom Fragoso ordered me sternly to take care of the people. I was very much ashamed not to have thought of it myself. It seems to me that I was doing something with them, perhaps saying the Rosary, and that they all calmed down and started praying peacefully.

Wednesday, June 13, 1979: Munhoz

This morning I was interrupted almost continually.

First by Chico, who lives in a *barraco* on the other side of the gutter; his family had given shelter to an eighteen-year-old boy in the tiny room that is all their dwelling (five grownups, one baby). The young man had "incorporated" a spirit "Exu," a messenger who reveals the future and the past; he fell into a trance and threatened to kill the eldest son. He had become the "horse" for the spirit "guide." Spirits make use of persons as mounts to act among human beings and convey their predictions. Under the control of the demon, he revealed also that he had been the one who had taken the 500 cruzeiros, which disappeared two days before. The family moved onto the offensive: they planted two big crosses by the two doorways and threw salt on the one possessed, who fled. Hilda, twenty, sick, was completely upset. Cida, the other sister, seventeen, child-mother and prostitute, laughed a little at the whole proceeding and half believed it. Chico had come to ask me if I would pass by their way to bless the house. I went and talked with them for twenty minutes, and had a cup of coffee. We prayed together.

Ten minutes later, it was the turn of Maria Isabel (mother of five, abandoned by her husband) to knock on the door, to talk about Nilson, her eldest son of fifteen; I had told him that we could find him a garage where he could work as a mechanic, and also find him a tutor so that he could get into the professional school (SENAI). Nilson has never got tall (1.4 meters). He is very intelligent and already has a most busy night life. (Some years later, in 1984, Nilson was murdered.) The whole family lives in a tiny *barraco* on the edge of the sewage gutter of our *bairro*. Dona Maria Isabel wants to take in her sister who has five or six children: "My house is little but my heart is big. We are one big family. If my sister comes and lives with us, she will do the cooking and I can go and work. My sister is amazingly resourceful, she'll put food on my plate. That's how you get out of feeling sorry for yourself, by all being together again."

I ask myself how fifteen of them are all going to live together in this tiny shanty (10 square meters). Dona Maria Isabel was very happy because a neighbor who knew her when she was in the country said that she had straightened out her life after two years in São Paulo: "You've become a different person. To think that you've even found a job mopping floors in the hospital!" She still speaks in the country language.

Toward the end of the morning Marinete and Ione arrived, the two right hands of the Pastoral Operária (Workers' Pastoral Center) and the Centro (for human rights). We talked about the monthly Mass to be celebrated with the militants. The worker militants are a very special group. They have acquired tools of political analysis, but a number of them no longer have communities able to understand them. How can one go on being Christian if one no longer celebrates the memorial of Jesus? The church, the assembly of disciples, has a character that is baptismal and eucharistic; it gives thanks.

I went out and took a stroll to Adalberto's house where I had never been. His son of fifteen looks like a larva of 50 centimeters high, only his head has a normal appearance. This head talks (he had a siege of polio when he was a baby). Adalberto hasn't had a job in six months now; he has five children and a wife, who isn't the mother of the three oldest.

Before this, Zé, the sixteen-year-old, had dropped by to ask for news of my trip and to talk English with me. He is devoured by sex. There's an inexorable sequence here: sex—violence—pistol-shooting—*maconha* (marijuana)—police—armed robbery. Once you get into this cycle, it's almost impossible to get out. Evil has incarnated itself in a social structure that, so to speak, renders love impossible, structurally impossible.

Dona Nair (who had the *quadrilha* in her house) came by with a box of perfume bottles in her hand that she sells in the streets. She told me that her daughter-in-law, Elisa, had been hung up by her feet by two policemen, from the top of the outside wall of the house, which is quite high here; they threatened to let her drop if she didn't talk. Elisa is pregnant. Her husband, Jonas, all that time was fastened to the feet of the bed, I think with handcuffs. Two days later the police realized that the two were innocent and released them. The police had originally wanted 30,000 cruzeiros to release Elisa. Dona Nair told me that her house had been invaded at 4:00 o'clock in the morning in defiance of the law: "Nobody shall be arrested except while actually committing a criminal act or by an order of a judge." The police behaved like savages: they shot at the doors and walls; they made men and women get undressed and stay naked in their presence; they put their hands where you can guess, even with the fifty-eight-year-old grandmother, to see if they had something hidden. There were three little children present. Dona Nair assures me that there had not been any stolen goods in her house except for a packet that one of the members of the *quadrilha* had left there; it had got into the house against the will of the mistress.

So it seems that all the family members are innocent, since they were released. I am worried about the eleven-year-old boy who took part in the jobs along with his father. I am afraid the police will take him and beat him to make him say more than the truth. I tried to convince his mother to hide him and only to surrender him to the police in the presence of a lawyer. But this woman is afraid, and besides she is a member of a Pentecostal sect, a *crente*: she puts everything in the hands of God, which dispenses her from having to struggle.

In all this affair our community was incapable of doing anything: nobody reacted, nobody acted, nobody even went to notify the Centro. I had to do their job: making the investigation with the families, carrying out liaison with the Centro. All that "social" side of the struggle still is turned over to the "father," at least in this community. How can we manifest a first sketch of the kingdom—the new world, the sign of the definitive world that is coming—if we don't make the charity of Christ "operational"? And that presupposes a Centro for defense of human rights, among other things. It is difficult to create militants in this situation. And on the other hand, it also comes about that the militants no longer believe in "grace."

But in the end, it's the same sickness of being like Prometheus: to rely only on human forces to get out of our predicament. If those forces are weak, we don't do anything, we cross our arms and wait for a miracle (a distortion of the true sense of miracle, which is always a *sign* and not an infallible recipe). If the forces become strong, we rely exclusively on them and take justice into our own hands. I believe that human beings have inside them an *aversion* to God and God's grace.

Thursday, June 28, 1979

People might say that I make a game of noticing only the catastrophic events. But that's not true, I record what happens. . . . Last week a woman lodger of Dona Nair (the one whose house was invaded by the police) poured alcohol over herself and set herself on fire. She is in the hospital with severe burns. Her son Fernando is sleeping outdoors because he doesn't get along with his stepfather. Fernando in one of the known thieves in our *bairro*; he is seventeen. Yesterday the police descended on the street 500 meters away from the church. Shots. They killed Gerson, eighteen, a *trombadinha* (a young blackshirt who does armed robberies). The police also invaded Maria Isabel's shanty to recover a bicycle, which they alleged was stolen goods. The kids were ready to die of fright. Maria Isabel didn't dare tell me anything. Fortunately, Marlene, a member of the community of Mutinga, came to inform me. The police left the bicycle in her house under condition; now she is afraid that the *trombadinhas* will come and attack her.

Adivam, who is responsible for the community of Garden São Vicente, came to tell me that he had to go to the Centro. A young man of his *bairro* had not been seen for about eight days, after the police of the DIEC had picked him up. (The DIEC is the criminal police of the state of São Paulo; it was headed by the infamous torturer Fleury, who died mysteriously on May 1, 1980.) Nobody knows where he is. His parents, who are *crentes*, no doubt believe that God will solve the problem all alone.

This evening we shall have Mass at 8:00 P.M. in the community of Mutinga, that is to say, in the building next to my room. Zé and Maria Alves, from the community of São Vicente de Paula, will be presented to the community of Mutinga as the household responsible for the community center of this *bairro*. (Actually this choice will turn out to be a disaster. Zé himself was strangled during the night, in 1984, by a lunatic.) They are each about twenty-eight, with two children. Zé was baptized on Christmas eve; the same evening, the two were married and made their first communion. Before, they had belonged to a *crente* family and because of that had never been baptized. Of the six communities in this *bairro*, just three have a household that is their *animador* (animator) and responsible for the center: Munhoz-Centro, Mutinga, and São Vicente. It remains to organize Petrobrás, Eurico da Cruz, and Nossa Senhora do Desterro. The household that takes on the center is not automatically the coordinator of the community, but still it has an essential role, since it gathers the community together. These are the new "doorkeepers" of this church, which is being born from the bottom up. Each of these households lives in a little house built on the lot of the community center. They need to correspond so far as possible to the standards that Paul sets up in the pastoral Epistles.

One would have to be blind not to be aware of the hell that is blazing in the basements of humanity. From time to time a tongue of infernal flame and a gust of diabolical heat lick our feet and fill our nostrils: the death of eighteen-year-old Gerson, shot down by the police; Somoza of Nicaragua; Bude who came looking for me this morning, drunk as a lord, to baptize his little ten-day-old daughter, dead of dehydration. These are sparks from the conflagration, which always simmers in the depths, and which only the prayer and suffering of the just can drive back into the abyss.

This morning I thought that it was really absurd to imagine that a political organization, revolutionary in its own right, and with some real degree of power, could ever emerge at the end of such anarchy. One needs only to look at the innumerable political tendencies that divide even the smallest revolutionary groups. And furthermore, political instruments of analysis and action are indispensable.

It was the gospel faith that led me to the revolution. How can one tolerate the actual condition of the world and not rise up in insurgency, when one preaches the kingdom of God? *Resurrection demands insurrection.* An insurrection where the cohesion of the social body would depend more on inspiration than on laws. We need a new Montesquieu to write a new *Spirit of Laws.*

January 27, 1980

The hot tropic dampness is on the level of an emotion, on an *affective* level. The affective and the subjective are so intense here that one is nearly stifled. How can one draw clear outlines in this Amazonian vegetation of feelings?

What characterizes *Homo sapiens* is not a reduction of emotion ("affectivity") to the benefit of intelligence, but on the contrary a veritable psycho-emotional eruption, the swelling of *hybris*, that is, of whatever goes beyond proper limits. . . . Among the primates, and especially the chimpanzees, affectivity already starts to break all the barriers. But it is with the human being that it takes on a character that is eruptive, unstable, intense, disorderly. . . . *Homo sapiens* is a being that smiles, laughs, weeps; an anxious and anguished being; a being that is playful, drunken, ecstatic, violent, furious, loving; a being invaded by the imagination; a being that knows that death is coming and cannot believe it; a being that secretes myth and magic; a being possessed by spirits and gods; a being that nourishes itself on illusions and chimeras; a subjective being whose relations with the objective world are, always, uncertain; a being subject to error and vagrancy; a being without measure, which produces only disorder.[1] That is more true in Brazil than elsewhere.

April 1, 1980

Forty deaths at the funeral of Don Oscar Romero, archbishop of San Salvador. Of the five bishops who make up the country's episcopate, just one came to help bury his brother! The others were either in disagreement with him or afraid for their lives because of threats from the extreme Left.

This morning when I went out of my house I dropped by Maria Isabel's, this woman with seven children, abandoned by her husband; often she gets food to eat from the city's garbage. She gets $50 a month to live on. She was in a

---

1. E. Morin, *Le paradigme perdu* (Paris: Seuil, 1973), p. 125.

different mood, weeping quietly over the ills of the world and her own. "Today I sinned and this week [Holy Week] is a week of sadness. . . . What will happen to us?" Despair without bottom and almost silent.

She lives in the poorest *barraco* of the *favela*. I help her live, in part, with the money that the Trappists of Tamié have sent me. The garbage dump is 10 kilometers away. People collect old cartons and scraps of food to take back home. In the same city, there are people who earn $4,000 to $5,000 a month: a hundred times as much.

Maria Isabel makes me think of Anne Frank. She also, in a certain way, lived cloistered in an attic room or in the basements of humanity, out of which her voice didn't make itself heard. Maria Isabel's normal destiny is a concentration camp—these camps where the industrial world throws those who haven't got any strength to resist society.

April 2, 1980

When I was six or seven years old, I often dreamed that I was the driver of a miniature train like the one in the Jardin des Plantes. This train came out of a tunnel and went through the subbasements of an enormous and fantastic medieval chateau, full of dungeons, towers, and pinnacles that reach up to the skies. The little train wound through the moats of the chateau in the chiaroscuro of a kind of twilight. When I think about this fantastic chateau I feel peace and wonderment, mixed with terror as in face of a great mystery. I have always remembered this dream of my childhood.

It seems to me that the chiaroscuro of the corridor, the moats of the chateau, are the deep and unconscious part of myself. I put myself (the train) inside myself; I am even invited to share in the discovery of whatever is obscure and mysterious inside me. The tunnel is perhaps the moment of my birth or perhaps even earlier. (It is said that the experience of death is also that of passage through a long tunnel.) My "self" ("my soul," Saint Teresa of Ávila would say) is this fantastic chateau, which goes up to the sky. I remember that Saint Teresa compares the spiritual adventure to the progress of a person inside the seven dwelling-places of a great chateau. At the center is the king. At the center of the soul, there is God, who is the point of origin of my true self.

Each dream is a message that the unconscious sends to the conscious self with the hope of being heard. If the unconscious is not heard, then neurosis appears: the deep self resists the conscious self, which does not hear it, in order to save it from a great danger, by the subterfuge of a kind of madness. Madness permits one to live out in an imaginary way what the conscious self is not willing to live out in a real way.

April 3, 1980

Another very different dream: at the end of October 1976, in Switzerland, at the house of Manoel da Conceição. That night, I dreamed that I was in China, on foot, a sack on my back, having lost all my other baggage. Suddenly I see a train, which is passing at top speed; it is the train of the poor. Another train passes in the opposite direction; it is cursed by the people; it is the train of the rich. I am walking in the mud. I am leaving the suburbs of a city after having bought something in a shop, on the edge of the road. (The shop lady gives me the correct change with a smile.) I arrive in the countryside; in the distance are some houses in the curve of a valley at the foot of a slope. I retrace my steps. I have no desire to go on. Now comes the culminating moment of the dream. I meet an old man, accompanied by a little child whom he holds by the hand; he is good and wise with a gentle smile. He is wearing the traditional long robe of the Chinese. He tells me that everybody will know tomorrow that I was walking on foot like a poor man, in the mud; and that he was with me, a Westerner. I tell him that I am afraid of compromising his position. He tells me that this is not important. He takes up a packet of pieces of red-orange jade, which I had hung at the side of my waist. Then he draws the map of China. The south (Portuguese *sul*) is colored blue (*azul*) and he asks me if somebody has prevented me from going to the south. I say No, it is just a matter of itinerary which accounts for my being here. Then it seems to me that I am in the south, in the blue. Afterward, the dream comes to an end by my being in a train, somewhere else, in a different region, perhaps outside China, toward the north; it is carrying me at high speed.

May 8, 1980

Now the story of Nair's brother Noé, who died a few weeks ago leaving six children, has become clear. In fact, he died of exhaustion and hunger. He was the custodian at a school on Avenida Paulista, a fashionable street in the center of the city. He worked sixteen hours a day: two days' work per day to double his wages. Once he confided in his mother, who was passing through: "How many times I have left my house dying of cold and hunger! I used to take the train with my stomach empty. Now what has happened is that I can't go on any longer because my head is out of control"—from lack of sleep.

The youngest child, a baby a few months old, crying with hunger all night long because they couldn't buy him milk, and he couldn't assimilate *caldo de feijão* (kidney-bean soup).

One day Noé fainted. They had to try several hospitals before they could get him admitted; it was all done by bus: literally they had to drag this exhausted man on and off. When they got him in the hospital, nobody recognized that he had advanced tuberculosis, with one lung wholly wasted. They gave him an injection; he couldn't support the shock and died.

Thursday, September 11, 1980

This morning Odete, Lourdes, and Albertina came by my house to wash the dishes and sweep up. They are all mothers, between thirty and forty years old, with five or six children apiece.

I was getting over my trip: certainly over 15,000 kilometers. In Minas Gerais, I visited Teófilo Otoni and Belo Horizonte; in the northeast, Recife, João Pessoa, Campina Grande, Petrolândia, Juazeiro de Bahia, Bonfim, Antônio Gonçalvez, Jacobina, Rui Barbosa, Salvador, Fortaleza, Crateús, Teresina; in

Amazônia and the north, Manaus, Itacoatiara, Rio Branco (Acre); in the center, Brasília and Conceição do Araguaia.

Twenty cities! and in every place, or nearly so, Alamiro and I had visits with the diocesan or parish cadres to understand the local situation with its conflicts and to present the nonviolent alternative. Brazil is a land of conflicts. They spring up everywhere, and everywhere it's just about the same story: big international capital is buying up local resources (land, minerals, water impounded in dams, the fish of the rivers) and exploiting them industrially. The farmers, who in general have no title to their property, are dispossessed and emigrate to the cities. Out of Brazil's total population of 120 million, there are probably 40 million migrants across the country—unstable populations trying to resettle after being dispossessed. In fact, the farmers here in most cases are tenants; they "hold" the land, sometimes for generations, but they are not its owners. It is hard even to find out who is the landowner. But when the rich arrive—that is, the great landed proprietors of the national bourgeoisie or the financial groups representing "transnational" capital—they go to the notary and get themselves written title deeds. The national bourgeoisie and the transnational capital are in fact closely allied. Here the national bourgeoisie, contrary to the way it is (or used to be) in Europe, has no effective autonomous existence. The old Brazilian Communist party (one of the twenty-seven organized Marxist tendencies in the country—the most important, it is true) never understood that; and the tactical alliances that it made with the national bourgeoisie to confront big international capital have always been a snare and a delusion. At the critical moment, the national bourgeoisie, almost totally dependent on big international capital, succumbed to external pressure and turned the country over to foreign influences. However we judge the numerous blind spots of the Brazilian Left, the result is that Brazil is a country of conflicts, where it is urgent to find an adequate strategy. We are trying to mount a nonviolent strategy.

Thursday, November 13, 1980
Florensky describes an experience that was an anticipation of hell:

The problem of the second death is a great problem. Once in a daydream, I lived it in a wholly concrete manner. It wasn't a matter of images but only of interior sensations. I was surrounded with deep shadows, so thick it almost seemed they were made of matter. I was so to speak drawn by strange forces toward a boundary; I knew it was the boundary of God's creation, and that beyond there was only absolute Nothing. I wanted to cry out but I couldn't. I knew that in an instant I would be expelled into the outer darkness; in fact it began to invade my being. I had almost completely lost consciousness, and I knew that this loss was an absolute metaphysical annihilation. At the point of despair I said, "From the depths I cried out, *de profundis clamavi.*" Into those words I put all my soul; something seized me with strength just before I foundered, and removed me far from the abyss. And immediately I found myself in my room, in my familiar setting; from the mystical Nothing I found myself in the normal course of life. And I felt myself before the Face of God.[2]

The other day I was on my way to visit the family of Bouca, the great bandit of the *bairro* who had been shot a couple of months ago by a buddy in a question relating to a woman and a revolver. I saw a sight that turned my stomach. A gang of urchins, all of whom engage in armed robberies, had submerged a rat as fat as a kitten in gasoline. When the rat was saturated with petroleum inside and out, they took it out of the jar, tied a rope to one paw and set it on fire. The rat ran like mad, all the time throwing a jet of fire out of its mouth like a flame-thrower. Everybody found it charming and the little children couldn't take their eyes off it. I told the boys they were behaving like torturers. "Today you do that to an animal, tomorrow you'll do that to a human being. Even an animal doesn't make another animal suffer needlessly; an animal doesn't know how to torture; you've sunk lower than an animal . . . ." I didn't persist. (Even so, the next week I found a dead rat on my bed.) I invited the bandit's family to the Mass that will be celebrated next Sunday.

During the last fortnight seventeen young men have been shot to death in the streets of Osasco in revenge; by the police; one way or another. . . . Ten of those were last Sunday, seven the preceding week, the day when Henry left. I showed him the newspaper at the airport. A month ago, a fifteen-year-old bandit was lynched by the people of the *favela* in another *bairro* of São Paulo. He had killed his cousin of thirty-five, the father of three children, for refusing to lend him his car. Even after his cousin was dead, during the wake, he came back to provoke the family and neighbors: "Really dead, still dead?" Explosion of popular anger. The women were in the front lines with bricks and planks. The guy's head was squashed flat as a pancake. I entrust this boy's name to you who read this journal: Nilton da Conceiçaõ, fifteen. His mother mops the floor in a supermarket; every night she gets home from her work at midnight, she lives in a *favela* and certainly has a number of other children.

It's unbelievable how in these times the violence in the *bairro* has increased. Every year hundreds, perhaps thousands, of people die like this. The principal cause of this explosion of violence is hunger. In October the annual inflation rate rose to 109 percent. It corresponds to the global crisis of unemployment.

Friday, November 14, 1980

Last night I found an old man sleeping in the street, near my place, under the roof of the butcher's open-air shed. You don't see that very often in the *bairros* out here in the outskirts. On the other hand, in the middle of the city there are thousands of people sleeping under the bridges. But you don't see very much of them either. Misery is hidden in the factories, in the prisons, under the bridges.

---

2. Florensky, *La colonne et l'appui de la vérité*, p. 205.

Even the *favela* is "physically" small: doll-huts hidden in the lowlands, outside the city or under the viaducts. Still there are a million *favelados* (shantytown dwellers) in São Paulo. Affluence takes up a lot of space, misery is huddled in corners; and so the world's suffering doesn't pain the individual conscience. You can't *see* the poor any longer, those who suffer. You can't even have any regrets. The task of the church is to proclaim from the rooftops what nobody says, to bring out into the light what has been relegated to the background.

This old man was a deaf-mute. He went off this morning "saying" energetically he knew where he was going. A big pack on his back. I thought of a Russian pilgrim.

Joseph Folliet wrote in *La Croix* for November 9, 1972, a week before his death:

> In connection with drugs and the role of artificial ecstasy among certain young people, a hippie upon being questioned tells about a spiritual experience in which drugs play no part. "I'm a believer. I had the experience of a frightening encounter with the absolute. It was an encounter with something so big that I asked myself who I was. What saved me from fear, what still saves me today, was the reassuring conviction that God loves me and I am one of God's children."

Thursday, November 27, 1980

As I was going to the bishop's, I met a fairly young bum who was drinking as he walked, with his shoes down-at-the-heel and his clothing in tatters. I went up to him, talked to him, and offered him 100 cruzeiros. (Ordinarily we make it a practice not to give money, even in private, for receiving charity humiliates people and inhibits them from organizing.) He answered: "Go off, child of God, with a blessing; take care of your little bit of money [*dinheirinho*], you may need it." It's very rare to meet people who live "by the grace of God." Certainly they are mad, and this one looked a little haggard. But what is madness? Who is really mad? Who is out of his senses, he or I?

Last Monday the tally for the month to date reached thirty-six dead: thirty-six young men shot down to settle an affair, in the streets of Osasco—our western suburb of São Paulo with its 1½ million inhabitants. And that in three weeks. I have never seen such a blaze of violence. In my *bairro* one more died last Saturday, at least the sixth in three months. Dínio, the brother of Bouca who was killed two months ago, has been locked up again: he had two bullets in his belly six weeks ago, now a bullet in his head a fortnight ago and he's still alive. And also he was beaten up by the police.

We are trying to pull off a collective action of the Centro in resistance to this wave of violence, but it's going to be difficult.

Friday, December 12, 1980

Last evening, as we do every Thursday evening, we celebrated the Eucharist (at 8:00 o'clock, after work). Generally from twenty to fifty persons participate—nearly all of them the most committed of the community. A lot of them are young. It's the truly Christian Mass of the week. I think that angels fill the church and celebrate along with us whenever Thursday evening comes around, for everything happens in a great calm. All say in turn what they have got out of the gospel, pray out loud, sing with faith; their faces are illuminated, two penny candles are burning in front of the statue of Nossa Senhora Aparecida. Before communion everybody embraces. Afterward a few words, then everybody goes home, into the night, in peace.

The patroness of Brazil is a black Virgin. Some black slave fishermen found the body of a statue of the Virgin in a river, about a hundred and fifty years ago. A little later, when they cast their net again, they brought up the head. The two made up a little statue about 50 centimeters high, black from head to feet. (Perhaps it was the water that made it black; it's quite likely; its style is Portuguese Baroque of the eighteenth century, if I'm not mistaken.) Popular piety took over this discovery, this "apparition" (hence the name *Aparecida*) of the Virgin in the river. For a number of years the statue was venerated in a poor fisherman's house, a hut. People from the neighborhood came on pilgrimage. Then the priests took over the devotion, and a cardinal (Leme) built a basilica (to have his Lourdes or Fatima in Brazil). It was in the city now called Aparecide do Norte, and the Aparecida was proclaimed patroness of Brazil. I don't say that the ecclesiastics did wrong; but history doesn't come from above, but from below, from the "base," from whatever is butchered, from the black slaves, who somehow or other created a prophetic and evangelical "counterreligion," in the interior of that official and dominant religion that is foreign to their African mentality. You have to take into account the mysterious acts of complicity of what Christians usually call Providence. "Gospel Providence" always uses impoverished means, signs that one must know how to decipher. Who could have guessed that Mary's son, born at Bethlehem, under precarious circumstances, right at the end of a long journey, was an *aparecido*, an apparition of the divine in history?

Friday, December 19, 1980
About Marx
The critique that Karl Marx makes of religion has to do with its social function. Marx studies the phenomenon of religion to the extent that it reflects, on the ideological level, the position of the different social classes in the class struggle. The contribution that he and Friedrich Engels made to the history of religion was to demonstrate in particular cases how religion can be manipulated by the dominant classes to become a means of exploiting the oppressed. Nothing less than that—and also nothing more. To go beyond—namely, to raise on the level of principles the question about the existence or nonexistence of God—is to formulate a metaphysical query that forces Marxism to enter into a type of reasoning that doesn't belong to it, for it is neither materialist, nor scientific, nor dialectical. It is strange to see certain Marxists—and perhaps Marx himself—defending in practice a *metaphysical materialism* that places them in contradiction with their own fundamental intuitions.

About Freud and Reich

Every ideology, when it claims to become the final and total explanation of things, becomes a scourge, an Antichrist. Profit becomes the decisive criterion of economic choices; technique is celebrated as the source of salvation; the proletariat becomes the Messiah of humanity; the libido becomes the final explanation of psychological dynamics; national security is the goal of development; and so on (so Leonardo Boff in *Vida para além da morte* [Petropolis: Editora Vozes, 1973]).

The soft sexual liberation of Wilhelm Reich and the superficial atheism of Marx are making disciples here (Marx never studied the question of religion, he just picked up Ludwig Feuerbach's critique; he had no notion of gospel transcendence)—at least in sectors of the middle class and among some worker militants contaminated by the middle class. Culturally, they don't observe the profoundly original things happening here; they are still being towed along by Europe and its intellectual fashions.

I know very well that Marx, Reich, and Freud are great men or, rather, important men, and that it would be absurd to execute them in a few lines. But how can one not be irritated by the people who repeat the obscurantist slogans that pseudo-scientific ideology keeps solemnly pronouncing against Christianity: "it has a morality that is repressive, archaic, designed for a patriarchal civilization. . . . " The Freudian-Marxists consider that sexuality is good in itself, which is true, and innocent, which is less true (for nothing in the human being is totally innocent); and that the relation between men and women would present no problem if there were no "repression" in the realms of family, society, religion, created by a mountain of rules no longer useful in the psycho-social phase that humanity has reached. This archaic survival is (they say) the cause of anxieties, neuroses, all the destructive impulses such as war and the rest that regularly devastate humanity. They accuse Christianity of participating in this repression.

Here a general observation emerges. Among living beings, death appears only along with sexuality. An animal without sexual differentiation does not die; it reproduces by division. Sexual differentiation increases the quality of life, which thus becomes infinitely more complex and intelligent—see Pierre Teilhard de Chardin's law of complexity and consciousness. But, at the same time, every sexual being is separated and incomplete. It lacks its "other half." And thus there appears, along with sexuality, an insurmountable weakness, which is at the heart of each of us and is made concrete by death. Isn't this the deepest reason for sexual relations: joining the two halves to overcome death? But neither sexuality nor politics—nor Marx nor Freud—is able to overcome death. The union of lovers and revolution go a long way; their powerful waves shake the power of death for a moment, but come to a halt, defeated, at the edge of the grave. Here Christianity has a decisive word to offer. The main axis of its message is resurrection: life that triumphs over death. Those famous "moral rules," so easily condemned by the Freudian-Marxists in the name of nineteenth-century scientism, have nothing to do with moralism: *they are not rules but exercises, exercises to teach people how to come back to life.* People do lots of yoga, why not do exercises in gospel morality? By baptism we are grafted onto Christ; resurrection is in us. But we have to develop it. Whenever people take a lover, abandoning the companion of their youth ("I am frustrated, he is no longer pleasing to me . . ."), when they do not forgive, when they lie down with anger in their heart, when they slander their neighbor—then they lie down with death and delay the process of resurrection, which has already been thrown into gear in them.

Barbarians don't see that: they sweep away with the back of their hand the wisdom, an art of living, which comes to us from Abraham and thousands of saints and prophets, who, down through the ages, have built up a "knowledge" and in particular a science of the resurrection of the flesh, of the complete human being.

Before the heirs of the great Judeo-Christian tradition, two possible roads stand open: the monastic life and the life of marriage. They can either renounce the genital life or assume it, but in either case in the interior of a spiritual discipline that leads to resurrection.

The monastic life is the testing-ground or laboratory of the new human being in Christ: it is where the ultimate modification of the human being is worked out, which will permit one to attain a higher life capable of overcoming death. All the spiritual masters know that the monastic life is sown with ambushes and that one can't venture there by oneself.

The life of marriage is an *encounter* with a partner, thanks to whom one can find the source of resurrection. But it takes a lot of time to encounter somebody. That is why a man and a woman can't be the lovers of a single night or of brief rendezvous. The passion of love can become the road to an effective meeting if, thanks to ongoing patience and through successive crises, one finds out that the lover is different and, in a certain sense, *inadequate* to complete one and to make the leap beyond death. It involves not demanding the impossible, not turning the other into an absolute, but through the other and thanks to the other, being on the way to the Absolute. Then there is born a type of love that is very humble, full of compassion and respect. One's lover is not possessed by one, but received like someone who, through one's person, is looking for a higher unity, that *one cannot provide*, but which passes through one. Love stops being a totalitarian demand and opens up to God. That is the moment when the other is revealed as another person, in that person's fragility, irreducible originality, difference, insufficiency. A person can never possess or annul or satisfy the other totally. One is not the Lord of the other's life; and resurrection, if it passes through a person, does not come from that person.

It is evident that this perspective on marriage presumes conjugal fidelity. Certainly "marriage in Christ is not a law but a gift of grace" (so states Olivier Clément), and one may simply not be capable of receiving this gift. Separation can become inevitable. But the catastrophe of a marriage, always possible, remains a catastrophe. So it remains true that the *encounter* with one's partner can be nothing less than a long adventure, which presumes a promise of fidelity, a discipline of ascetic type, if one wishes to go to the end of experience, that is, to open oneself up to the Absolute of God and of Christ resurrected, through a companion in struggle, one's spouse, who becomes little by little the privileged place of the revelation of a superior unity, stronger than death.

December 26, 1980; January 1, 1981

Happy New Year to all! Since I was speaking about death, I can say that my brother, Marc, who came from France to spend Noël with me, was a witness of the death of Aderbal José dos Santos, father of eight children, the oldest seventeen; he himself was forty-five. Aderdal died when he came to the end of his lungs, after having gone through ten hospitals in two months. I do know that, even in France, hospitals don't always keep those who are dying; they get sent back home. But, in the first place, Aderbal was very recalcitrant in the face of death. The next to last hospital where he stayed sent him home without a penny; this man at death's door covered at least 15 kilometers on foot to get back to his house. He should have refused to leave the hospital, or insisted on an ambulance, or money for the bus; but the poor have sudden fits of independence, incomprehensible to those who are well provided-for. . . . Anyway it's not at all certain that he would have got what he was asking for. Administrative inertia, bureaucratic cruelty and incredible! All the rich countries have social services. It would seem always possible to send those who are dying back home with a tank of oxygen, or to put them in a hospice, as Mother Teresa does in Calcutta. But Aderbal lives in a *favela*, in a *barraco* where he is crammed in with his eight children and his wife. He got 8,000 cruzeiros per month from the Social Security (533 francs; $65). One of his children, Joel, fourteen, washes cars for 250 cruzeiros ($2) a day. His oldest son is at the age for military service, and like all the young men in that situation can't get a job. The whole base community took it on itself to help Aderbal die. Finally the Centro found a hospice 25 kilometers from here. Strings had to be pulled in high places to locate this filthy hospital. Aderbal died Saturday at 10 in the morning, the day after his admission: epilepsy, acute gastritis, perhaps lung cancer or else a vascular disease. At forty-five this sturdy man ended his life, leaving behind eight children without resources.

One inevitably comes to the conclusion that this local drama has a political side. We don't need an economy here built around cars (Ford, Volkswagen) or electrical appliances. We need an economy that will carry out reforms on the base of society: health, hospitals, schools, agrarian reform. There are 1 million *favelados* in São Paulo. The number has more than doubled in the last ten years. We are backed into the corner of revolt, revolution.

Still, Noël went very well. Lots of rain and mud. Last night, December 31, a very lovely prayer vigil until midnight with many people in attendance. The young people collected 20 or 30 kilos of food in the *bairro* for those who are poorer than they are. That's admirable, because they live themselves under very precarious circumstances, many of them in the *favelas*.

I thank Marc warmly for having come to "live" here a little. There are some things that it is necessary to see with one's own eyes. One can have only the faith and the experience that come from the place where one lives.

2

Theology of Liberation and Theology of Oppression

RELIGIOUS SENTIMENT

Religious sentiment is highly ambiguous. It can produce the best and the worst: Francis of Assisi or the Inquisition. Furthermore, it is a very subtle and violent sentiment. At least it can become such, both for the best and for the worst. Either Teresa of Ávila or the Wars of Religion. We shall get either Grand Inquisitors or seraphs. How could it be otherwise? For what else is the religious part of a human being but the capacity to *worship*? Either one makes an absolute out of something limited, and in this case falls into the idolatry constantly denounced by the prophets of the Bible; or, by an unimaginable grace, one finds the true Absolute, the humble and living God, and bends one's knees before that Absolute. In true worship one does not have the option to prescribe either the form of the Absolute (who comes to one as it is and not as one imagines it) or the knowledge of the Absolute (who reveals itself as it chooses). The problem consists in encountering the Absolute through the mediation of the relative and the limited. Hence the need of a spiritual adviser to find one's way.

The capacity to worship is simply the capacity to absolutize. To absolutize country, science, party, a loved one is to idolatrize them; and then one becomes blind and sometimes fanatical. On the other hand, to worship the True God means becoming more and more human. Sex and emotionality, politics, religion—these are three giant forces that traverse the heart of every human being, both entire and in every part; but the most formidable of the three is certainly religion. That is why we need spiritual advisers—and not professors —to venture out on these burning soils.

A DEFINITION OF THEOLOGY

Before talking about the theology of liberation, we need to have a definition of theology, however brief. *Theology is nothing but organized discourse on the data of faith.* "In that case what is the need of theology? Will not the simple gospel be enough?" Actually, no. Every age is different and the course of time brings new problems at every moment. The questions of an industrial society have their own special character; so do those of the Middle Ages, so do those of the third world, so do those raised by the anxieties of the advanced and overorganized societies. The essence of the gospel is to be good news. The first condition of preaching the gospel is to be heard. We do not have the option of being pre-Marxist, pre-Nietzscheans, pre-Freudians. So in every age we have to reorganize the data of the faith so that they will really be an answer to the problems of a contemporary human being; otherwise the gospel will no longer be good news, no longer an answer to anything. We must draw out of the tradition we have received: that is, ask the right questions about the "practice," the way of life, and the words of the great saints and prophets, above all of Jesus. We must study their existence to learn how we also may position ourselves in life, in order to overcome the evils that cripple us, to find joy and then happiness. So our reason will make use of all the scientific means at our disposal—philosophy, philology, economics, history, sociology—to render our religious discourse more penetrating, more complete, more organized. Saint Thomas Aquinas has already said that philosophy—rational discipline—is the servant of theology. It is the same today with the other scientific disciplines, and in particular with sociology.

We wish constantly to confront our life with the life of Jesus, that is, to renew his memory. And so we constantly study not only the sacred text, which transmits to us the record of his actions, through our philology and exegesis; but also the social conditions in his time, through our sociology, to understand how he lived his struggles and how we can live ours. Psychology can also help us understand the mutual relations among the persons of the gospel. But we do all this from the standpoint of a religious given, which we accept as such, and in a religious perspective. We are interviewing actors of the past, still living for us, who are religious persons; we share the same faith. That is why our discourse is theological and not merely philosophical. We are to accept this state of affairs as the point of departure for our reflection.

THEOLOGY OF LIBERATION AND THEOLOGY OF OPPRESSION

Theology may be put at the service of oppression, death, and destruction. For example, there was a theology of slavery. The theologians of Salamanca with full seriousness, at the time of the Spanish colonization of Latin America, raised the question whether or not the Indians had souls! If the answer had been No, that would have been a fine ideological justification for massacring the native populations without remorse. Fortunately, great theologians, and in particular the Dominican Bartolomé de Las Casas, answered Yes, and with such energy! And the pope supported them. Further, in opposition to the prevailing sentiment of his times, Las Casas affirmed in effect with a martyr's energy: "Better an Indian, infidel but alive, than a Christian baptized by force and executed. Let us not forget that the emperor of the Incas was baptized before his murder." What a bloody theology! It is true that Las Casas was never able to prevent the massacres; he could barely moderate them.

Each time that the gospel is preached in an authentic manner, it encounters fanatical resistance, not least in the interior of the churches. The church is holy; but within it there implant themselves cabals, interest groups, synagogues of Satan. But in the end the Christian conscience will always remember that the human beings of the whole world, whatever their race and the color of their skin, are immortal beings created in the image of God, children of one God and brothers and sisters of each other—including their torturers. We stand in a biblical pattern, that of Cain and Abel. Fratricidal wars do exist; and they are abominable to the degree that they are fratricidal. Thanks to the theology of Las Casas, in the place of justice at least there remained remorse in the Christian conscience, and consequently repentance was possible. The results have not been as meager as they might seem.

Jesus himself constantly had to deal with a theology of oppression. Let us see how he undertook the restoration of truth.

Example No. 1: "Let your Yes be Yes, and your No be No; for whatever is more than these comes from the Evil One" (Mt. 5:37, interpreted by Jas. 5:12). It is presupposed that the teachers of the law twisted the word of God so as not to have to carry out their promises. Jesus restored the revolutionary truth of the divine word when he said that there was no need of oaths to commit oneself; a simple Yes or No was enough, for every word spoken should correspond to the secret intentions of the heart. If only an oath will commit one, it is a sign that one's Yes can be a lie; and that falsifies all social relations.

Example No. 2: "You always have the poor among you" (Mt. 26:11)—the verse of Scripture that has been the most "rediscovered" by a certain middle class. Their interpretation: "If there will always be the poor, it is because Jesus himself foresaw inequalities and social classes; therefore it is our duty to help the poor, but not to change the social order in effect." But in reality, this interpretation forgets the context in which these words were spoken by Jesus. A woman came to break a flask of perfume to anoint his head or his feet; and over the objections of those present, Judas Iscariot in particular, Jesus quotes a phrase of Deuteronomy (15:11) to the effect that one should constantly come to the help of the poor and not wait for the Jubilee year. (Every seven years, the Jews had the duty, according to the law, of restoring social equilibrium by returning to the poor their goods, which economic relations had succeeded in taking from them. However, history records no clear instance of this duty being fulfilled.) Jesus says: "When my body is no longer with you, when I shall no longer be visibly there, the poor will take my place and it will be they whom you must perfume, that is, help in every way and overwhelm them with the perfume of your love." The saying is poles apart from an encouragement to maintain unjust social structures.

Example No. 3: The multiplication of the bread (Mk. 6:30-44). This text is especially instructive because it shows two religious ideas silently confronting each other. The crowds follow Jesus. And the apostles, as always "reasonable" with that reasonable common sense that dispenses one from taking on the problems of others, tell him: "It is already late; send them away . . . so that they may buy themselves something to eat" (vv. 35-36). Isn't it true that when others become burdensome, we try to get rid of them on whatever grounds, if necessary by sending them off to a professional agency! But Jesus answers them: It is you who must solve the problem of this people; "Give them something to eat *yourselves*" (v. 37). The apostles live in an economy of buying and selling and their answer is the one of a person deformed by a system where already nothing but money matters. "But how can we take care of them?" they say in effect; "it will take at least two hundred denars' worth of bread to feed this crowd" (v. 37). But Jesus answers them: I didn't ask you how much money you have, but how much bread you have. That's very different! "How much bread do you have? Go and see." "Five loaves and two fishes" (v. 38). While this gospel text has also several other meanings, in particular a eucharistic one, its meaning on this level is clear: we need to share in common the little that we have in order for God's omnipotence to feel at home among us. Sharing, which means love, draws down grace; and grace awakens love. There is a mysterious dialectic there. We must understand clearly that miracles do happen. But in Christian theology the miracle is never a recipe but a *sign,* a sign that God approves an attitude of the human being. In the case of the multiplication of the loaves, there may have been an extraordinary sign, a multiplication of matter—but only because the actors in this scene, kindled by Jesus' word of love, agreed to share the little that they had. The apostles were able to find a boy with five loaves and two fishes (Jn. 6:9); perhaps others chose to add their scrap of food. Anyway the miracle happened—a sign that God approves this human attitude and feels comfortable with this crowd. Then God's omnipotence, which is manifested only in love, breathes on these poor and humble ones who have learned how to share. Certainly a miracle is not generated solely by the attitude of human beings. It is an unmerited overflowing of the love of God. But its sign can be given only to hearts in harmony with the God who gives of self. Remember the *powerlessness* of Jesus at Nazareth: "and he could not do any work of power there . . . because of their lack of faith" (Mk. 6:5-6).

It is possible also to do a different reading of this text and come out with an authentic theology of oppression. Thus: *(a)* Jesus is the Son of God and endowed with supernatural power; *(b)* I am not a Son of God and I do not have any supernatural power; *(c)* therefore I can do nothing to solve the problem of the others, it is beyond me. That is a syllogism of the devil.

Here then, in two columns, this text generates the theology of liberation and the theology of oppression:

Theology of Liberation	*Theology of Oppression*
1. The nature of God is love. God can act only in love and sharing.	1. I am not Son of God. I am only a human being.
2. At the time of the multiplication of the loaves, the word of God convinces the boy to share what he has.	2. Therefore I do not have any supernatural powers.
3. In this case, God, with all power, is with us to solve the problems with which human beings are faced. We need send nobody away on the grounds that we don't have the means.	3. Therefore, unfortunately, I can't do anything for the others. Only money solves the problem.

It is clear how strongly the theology of liberation is liberating—how strongly it pushes fervent believers in God to act, to take history into their hands. It is the opposite of passivity and alienation. It is, as we said, fervent. It relies on the power of God, but it knows how this power works. Never by a "magical" miracle like the sign from heaven demanded by the Pharisees (Mk. 8:11–13); it is only in love *willed* with energy that it manifests itself.

Example No. 4: "Blessed are the poor, for yours is the kingdom of God" (Lk. 6:20). The theology of oppression, as we all know, consists in saying: "You poor, live now in resignation, with the assurance that you will be happy in heaven." But the text doesn't mean that; the text doesn't say that poverty is blessed, but that the poor are blessed. Why? Because the poor are less hypocritical; living huddled together in the *favela*, they cannot hide their faults— drinking, arguments, crimes. Being poor, they are obliged to share, to help each other. You constantly see that in the *favela*; the *barracões* are crowded one on top of another and it is much easier to maintain human relations with one's neighbor than in a big apartment building. You can't let somebody die next to you without doing anything, for the walls of the huts that serve for living are so thin that nobody can miss the groans of the dying one. There are many horrors in the *favela:* hunger, despair, violence, drugs, sexual abominations. Nevertheless, there are more encounters between human beings, more mutual support, therefore more "humanity" and—let us speak the word so much devalued— more "love" than among the rich. And that is why the poor are blessed: the kingdom of God has already begun among them, because the presence of the kingdom consists in the awareness of charity. God moves with more ease and feels more at home in the middle of the *favela,* under the viaducts, and in the poor districts, than in the rich quarters; because God finds there something that corresponds to the divine nature: love. God's name and power are revealed more easily there than elsewhere. God's grace is *felt*. Therefore it is easier for a human being to undergo a spiritual experience and to acquire the faith. Furthermore, the poor are blessed because, since their situation is unsatisfactory, they want to change the world, they have hunger and thirst for justice, for harmony. The rich are replete and wish to maintain the fragile equilibrium that benefits them. The poor are committed to a project of hope. . . . You poor are blessed because you do not resign yourselves to evil, whether in yourselves or in society. You wish to change the established disorder. You are the combatants of the kingdom—in the sense in which we shall later speak of combat. You weep now, because the struggle is hard, but you will be comforted.

THREE FUNDAMENTAL PRINCIPLES
FOR THE INTERPRETATION OF A TEXT

How, one may ask, is it possible to make one and the same text say so many different things? Our answer is derived from the theologian and interpreter Carlos Mesters, who, with much more talent and accuracy than this writer's, has given us in Brazil these keys for correct reading. Opponents always say to each other, "You read the text through your own glasses." Such disputes over interpretation are evident in all ages, in particular during the time of Jesus or of the apostles. One example among a thousand: the apostle Paul appeared before the Sanhedrin to justify his Christian positions, which were arousing opposition and hatred among the religious authorities of his people. With a master's skill he divided his audience. Paul knew that there were present representatives of the Sadducees as well as of the Pharisees. And so he cried out, "It is because of our hope in the resurrection of the dead that I am brought to judgment." He had hardly finished speaking when a conflict broke out between the Pharisees and Sadducees, and the assembly was divided. The Sadducees, in fact, said that there was neither resurrection, nor angel, nor spirit, while the Pharisees affirmed each (Acts 23:6–8).

The same biblical texts, supporting the faith of the Pharisees as well as of the Sadducees, therefore do not just by themselves create unity. It was ever thus. At the Diet of Worms, Luther debated for some hours with Cardinal Cajetan on the Real Presence in the Eucharist: each claimed for himself the same words in certain verses of the Gospels. Today we observe the enterprise of the archconservative Bishop Lefebvre who questions the interpretation given by Vatican Council II to the sacred texts and to the Christian tradition.

What then is needed in order to interpret a text correctly; that is, to give it God's sense? We say that in Holy Scripture, the Bible, God *speaks* to human beings. The Bible is the word of God. In it God inspires the author to say or write things that cannot deceive us; it is something sure, true, solid (that is the meaning of the word *Amen,* "truly"; "Truly, truly I say to you"). Now, how and why does God speak? God speaks to answer real problems that have been raised in this or that age; the word of God always needs to be put back into its historical context. The prophet Jeremiah is much better understood when one realizes that during the time of his ministry Babylon was in the process of invading and destroying the remnant of the Jewish nation, and that the people had doubts about its God. Restoring the context does not imply that the word of God lacks any universal value. In fact, the universalism of the text arises precisely out of its particularity. Thus to grasp its exact sense, to discern the grain of the wood, we have to know *out of what circumstances* it was pronounced. By following that procedure, we shall be able to apply the text with much more strength, because with much more accuracy, to our own age and its problems. Only so shall we be able to make the necessary transpositions. We need always to be on our guard against both fundamentalism (taking the text in a merely literal fashion) and "concordism" (creating an artificial agreement between the biblical data and scientific truths).

It is not, however, sufficient to know the historical context in which the word of God was pronounced. Every word is spoken *out of a community* and in its midst. The community of the Pharisees was one thing and that of the Sadducees another; one was the community of Christians of Paul's type, another that of the Judaizing Christians of the school of James, "the Lord's brother" (Gal. 1:19). The community that inspires Bishop Lefebvre is one; that of the archbishop of Paris or of São Paulo is another.

Thus the original sense of the word of God has three components: the biblical text, its original historical context, and the presuppositions of the community from which it emerged. In French or Portuguese "pre-text" has a good sense, so that we can say neatly:

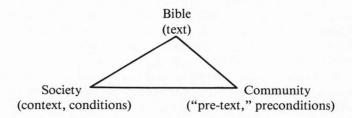

Bible
(text)

Society   Community
(context, conditions)   ("pre-text," preconditions)

Every community has a point of view on the answers required for the questions being asked at a given time. Generally, the communities that live *in the midst of the poor* and out of the situation of the poor, the oppressed of this world, have a different answer from the answer given by groups with a different social, economic, and political origin. The intellectual production of a group changes color in accordance with its role in the process of economic production. These general observations hold both for the original situation in which a text was produced and for a later situation. Our interpretation, then, is faithful to the original. It represents the word of God for us only if both *(a)* our historical conditions are continuous with those that generated it and *(b)* the preconditions of our community are parallel to those of the community from which it emerged. But condition *(a)* is in fact automatically satisfied in the present world, for we live in a world of oppression, the model and antecedents for which are to be found in the Bible and which constitute the universality of its historical situation. It remains therefore that the presuppositions *(b)* of our community should correspond to those of the community from which the biblical text emerged.

Thus it is not the case that we can interpret the Bible any way we please, according to the community we belong to and the historical situation in which we live. We can interpret the word of God only if we live it, or try to live it, as God wishes it to be lived—that is, in accordance with the pattern of the community from which it first came. The *lectio divina,* the "divine reading" of the monastic tradition, the slow and long meditation of monks nourished on the sacred texts throughout their life, especially during the liturgy, is much more than an exercise in recitation; it is an exercise in life. A community that is arrogant, divided, distant from the poor and humble, which severs its link with other communities united in the universal church, will have a bad spirit, a false interpretation of the sacred text, precisely because its life is not in accordance with the original and ongoing presuppositions of the text. Carlos Mesters thus presents by the following diagram the components that must be taken into account to read sacred Scripture as God wishes it to be read.

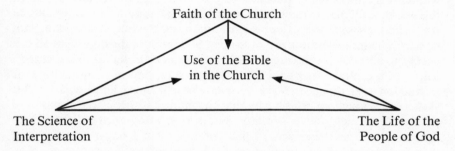

Faith of the Church

Use of the Bible in the Church

The Science of Interpretation

The Life of the People of God

Thus three forces enter into action in the explanation of the Bible. (1) The faith of the simple, with a special intuition to perceive what the word of God means; this gift of discernment comes from their baptism. (2) The science of interpreters, specialists in the sacred text, which is necessary to discern the continuity between past and present historical situations. (3) The faith of the universal church, which receives or does not receive this and that interpretation.

The theology of liberation is a fresh reading of the Bible springing from two components. First, it asks the questions raised by industrial society in the late twentieth century—questions continuous with those raised by contemporaries of Moses, the prophets, or Jesus. Second, it asks them from the situation of church base communities, which live in the midst of the oppressed and come from their situation, just as Moses, the prophets, and Jesus did. It is a reading from the point of view of the oppressed; that is why it is a theology of liberation.

THE THREE GREAT AXES OF THE THEOLOGY OF LIBERATION

There are three words in the Christian vocabulary, among the best known and the most traditional, which allow us to summarize the Christian message and to balance the different aspects of the theology of liberation. These three words are "charity," "cross," "grace."

Charity

This is the dimension of our faith that determines the final objective of the Christian mission and ensures our keeping that objective always in view. We are well aware that the mission loses its center when it is reduced to simple religious instruction or to sacramentalization. Reflection on the faith through instruction and theology, celebration of the faith through prayer and liturgy are indispensable to awake and strengthen the gospel energies that lie dormant in each of us. But to attain the final objective of the Christian mission in the world we must not stop short at that point. For the goal is, now and immediately, to install love on earth so that tomorrow, in eternity, the new creation may arise, without wrinkles or tears. We know very well that at most we can only sketch this world of solidarity; right now the terrestrial paradise is only beginning. In this current phase of the divine presence among us, the fully realized kingdom of God remains on the horizon of history. Still we have the duty, with all our energy, to initiate the construction of the kingdom by installing love on earth. This is the central axis of the Christian mission, and not cult, liturgy, or instruction, even though they are indispensable to it and an integral part of this sketch of the kingdom. This is why charity, among its other effects, leads us to politics. If our duty, our missionary task, is love, we are then obliged to help bring it about that the citizens of this world, without a single exception, can effectively become the children of one God, brothers and sisters of each other. And that will not happen with words alone. In a society whose inequalities cry out, no love is possible; rich and poor are separated from each other by fear and envy. How can we speak of love in a *favela* trembling with cold and hunger, when the houses of the city around it are muffled up to their ears and do nothing?

Love demands a radical social transformation. This transformation passes through the door of each one's conscience. It is impossible to act solely on the level of structures without reducing politics to a battle of reciprocal forces. We cannot reduce the dialectic of human history to the dialectic of nature. Struggles of force govern cosmic and animal energies. But with the human being there appears a new phenomenon: the emergence of conscience and reason. The human conflict must remain *human*; if it does not, it can bring a human being down lower than an animal. An animal can eat another but does not torture it. Humanity can use its reason either to torture or to enlarge its love in a sublime manner as far as to love its enemy. Ethics must appear in human conflicts at the risk of destroying the nature of humanity.

Still political action must be, almost by definition, an action on social structures. Hence there arises the Christian necessity of engagement in politics, since politics is nothing more or less than the art of organizing society so that its members should be happier. Pius XI said that politics is the "higher form of charity." And Paul VI dedicated his great encyclicals to "the construction of a civilization of love," that is, to the construction of a just social organization and of a culture, human even in the economic sphere, which permits love among human beings. John Paul II speaks of a "social charity." Such objectives are impossible of attainment without the highest form of politics, inspired by a refined and intelligent humanism. Certainly it is not by politics uniquely that love will be created on earth. Many other activities are also indispensable to love, as for example, art, prayer, and science. Still politics is a privileged arena where, Hegel said, the Absolute Spirit emerges and human destiny is determined.

For us, Christians, the political struggle is much more than a struggle for social justice and human rights. It is a theological struggle. We wish to have God brought back to earth. Listen to this text quoted by Saint Luke (3:4–6):

> The voice one crying in the wilderness;
> Prepare the way of the Lord,
> Make his paths straight.
> Every valley shall be lifted up
> And every mountain and hill made low;
> The crooked ways shall be straight
> And the rough places plain;
> And all flesh shall see the salvation [the glory] of God [Isa. 40:3–5].

We have there, in a symbolic fashion, one of the keys of the gospel "Prepare the way of the Lord": that is, make possible the return of God to the divine creation, among God's people, by eliminating the abysses of all sorts that separate human beings from each other—abysses of money and misery, of pride and jealousy, of despair and self-sufficiency. And then, if people do so, again God can manifest the divine name, reveal the divine glory, show salvation. There is a great mystery here. God is love; God's nature, Saint John says, is love and God can reveal the divine self only in love. A beautiful saying of the primitive church tells us: "Birds fly, fish swim, God moves in love." We struggle with all our might to "draw" God to us, conforming our world to God's nature. Certainly we cannot do that by ourselves, but under the impulse of divine grace. Nevertheless, our lack of mutual openness to the other, our softness, which denies us the energy necessary for the active struggle to break breaches into this world barricaded by the concrete of egotism and pride—these are the things that can prevent or delay the return of Emmanuel, the name that means "God with us" and also designates Jesus. Thus our Christian struggle, our life in militancy goes infinitely beyond a combat for social justice. It intends to draw the Spirit of God onto the earth, for there is no greater happiness than to love and be loved.

The Spirit of God fills everything that it touches with joy, for it is purity and fullness. It is not surprising that atheists should exist. It is not the fault of this or that atheist, but of the world, which in its totality has become insensible to grace; God is no longer "felt." Saint John tells us that the Word was made flesh, that the Word of God came to live among us, but that its own did not receive it (Jn. 1:11); and that human beings preferred darkness to light (Jn. 3:19). God can do everything in you, said a contemporary monk, but only if you wish it. And on the verge of paradox another father of the church cried out, "If there were more saints, there would be fewer earthquakes!" It is certain in any case that the saints, beings who are good, are breaches by which the grace of God enters into the world; and that through their touch evil flees away, even physical evils. They pacify nature. Remember Saint Francis. But a world of nonsharing and nonlove is, by essence, atheist.

It is discouraging to see how deeply Christians have fixed in their heads a pagan theology not much different from that of a Roman at the time of Julius Caesar. They think unconscioulsy that God is all-powerful in the sense that Jupiter was supposed to be. In that view God need only cast a lightning-bolt from divine omnipotence for all the problems of humanity to be resolved. Under these conditions, the existence of evil becomes incomprehensible. If God can do everything, why does God let babies die of hunger? But in fact the omnipotence of the God of Christians has nothing to do with the omnipotence of Jupiter. Certainly, God can do everything. By nature God is all-powerful. But God's love limits that power. God's love, like all true love, does not impose itself. In a manner of speaking, love is weak. It can do everything, even overcome death, *if one opens the door to it.* The Apocalypse says, "Behold, I stand at the door and knock; if anyone hears my voice and opens the door, I will enter into him and dine with him, and he with me" (Rev. 3:20). The evil will of human beings limits the power of God. At Nazareth, the gospel tells us, Jesus could not do any miracle because of the people's lack of faith (Mk. 6:5-6). In a manner of speaking, *God has been expelled from creation.* Grace has taken flight from the earth, not because it wished to, but because human wickedness left it no more room. The prophet Ezekiel, in chapters 8 and 11, describes how the glory of God, the *kabod Yahweh,* abandons Jerusalem because there is no longer a place for it in this corrupt city. And so humanity is plunged into darkness, into shadows, into sadness, into despair. No politics or human force by itself is able to bring the grace and the glory of God back to earth. Only love can draw it.

At the end of the day, the struggle of the Christian, the struggle for the kingdom of God, looks like a hard-fought battle, an agony, to destroy those obstacles that are blocking the return of grace. For John the Baptist, the Christian is a "bulldozer" which must make straight the ways of the Lord, fill up the valleys, and make the mountians low (Lk. 3:4-6).

The Cross

Let us speak now of a second characteristic of an authentic theology of liberation: the cross. The Christian hope turns with all its heart toward the transformation, or rather, the transfiguration, of this world. But on the earth rises also the cross of Christ. This means that the salvation of the world has come up against fanatical resistances. Jesus wished to draw human beings out of their egotism, to open them to the grace of God and thus to release a great movement of love, which would also have changed structures. He gave it the name of the kingdom of God. To do that, he wished to rectify his people's religion; to recall it to its original meaning, that of the prophets; and also to complete it. But he came up against the hatred of the rulers and the incomprehension of his disciples. Finally, isolated, he ended his life on the cross, assassinated. The disciple is not above his or her master. To be a disciple, to follow the way of Jesus, is to occupy oneself with this world, with all its carnal stupidities, to teach it how to come back to life. The zeal that pushes us to occupy ourselves with the unloved, the mistreated, the oppressed of every sort who fill the planet has no other motivation. We wish also to save the rich and powerful ones of this world so that all people, abandoning positions of superiority or inferiority, should become sisters and brothers. But all those who stretch their arms around the entire body of human problems inevitably embrace the cross of Christ. To change the established disorder, whether in politics, economics, or morality, is forcibly to disturb, irritate, provoke; then comes opposition, hatred. Thus the prophets also were treated.

Among the first Christians, the Corinthians, brought into a high pitch of enthusiasm by the spiritual gifts they had received (the famous charismata: speaking with tongues, prophecy, healing the sick), almost succumbed to the temptation of forgetting the cross of Christ. They thought they were already in paradise, and supposed that their mission in the world was to be accomplished in this false enthusiasm, this spurious fervor that ignored the harshness of sacrifice. Corinthians, how quick you are to forget this earth where the cross of Christ is implanted! The same is true for us today. And so that we should never forget the struggles of this earth in a false mysticism, the apostle Paul preached to the Corinthians and preaches to us today what scholars call the eschatology of the cross—the understanding of the last things, which come about through the cross, as in Jürgen Moltmann's "theology of hope." So Paul writes, "For I determined to know nothing among you except Jesus Christ and him crucified" (1 Cor. 2:2); "But I preach a Christ crucified, a stumbling-block to the Jews and folly to the Gentiles, but to those who are called, both Jews and Greeks, Christ the power of God and the wisdom of God" (1 Cor. 1:23-24). That is, apparently the cross is the opposite to what Jews and Greeks expect from God. The first believed in a glorious revelation of the Messiah, and the cross is an apparent defeat; the others are wholly turned toward a higher wisdom, and the cross seems an absurdity, which brings no solution derived from wisdom to the problems of this world. So we must rise above a superficial idea of our mission. It will not be with a few embraces or a sentimental prayer that a resolution will be found for the class struggle or the war in El Salvador, for example, or more generally that the children of God, scattered by sin and abandoned like sheep without a shepherd, will be gathered together.

Grace

Finally, we come to the word "grace." There is one further excess that can derail our mission of liberation and good news: to presume that human force alone (through a political party, a trade union, an organized class, the good management of society, scientific knowledge) will be able to overcome the structures of oppression that crush us. For according to our Christian understanding, the human being is like a great tree. By its taproot it is united to the source of being: God. Just as the human body receives blood from the heart, so the human being receives the flux of its most intimate existence from its creator. For us Christians and for many followers of other religions, in the end the human malady is religious: that is, so long as the relation with God for all and each one has not been restored in all its intended depth and correctness, new structures of oppression, individual or collective, mental or physical, will inevitably recur. That is why without grace, without a spirit of communion and a special civic generosity, socialism falls inevitably into bureaucracy.

We name "egotism," or better, "ill will," the refusal to enter into relation with others and to create communitarian structures in which each one slowly learns not to profit from the other. A social structure can be materially efficacious, but without this spirit (or grace) of communion, it will be inevitably destined to a dead end. Hence arises the need for an extreme zeal and for the attention at every instant to remain open to God, to search for God at every hour, like one who is searching for the source of life. That is only a sane realism! We are well aware that we can restore neither our relation to God nor our social relations ("making straight the ways of the Lord"), unless the creator takes the first steps in our direction. Certainly we do a lot of work, we are not passive or inactive; but how shall we find the right way unless the maker comes to search out the creatures who teeter on the edge of the abyss, and who constantly slip and stumble in their difficult ascent? This is what we call "grace": the antecedent act of love by which God takes the first step in our direction, if we call upon God ever so little and let the divine enter our life. Grace increases good will, and good will calls on grace.

So love, the cross, and grace mutually attract and complete each other. Many theologians and pastors insist with exaggeration on one aspect or another and fall into imbalance. To try to transform the world without grace leads one into the will to power. Mysticism without struggle falls into sentimentalism, a spiritual addiction. A demanding moralism, a militancy that sacrifices everything to the cause, ceases to be love and therefore ceases to be good news.

THEOLOGY OF LIBERATION AND BASE COMMUNITIES

The places where this theology of liberation exists in practice are the church base communities, especially flourishing in Brazil. Perhaps here we can make a helpful comparison. Europe was evangelized first by the Irish monks of Saint Columba, then by the Benedictines, between the fifth and tenth centuries. At that time, vast stretches of Europe were covered by a thick forest. Celtic or Germanic tribes occupied its territory. This European vegetation was a wild and savage one. What did these monks do? They built their monasteries where routes of communication crossed, at the confluence of rivers, on the cols of mountains. They cut down the forests with prudence, they broke up the ground and cultivated it, and *also* opened hostelries for travelers and pilgrims, infirmaries for the sick, libraries, schools. If we think about it, we may say that those monasteries had a role not unlike that of our base communities. It is true that not all monasteries today are necessarily models for the renewal of the church, nor the most inspired ones. But still in our own days the monastery is a group of fifty to a hundred persons, men or women, who practice the complete sharing of goods, after the pattern of the Jerusalem community (Acts 2:42–47; 4:32–34)—the model and inspiration for every renewal of the church. These men and these women seek to follow the gospel *au pied de la lettre*. Their monastery is nothing other than an association of the baptized, not necessarily or for the most part priests; originally there were only a few priests in the monasteries to conduct the liturgical service, the majority of the monks being lay. They have freely decided to commit all their strength to carry each other along and to help each other learn how to live as ones risen from the dead, beginning always from the present hour.

In fact, the objective of all Christian life should have been none other than this. It is clear, then, that the monastery has an essentially religious goal. True religion always seeks to incarnate goodness, bounty, and beauty in history so that all may be happy. The religious dimensions of a human being is the one that most promotes creative dreaming, imagination, above all the hope of a new world, which we are commissioned to build through life with our creator. True religion does not limit itself to celebrating in the liturgy what it hopes for. It also acts: it arouses, strengthens, and organizes the transforming and evangelizing energies that operate in every human being, to focus them on a historical project. We may say most correctly that the roots of great civilizations are mystical before they are political.

Today's communities are centers of integration in the midst of disintegration! Like the monasteries of other times, our base communities are "religious events," which seek to arouse human beings to the enterprise of building a new world. But the insane vegetation that we are trying to humanize and civilize is not a mere impenetrable forest like the European one at its historic origins. The Amazonian forest has been called an *inferno verde,* a green hell, partially in error. The true green hell we are called on to humanize is the industrial world, which has grown up beside the Amazon and elsewhere, the savage jungle of devouring industries, which at the same time utilize and crush the human being. Our adoration and meditation in face of the word of God, the celebration of our faith in the heart of our base communities afford us a glimpse of the new world whose rosy fingers dawn on the horizon of history; that hope is what impels us to raise up great popular movements; to demand clinics, day-care centers, sewer systems; to create a Centro de Defesa dos Direitos Humanos, trade-union actions, political actions. Behind these modest steps of those stumbling as they try to find themselves lies a great ambition: to save the industrial world from destruction—or, with greater accuracy, from disintegration.

Dom Helder Camara says that there are two bombs that can annihilate humanity: the A bomb and the M bomb, the atomic bomb and the misery bomb. It is instructive to note that a nuclear weapon generates physically the effect that industrial society, as it is organized today, generates spiritually. Both *disintegrate*: they make atomic constituents explode and send out insane fission products in every direction. Now our human reality is like this: it has been built up little by little into a highly specialized cultural, social, and ethical organism. It is complex but not necessarily complicated. Something can be simple and complex at the same time—in fact the two go best together. The more life and consciousness there exist, Teilhard de Chardin says, the more complexity we find, delicate balances, masterworks of harmony. The result of synthesis (at once complex and simple) is the opposite from that of syncretism (complicated and built of elements arbitrarily juxtaposed).

Our industrial society, overwhelmingly oriented to the economic side of production, takes into consideration far too little the *quality* of human relations in work or in consumption. To stuff oneself full is not a human act. Its twin results are misery and affluence. The miserable have nothing to live by and the affluent no longer know why they live. To the first Marx opens his mouth to speak; to the second, Nietzsche.

Even worse, the specialization of labor, the endless dissection of tasks breaks up time, breaks up actions; it brutally uproots the rural masses of the third world from their land and their cultural heritage; through arbitrary work-shifts it separates the father from his children, housemate from housemate; above all it creates a really tragic separation between production and consumption, where the goods produced bear no relation to the basic needs of the largest part of humanity. In short, such a society "atomizes" everything. This social disintegration creates unsupportable tensions; and atomic weapons (as Olivier Clément has written) merely translate visibly this perverse tendency to disintegration hidden at the heart of history. We were just speaking of Marx and Nietzsche. What do Christians have to say? Their response is more relevant than ever. They say that at the heart of reality exists that divine which is this indispensable power of synthesis. With the great Feodor Dostoevsky they speak of the "synthetic" or unifying nature of Christ. They explain further that evil cannot be reduced to its economic, psychological, or political dimensions, although each of these is real.

Certainly the world is good, so is industry, and good is greater than evil. The invention of the machine and great scientific discoveries are good in themselves. They have prolonged and aided life everywhere. There are more persons on earth than ever before, above all in the third world. But at what a cost! The current tensions in industrial society are so great, in both East and West, that it has become obviously necessary, at the risk of death and explosion, to change the regime. There exists then, Christians say, a mystery of iniquity, demonic forces of disintegration hidden in the heart of history. Christians are not Manichaeans and they do not believe in a principle of evil equal in power and existence to the principle of good. Evil in the biblical understanding is only a parasite attached to a living thing, nothingness attached to being. But still with power. "Devil" in Greek is *diabolos,* the one who throws false accusations, who destroys unity. Paul writes, "Our struggle is not against flesh and blood ['normal' human powers], but against Principalities, against Powers, against the world-rulers of the present darkness, against spiritual powers of evil in heavenly places" (Eph. 6:12).

This book, wherein are collected some texts born haphazardly from the urgencies of apostolic action in Brazil, could also be called *The Battle of Jesus*—a battle against the demonic forces of destruction. These pages, and others (See Barbé, *Teologia da pastoral operaria: experiencia de Osasco* [Petropolis: Vozes, 1983]—a Christology in simple language for worker-activists), intend to prove that Jesus' struggle was above all a religious struggle, so that the creature might, so to speak, through a free gift and a desperate struggle, acquire grace. But this battle to acquire grace, far from loosening our links with history, on the contrary integrates the human being in a manner at once intense and harmonious, and also painful, with the struggles of this world. The "strategy of grace" is extremely original. It embraces, in a unique power of salvation, the flower and the electronic brain, the amorous passion of man and woman, atomic energy. It forgets *nothing* of the fundamental necessities of the human person and adapts itself to each and to all, in a manner at once gentle and strong. How could it be otherwise when grace, having created humanity and all else, is by definition that which is most human in the earth?

FAITH AND POLITICS

We can now enter on a last question in this preliminary chapter, a question around which much ink has already been spilled. We shall do so by means of a diagram and very simple words, which we use in the base communities of Brazil when we speak of these subjects.

Commentary on " 'Theological' Diagram of a Base Community "

In this diagram we see the pyramid of misery in Brazil. Bread, with everything that it stands for, is not shared; and without bread, life is not possible.

The Messianic energy of the risen Christ, who confronts and surmounts death, is concentrated in the bread of the word, the bread of the Eucharist, the bread of fraternal love. The energy of Jesus always passes through his brothers and sisters, "When two or three are gathered together in my name . . ."; never outside fraternal love through an individualistic channel. This Messianic energy is what gives us the strength to sacrifice our life to arrive at the sharing of everything that bread represents: nourishment, the necessary goods of life, whether material, ethical, or cultural.

The community is the *place of celebration of the faith.* There we renew the memory of Jesus; there we receive the strength of his sacrifice, the luminous awareness created by his word and his "ideas," as well as the strength of our brothers and sisters with whom we speak after the Mass. This strength must not stay contained inside the community. It goes out to a battle in the streets, to arrive at this civilization of love of which Paul IV spoke. The *place where one's faith is lived* is not the temple, but one's group in the *bairro,* the factory, office, street, family, union, political party. It is with these instruments that we try to transform history and society so that they should become a sketch (and of course no more than a sketch) of that kingdom of God, which Jesus came to announce and for which he sacrificed himself.

It is useful to distinguish the celebration of faith and the practice of faith without separating them. We practice what we celebrate, not in the church but in daily life. But it is indispensable to celebrate what we practice, in the church or elsewhere, constantly renewing the memory of Jesus with our Christian brothers and sisters, combatants for the same kingdom. If we no longer celebrate, no longer pray, if we abandon the celebration of the Holy Supper, little by little gospel energies die in us and the battle for the world ceases to be a battle for the kingdom. We begin with much energy to build the tower of Babel.

The question about the relation between faith and politics is often wrongly asked, and that is why it is insoluble. At the beginning of this chapter we recalled that the axis of evangelization is charity—that is, action and battle, under the impulse of grace, to render love possible in this world. In the diagram we have symbolized the world by material bread, which is here the sum total of goods of every kind necessary for life, including symbolic goods, but with physical nourishment first of all. The spiritual act (that is, one enabled by the Spirit), which consists in loving one's counterpart, makes greed impossible. We want to give everything; we do not seek how to do good but how to love, which is quite different, as Iribarne has said. Those who do good to others "already have their reward," because they correspond to the ideal image that they have formed of themselves. All the Pharisees of all times are in that camp. To love, however, is an impulse of sympathy and communion where we no longer are in search of ourselves. This sympathy is what leads a human being with a heart to become a revolutionary. Such ones wish that they themselves could share and that society also could share. As soon as they feel that, they enter into an obstinate struggle where they meet fanatical resistances; because, structurally, our society is not one of communion.

Thus the act of evangelization includes politics but goes far beyond politics. No means are excluded for letting love invade the earth, to change society: among them of course are political instruments, and many others as well.

"Theological" Diagram of a Base Community

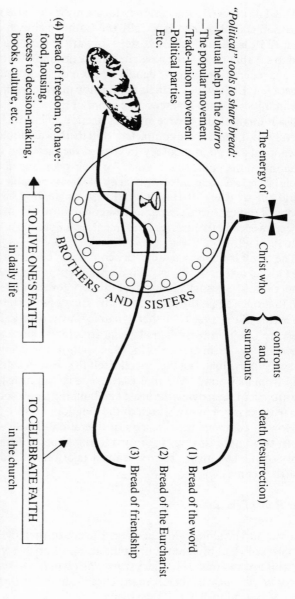

The energy of

Christ who { confronts and surmounts } death (resurrection)

(1) Bread of the word

(2) Bread of the Eucharist

(3) Bread of friendship

BROTHERS AND SISTERS

TO LIVE ONE'S FAITH

in daily life

TO CELEBRATE FAITH

in the church

The energy of the risen Christ, who confronts and surmounts death, passes through the three types of bread—the word, the Eucharist, and friendship—to give us the strength to share material bread and to found a civilization of love

"Political" tools to share bread:
— Mutual help in the *bairro*
— The popular movement
— Trade-union movement
— Political parties
Etc.

(4) Bread of freedom, to have: food, housing, access to decision-making, books, culture, etc.

1 %
4 %
15 %
30 %
50 %

} 20% with 80% of the wealth

} 80% with 20% of the wealth

The division of bread in Brazil: a civilization of nonsharing

THREE STEPS FORWARD OF THE CHURCH

May I be allowed a digression to locate my reflections more accurately? The Christian churches, and especially the Catholic church awakened by Vatican Council II, have taken decisive steps forward in recent years. It is no exaggeration to say that these steps have shaken the ground of our society and continue to have repercussions in the depths of our individual and collective existences. Nicaragua, El Salvador with its archbishop martyr, Latin America and its base communities are in a real sense the proof of this.

No human effort is free of imperfection. That includes the theology of liberation. It needs to be completed. Still there is no doubt that it is "holy." It is a beautiful and good theology, in view of the facts that it was born out of the situation of the poor; that it exists for their sake; and above all, that its major intention is love, to render the charity of Christ possible on earth, to make the world the dwelling of the children of a single God, wherever necessary by means of radical social changes. How could those who make love their essential objective deceive themselves fundamentally? For God is love, and in God there is no lie at all.

The result is there. A systematic, conscious, and critical effort to "recover" the Gospel text as Jesus spoke it and thought it has been shown adequate to ensure that the gospel and its revolutionary force will be restored to the poor; and that once again the dynamic of the kingdom will be visible in the midst of the events of our age. Then that dynamic shakes off the dust that concealed the presence of sin in persons and social structures. Once again the beast of the Apocalypse, the sin of the world, which puts its roots down into the conscience of every individual, but incarnates itself in social structures, begins to howl in pain from its wound. And thus is awakened a fantastic hope, a Project Hope: the project of destroying the beast and building a new society, which will never, it is true, be more than a sketch of the kingdom.

How to *complete* the theology of liberation? I believe that the church has taken two important steps forward in this time, but that now, in these final years of the twentieth century, it must take yet a third, and possibly also a fourth. Let me explain.

The Role of the Laity

The church, along with the great European theologians, inspired by their peoples who had just come out from the most horrible war of all times, first of all rediscovered this elementary truth: *the church is in the world and the world is not in the church.* Therefore the church should serve the world and not the other way around. That was the theme of the conciliar constitution *Gaudium et Spes.* It marked the end of the concept of "Christendom": that is, a society where political institutions are directly picked up by religious ideology and pressed into its service.

Furthermore this church, which is in the world, is also the people of God:

here also we have taken from our biblical inheritance an extremely simple idea. That means that every baptized person, by baptism, has a task, a responsibility, a ministry. Baptism is our diploma for mission. Just like all citizens in a free country, all baptized persons can ask for the floor in the assembly and express their opinion. It is no longer the case that the bishops (or the priests) alone have the right to speak or give basic directions; in the domain of thought as well as of action the door is thrown wide open to those who are called "lay," collectively the *laos,* the people of God. The combatants for the kingdom are rediscovering an individual equality, even though the gifts and tasks of each are different. This discovery marked the end of clericalism, at least potentially. Let us hear the texts of Vatican Council II:

> And if by the will of Christ some are made teachers, dispensers of mysteries [the sacraments], and shepherds on behalf of others, yet all share a true *equality* with regard to the activity common to all the faithful for the building up of the Body of Christ (*Dogmatic Constitution on the Church,* no. 32) (See *The Documents of Vatican II,* ed. Walter M. Abbott, S.J. [New York: Guild Press, 1966].)

And again:

> The laity derived the right and duty with respect to the apostolate from their union with Christ their Head. Incorporated into Christ's Mystical Body through baptism and strengthened by the power of the Holy Spirit through confirmation, they are assigned to the apostolate by the Lord himself [and not by the hierarchy!] (*The Layman's Call to the Apostolate,* no. 3) [Ibid.].

The tone was exactly the opposite in official texts of the Catholic hierarchy at the beginning of this century. Pius X, in the encyclical *Vehementer Nos* of 1910, wrote:

> The church by nature is essentially an *unequal* society, that is, a society comprising two categories of persons, the Pastors and the flock; those who occupy a rank in the hierarchy and the multitude of the faithful. So distinct are these categories that with the pastoral body only rests the necessary right and authority for promoting the end of the society and directing all its members toward that end. The one duty of the multitude is to allow themselves to be led, and, like a docile flock, to follow the Pastors (Claudia Caren, ed., *The Papal Encyclicals,* 1903–1939, vol. 3 [Raleigh, N.C.: McGrath Publishing Company, 1981]).

And Dom Guéranger, the renewer of the Benedictine order, wrote in turn:

> The faithful people has only the duty of submitting itself to its hierarchical leaders. The mass of the people is in essence subject to government

and radically incapable of exercising any spiritual authority, either directly or by delegation. . . .

In fact, attempts at a restoration of clericalism are constantly underway, especially at this very time. Nevertheless, those attempts cannot alter the fact that the impulse has been given to a great missionary effort for which all the baptized are responsible as an integral body.

The Latin American Contribution

There is blowing through the world and through the church an impetuous wind that some call a tempest and would like very much to abate. As a result, the churches of Europe have lost a little breath; they have handed the torch (one might say) to the churches of Latin America. European Christianity, especially in Western Europe, is in the process of giving an answer to its own fundamental questions. Not many are aware of it. If the Christians of Latin America are more responsive to the questions of Marx, who challenges Christianity to build a more just society, the Christians of the "rich" countries are trying to respond to the challenge of Nietzsche about the meaning of life: is it truly nothingness that is at the center of the world—or the divine, the fullness of being? France is neither Latin America nor Poland. The hour of Africa has not yet struck. Much further ahead yet lies the encounter with Asian cultures, especially the Chinese, and then we shall see other revolutions in Christian thought and action. And what revolutions!

What then have the Christians of Latin America contributed since Vatican Council II? Here also an elementary truth, which we have tried to lay out in this chapter: evangelization does not consist solely in explaining the word of God, in praying or receiving the sacraments: *evangelization consists of transforming society* so that it may become in reality the home of the children of one God, so that charity may become possible on earth. Evangelization is love. This "rediscovery" inevitably threw Christians into the "obedient and radical discipleship" *(discipulado obediente e radical,* Meeting of the Evangelical Churches at Uaxtepec) made concrete at the Medellín and Puebla conferences. I shall always remember Ernesto Cardenal at Puebla, answering the question of a woman journalist about his political commitment as a priest: "Madam, it was my religious faith that led me to the revolution, not my politics." What he meant can be understood. It is mere truth: in Latin America revolutionary discussion is religious discussion and not primarily political discussion. God said, "Let us create heaven and earth and let human beings increase there." Then the earth (factories included!) belongs to all. The first Christians put everything under common ownership; let us put the riches of the industrial world and the means of production under the control of all. That deeply disconcerts both Marxists and ruling classes. Our current task is to move on to readjustments on the philosophical level in order to arrive at a true union of the democrats of the Left. In particular the Marxists must reevaluate, by another standard, the religious phenomenon if they wish to participate in the revolutionary movement.

Nonviolent Revolution

At this point the necessity arises of taking a third step forward, and of taking it without delay if we wish to follow the Way (the first Christians called themselves the followers of the Way) that the gospel seems to indicate. Here is the problem. Whoever seeks to transform society is in effect getting ready for a social war. In any war weapons are necessary. It would be naïve not to inquire about the means of conflict, and irresponsible not to learn to wield these arms. Earlier in this chapter we were speaking about the necessity of a theology and a pastoral practice of conflict to complete the theology of liberation. This must mean that, for us, there are weapons that belong specifically to the poor and the little ones of the world; and that the *political* translation of Jesus' commandment "Love your enemies" must be implemented as an intense preparation of the people's cadres, which emerge from the base communities, in view of the coming struggle. A war cannot be improvised. If we throw ourselves deliberately into a social war, *as we are doing,* everything tells us we must prepare the arms of this combat—and with the utmost urgency.

As for myself and my colleagues, we have made the choice of active nonviolence, *firmeza permanente* (unceasing firmness), as we call it in Brazil. Dom Helder Camara translates it "liberating moral pressure." Toward this end, we have invested much time, and many efforts and reflections have been made by many other groups, to work out the manner of living our conflict. For example, to the best of my knowledge, Paz Y Justicia was the only organization to propose an international action in El Salvador *before* the war broke out. (This body coordinates the nonviolent groups of Latin America; its principal organizer is Adolfo Perez Esquivel, Nobel peace laureate in 1980. The action was the "international days" planned for July 1979. Unfortunately, and in my opinion erroneously, these days were canceled.)

Active nonviolence, as Mahatma Gandhi and Martin Luther King, Jr., practiced it, at present is generating many actions in Latin America, although of limited and sporadic character. It is also generating a body of theological reflection. We shall speak about it in a later chapter. In any case, the theology of liberation must think about nonviolence—that is, about the theology of conflict—if it is to press its original intuitions to the end.

Without beginning this discussion, we note merely that very frequently the Brazilian peasants, descendants of Indians and oppressed blacks, have spontaneously been living this theology of nonviolence in practice. It is the only way that they have survived. For how could they have confronted with their few weapons an enemy infinitely better armed? It would not have made sense. Certainly, there are today and there have been people's wars; but this tendency to violent combat must not hide the other tendency, also very much in evidence—that of the nonviolent struggle of the poor of the continent. Let us take this fact under advisement: the prevalent theology of liberation is still too often a theology *about* the poor and not a theology *from* the poor.

Overcoming the Tendency to Domination

What would be the fourth step forward necessary to carry out a more complete initiative? The question can reasonably be put to us. Suppose that nonviolent struggle reaches its goal, suppose that the base communities generate people's cadres to arrive at a participatory society, suppose that new social structures permit a higher level of sharing and therefore of love. There still remains the question at which everybody stumbles. How build socialism that does not fall into bureaucracy? How create a society that in actuality overcomes the various types of domination? This was the topic of the fourth continental meeting for nonviolence in Latin America, held at Riobamba, Ecuador. Other groups also are concerning themselves with this question, to which there are no easy answers, no quick solutions.

3

Political Consequences of Redemption: The Trinity and Politics

Here we shall study the different theological aspects of salvation. We shall try to relate the theology of redemption to the theologies of the creation, of the resurrection, and of the Trinity, so as better to encompass the fullness of salvation in Jesus Christ, seen under its various aspects.

THEOLOGY OF REDEMPTION AND THEOLOGY OF CREATION

It is impossible that the political activity of Christians should not exist. It is a historical reality. In fact, how could so great a body of men and women not influence the course of events? But then, how does it happen that so often the political attitude of Christians has been reactionary as to its objectives and so unevangelical as to its methods? In my opinion, one of the reasons is a kind of ideological catastrophe that has been introduced into the world of Christian thought: *a separation or dichotomy between the theology of creation and the theology of redemption.* More exactly, the effects of redemption have stopped being applied to the "entire creation" (Rom. 8:22), which still "waits anxiously for the revelation of the children of God . . . groaning in travail together" (Rom. 8:19–22). This perspective of an integral salvation of the created order—flesh and spirit, cosmic and individual, human, animal, vegetable and mineral—which Paul renews in the most authentic biblical tradition, was progressively abandoned by Christians.

In fact, the connection between creation and salvation is energetically affirmed by the Bible. In the words of Gustavo Gutiérrez, in *A Theology of Liberation: History, Politics, and Salvation* (trans. and ed. Sister Caridad Inda and John Eagleson, Maryknoll, N.Y.: Orbis, 1973), "The Bible does not deal with creation in order to satisfy philosophic concerns regarding the origin of the world. . . . Biblical faith is, above all, faith in a God who reveals himself through historical events, a God who saves in history" (p. 154). The creation is the first saving act of God, who out of nothing brings Being into existence. This

41

creation presupposes a plan by God, which is to be realized by stages and therefore is to constitute the web of history: "He chose us . . . *before the creation of the world* to be holy and blameless in his presence, . . . having determined *in advance* that we should be his adoptive children in Jesus Christ" (Eph. 1:4–5).

At every instant the creation stands in need of the saving action of God. "Thus says the Lord who *created* you, O Jacob, and who formed you, O Israel: 'Do not be afraid, because I am occupied with your *redemption*. I have called you by my name, you are mine. When you pass through the waters, I will be with you, . . . when you walk through fire you shall not be burned . . . ; for I am the Lord your God . . . , your Savior' " (Isa. 43:1–3). This saving action is necessary because the entire creation is in process of giving birth, and is on a journey: "For behold, I am creating new heavens and a new earth; the former things shall not be remembered, they shall no more come to mind" (Isa. 65:17; cf. 66:22; Rev. 21:1–5). As in Romans 8, the work of salvation in the creation is beginning to happen here and now on this earth and in the interior of our history. To quote again from Gutiérrez: "By working, transforming the world, breaking out of servitude, building a just society, and assuming his destiny in history, man forges himself" (*A Theology of Liberation,* p. 159).

Unfortunately, Christians have had a tendency to forget the close link between creation and redemption. Theology has had a tendency to say that the material or "fleshly" aspect of salvation (this new earth and this new human being) belong to the future and to the other side of death. Without absolutely denying that the new creation begins here below, in fact traditional theology has not put the emphasis on this transfiguration, by the grace of Christ, of matter and flesh just we know them in this current phase of the creation. In practice, this tendency has resulted in an actual opposition between creation and redemption, as if the latter did not start to become effective until the moment when the former ceased to exist. "The victory of the Redeemer has seemed to require the defeat of the Creator," wrote J. M. Muller in *The Gospel of Nonviolence.* In fact, if the Messianic promises relating to the new creation and the new human being do not have in any way a beginning of existence here and now, if everything is reserved for the other world, then the sufferings of this life have no other meaning than to render it a valley of tears to put the souls of the faithful to test.

How did we come to restrict so drastically the biblical meaning of salvation? In the first place, the sphere of redemption has been reduced to the human being alone, as such; it has been forgotten that the totality of the material creation—plants, animals, cosmic forces, in short, the entire universe—also is part of the world saved by Christ. In some mysterious way, all these material creatures are subject to his saving action. But this truth is no longer a certainty for us. What all the great animistic religions knew—that everything has a soul—we have forgotten. We have forgotten the Holy Spirit. Do we any longer spontaneously wonder what value an animal has in the eyes of the Lord Jesus? The consequence is that if the material creation no longer belongs to the sphere of redemption for us, we are permitted not merely to use, but now to abuse the resources of nature. What then prevents us from destroying the forests and plains that still survive in the polluted outskirts of the great cities in order to build a monstrous airport there? The limitation of the effects of the redemption to human beings alone is, in this writer's opinion, the theological cause of all the kinds of violence that are done to our natural environment. If the material world is removed from the influence of redemption, it is then profane. If it is profane, no wonder that it is profaned! (So Olivier Clément, in *Questions sur l'homme*, Paris: Stock, 1972.)

Furthermore, Christians have forgotten that history and human society are the highest manifestations of God's permanent and ceaseless act of creation. All the more so, then, has it become impossible for us to imagine that these realities should be subject to the redemption of Christ. We have forgotten that history needs to be saved; and that it is holy, not because human beings are holy but because, even through the most disgraceful events and beings, there still is manifested the splendor of grace, that is, of the divine action that creates beauty. We have lost the understanding that, if God acted in history in the times of Abraham, Isaac, and Jacob, that same God must continue still to do the same today. It has become impossible for us to discern that politics and history, the realm of the collective, are also the place of divine revelation. We think that redemption produces its effects solely in individuals, in the privacy of their conscience. Centuries of preaching have put into our heads the false idea, expressed by Paul Ricoeur, that "Sin is abundant in the external, while grace is superabundant in the internal."

Hence this very serious consequence: if the redemption does not affect the creation in all its aspects—the physical world, history, human society—if it does not shine its rays into the entire cosmos, then God has absolutely nothing to do with the struggles of this world. God becomes the great truant from History; and consequently politics belongs exclusively to the domain of Caesar, who can exercise his power without any control, without subjecting himself to the divine. There is then no cause for surprise when the enemies of the Lamb cry out, "We have no king but Caesar" (Jn. 19:15). Why this astonishment when the heads of states use the weapons of Machiavelli to govern the human city? As soon as the social and political aspects of the redemption are no longer recognized, the kingship of Christ is limited by the disciples of Jesus themselves to the world of souls and of individual sentiment. An amazing castration!

For Christians, the separation between creation and redemption has therefore been tragic; for they have been forced to put their confidence much more in the weapons of this world (money, force, diplomacy), in order to fortify their positions in the midst of the nations, than in the royalty of Christ. And in fact, if the redemption of Jesus does not reach as far as politics, then the church must use the weapons of this world and not the weapons of faith to live in society. From this situation arise all the theologies about the "lesser of two evils" and about the just war of Saint Thomas Aquinas, which are not, as a matter of fact, Christian theologies at all. We have reached the point of which

Muller speaks: "Not merely did Christians acquire enemies, they became enemies to each other." Christian peoples passed their time in fighting each other "for a just cause," and their bishops passed their time in blessing the cannons.

Saint Bernard, oblivious to the fact that Muslims belonged to the creation of God, unleashed the Franks against Islam and undertook to justify the war by calling it a "crusade." Today, in Latin America, "Christian civilization" is defended by weapons in the hand; and the doctrine of "national security" is one of the final results of the theological catastrophe I have been describing. The tragedy of Christian history has been that the sacraments have been able to purify the disciples of Jesus of their evil thoughts, but not of their evil actions. Even Peter (the See of Rome) during the centuries frequently succumbs to the third temptation of the desert, that of power (Mt. 4:8–10): exercising the supreme magistracy, and a kind of spiritual dictatorship to "force human beings to do what is right." "We have accepted Rome and Caesar," said Dostoevsky's Grand Inquisitor, "we have proclaimed that we are the sole kings of the whole earth." "The Roman Empire," wrote Berdyaev, "became Christian in its symbolism, but, in recompense, the Church became imperial." So the work of Jesus was corrected in this fashion, and the church of the martyrs became the church of the torturers, in Muller's words. It was no problem for the state to take as its concubine a church that no longer dared to pronounce what things belonged only to God. The Beast of the Apocalypse was baptized, but not converted. They were not many who down through the centuries became aware of the imposture. And those who did nearly always paid with their blood for this crime of conscientization.

THEOLOGY OF REDEMPTION AND
THEOLOGY OF THE RESURRECTION

It is impossible to understand the motivation of the Christian's political activity, unless we draw the practical consequences from the major happening of Christianity: the resurrection of Jesus. If creation and redemption reach the culmination of their effects in the resurrection; if salvation presupposes that human beings are delivered from the ultimate evil of death; then it is necessary for us, in order to be consistent with our faith and hope, to act firmly in this world to help our society escape from the forces of death that oppress it. Political liberation is therefore an integral part of salvation.

Resurrection is the masterpiece of redemption and the summit of creation; it is identical with salvation when salvation attains its final objective: victory over death. By the resurrection, creation is in truth saved totally and in all its parts; and we see, in the light of what happened to Jesus, that matter and flesh are called to participate in a new life and in the glorification that the Spirit of God produces in things when it is given in its fullness. For one of the meanings of the resurrection of Jesus is to tell us that a particular segment of matter, namely, the body of Christ, has entered into the divine sphere, through the fullness of the

Spirit. Is it necessary to mention here that, in biblical language, "spiritual" does not mean "disincarnate, without body," but "filled with the Holy Spirit"? Thus at least in Jesus, who is this part of the creation that has arrived at its fulfillment, we see that the cosmos in its entirety is called, as Paul says, to escape from vanity and corruption to participate in the glorious liberty of the children of God.

And the same prodigious energy that snatched Christ away from death also made him "sit down at the right hand [of God] . . . far above all principality and authority and power . . ." (Eph. 1:20–21); that is, above all the forces of evil that dominate the world and bring it to death. And we who have been "rescued from the power of darkness" and "transported into the kingdom of his well-beloved Son" (Col. 1:13) therefore receive the force, by following Jesus our leader, to turn evil back and to rescue the world—our society, our history, our civilization—from the darkness and the anarchic forces that destroy them, that kill them.

It is obvious that this will not happen automatically. The Christian faith presupposes combatants. The Christian faith is not merely a "theory"—that is, a contemplation, a meditation, or the hearing of a message—but a "practice," that is, an action, a task of transforming the world where we live, a "praxis" as we often say today. And what can this praxis be? What does the resurrection of Jesus suggest on this topic? Without entering into details of exegesis, we can say that one of the truths suggested by the appearances of the risen Christ to his disciples is that in the new world, which God is starting to make together with us, there will be no further obstacles to *communication* and *communion* among human beings. In fact, nothing holds back the risen Jesus, neither distance, nor time, nor material obstacles, nor evil. He enters into the dining room when the doors are closed. He comes up to the disciples who are walking, discouraged, to Emmaus, and little by little makes himself known to them after having restored their courage and hope, that is, their faith. From time to time he appears visibly; and once recognized, when the "recognition" necessary for faith has happened, he disappears.

In all these encounters it is not a spirit that manifests itself in this way, but a being of flesh and bones, who eats, drinks, walks, speaks, allows himself to be touched. One thing alone presents an obstacle to Jesus: not distance in time or space, not even fragility of faith—we have seen how he tolerates it in the disciples of Emmaus and with infinite tenderness undertakes to heal them of their discouragement. The one thing that creates an obstacle is *being closed*: the proud self-sufficiency that refuses love—that is, which refuses the recognition of the other for what that one is, namely, another. In this case even God is reduced to powerlessness and cannot "approach" us as the disciples of Emmaus were approached. And even if we were approached, our eyes would refuse to be opened. Jesus did not manifest himself to the Sadducees and Pharisees, not because he did not wish to, but because he could not.

Without falling into a false mysticism, which would succumb to the temptation of "imagining," we can catch a glimpse, through the window on eternity constituted by the risen Christ, of this new world that we hope for and that the Apocalypse tells us of. It is a material world, but transfigured, a kind of terrestrial paradise, but an unimaginable one, where as we said the possibilities of communication and communion are infinite. The affirmation that the world which must come is at once terrestrial and spiritual is deeply rooted in the biblical tradition and gives our hope all its historical weight. We do not look for a salvation out of history or out of the world, but a salvation that draws this history and this world far beyond their present potentialities. This conception of reality confronts head-on our dualistic and Platonic notions that matter and spirit, the soul and the body constitute separate realities. No. Everything is one and everything is on a journey to a higher level or reality. This conception, so grandiose and so reasonable, will also shatter pettily "scientific" ideas.

The *political* consequences of this understanding of things are very considerable. For it means that we cannot accept a minute longer the present "shape of this world" (1 Cor. 7:31). We cannot be satisfied with its physical form (a universe that is thick, hard, insensible, where thought can emerge only with the greatest difficulty, full of terrible miscarriages, catastrophes). Nor with its brutal and unjust social form (a society where abysses separate rich and poor and render love structurally almost impossible). That is why the attitude of the Christian can only be critical and, in the true sense of the word, revolutionary. Science tries to transform nature, politics tries to transform history. By science we help thought to emerge. By politics we try to transform our society and to take responsibility for history, so that they may correspond better to the world of communication and communion that the resurrection lets us glimpse. Certainly, we are well aware that the effort of human beings by themselves is insufficient to cause the creation to make the qualitative leap that the resurrection demands. But conversely, we cannot deny that these human tasks of transformation are already in a real sense forming part of the energies of the risen Christ. This was seen by the intuitive genius of that great poet, Father Teilhard de Chardin.

"Heaven and earth will pass away" (Mt. 24:35) in their present form, but not what we have to say and to do. The more difficult a society makes communication and communion among human beings, the more it accumulates wealth, power, and knowledge in structures of domination; the more it multiplies the poor, those who hunger and thirst for justice, whether in the East or the West, to just that extent it distances itself from the world begun by the risen One, and demands from us a radical confrontation. Moltmann, in the introduction to his *Theology of Hope* (New York: Harper and Row, 1967), speaking of the world that must come, and which is the goal of Christian hope, says most correctly: ". . . faith, wherever it develops into hope, causes not rest but unrest, . . . Peace with God means conflict with the world, . . . (p. 21). He also suggests that hope makes of the Christian community a source of constant agitation within human societies, which otherwise would have the temptation of becoming stabilized as 'abiding cities' (Heb. 13:14) (Ibid., p. 22.). At least that should be the function of Christianity, if it played its role. To believe in the risen One is therefore to struggle with all one's energy against the evil forces that prevent a people from standing up and coming back to life in order to arrive at a society of communion.

Certainly, the drama of humanity is so deep and its evil so serious that politics by itself cannot effect this resurrection. No social revolution in the world is capable of doing away with structures of domination. It is a congenital evil in the human being that prevents the qualitative leap ahead on the basis of the resurrection, as we said above, which politics by itself cannot carry out. Still it would be false to separate insurrection from resurrection. Roger Garaudy correctly points out that there is a relationship of essence between them. In practice, to rebel is to show that one believes in the resurrection. To believe that social evil can be overcome and that societies can rise above the death that lies in wait for them—that is to be a Christian.

Christian insurrection escapes from both idealism and materialism. It escapes from *idealism* because the world that we want to transform is this very world in front of us with all its physical and historical texture. It is "matter" that is called to become the temple of God. Those that do not get their hands dirty will be excluded from this temple. "I was hungry and you gave me nothing to eat. . . . Go far from me, you accursed, into the eternal fire," Jesus will say on the day of Judgment. This is why genuinely evangelized Christians are dangerous persons. If it were the heaven that they were trying to change, they would be left in peace, but it is the earth that is the object of their preoccupations! We know very well in Latin America that the persecution that breaks over many Christians is due to their claim that they are making the kingdom of God germinate in economic and social realities, in the factory and in the fields.

On the other hand, Christian insurrection escapes from *materialism*, in the usual sense of the term, because our current world can in no way claim to become our permanent dwelling, whatever improvements we introduce into it. There is not a complete continuity between the present universe and the world that must come. There exists between them what we in our theological language call an "eschatological cleavage": that is, the break in the last times, the final "crisis," which the Bible calls the Judgment, when the new world that we are creating little by little under the impulse of the Spirit of God will succeed in being born. Hence the cry of the elect in Revelation: "How long, Lord, will you allow your elect to cry to you day and night? . . . Come quickly."

THE TRINITY AND POLITICS

It is rare today to ask questions about the mystery of the Trinity. Still, strange as it may seem, it appears to this writer indispensable to recenter Christianity on God! That should be one of the first tasks of contemporary theology. Christian reflection, rooted in the Bible, has arrived in the course of the centuries at the very surprising concept of a God who is three and one; a God at whose heart exists both difference and communion—and there no doubt is the entire secret of happiness. True union creates differentiations; authentic otherness leads to communion in difference, without confusion and without separation. Western Christianity suffers from a perspective that is exaggeratedly Christocentric. Father Bouyer, a wise scholar of the history of theology, speaking about the conciliar constitution *Lumen Gentium*, writes: "The ecclesiology of the [Vatican] Council which insists so strongly on Christology leaves practically no place for the Spirit, in spite of a few preliminary remarks in the first chapter." In a recent study by Maura da Conceição Marques, *Pneumatologia nas relações eclesiais entre Oriente e Ocidente*, we can read this perceptive observation:

> In the West we see both a doctrine of the Church and in general a theology that are very Christocentric. This fact has brought about a loss of dogmatic and practical equilibrium in the concepts that are held of the second and third persons of the Blessed Trinity. The indissoluble link between the doctrines of Christ and of the Spirit has received very little respect; thus Western Christianity has lost its secret center. Because of that, in the Latin church, after the break with the East, the Christological aspect of the church has been emphasized, to the detriment of its aspects that have to do with the Spirit and with prophecy.

This leads, for example, to an exaggeration of the papal primacy—and on another level, of the authority of the bishop and the priest—to the detriment of collegiality. Even the best contemporary theologians—Gutiérrez, Comblin, Boff (and Moltmann and Metz as well)—who are trying to express the faith in the perspective of the integral liberation of the human being, seem to show very little interest in reflection on the Trinity, and to limit their works to the context of Christology. These theologians, justly called "theologians of liberation," are perhaps among the most "spiritual" of the Western church; but still beyond question they need to explore more deeply the mystery of iniquity, and also, as we shall try to show, the mystery of the Trinity.

Without any doubt it was absolutely necessary, once again, to make a new presentation of the mystery of the Christ dead and risen, with all the consequences that that brings for our action, our *praxis* as Christians in today's world. But to center one's reflection exclusively on the second person of the Trinity creates grave theological disequilibria and dangerously limits our conception of salvation in Christ in all its dimensions, as this writer should like to show. Furthermore, if it be true that our reflection and action are hemmed in by almost insurmountable contradictions because we have forgotten the Trinitarian equilibria of the central theological tradition, nobody should be surprised if our concept of society, and therefore both our political action and our ethics, should feel the consequences. If the Christian interpretation of existence has to do with the entire human being and puts its finger on the deepest levels of reality, it should not be surprising that a defect in our idea of the Trinity should damage our whole doctrine of the human being—that is, should damage among other things our ethics and politics, whose functions are to translate into action what is believed in theory.

"POLITICAL" CONSEQUENCES OF TRINITARIAN THEOLOGY[1]

Let us take the example of Brazil. Behind the conflicts and problems that stir up the nation and the church, we find perhaps three great realities; as if there were three different great religions, three types of society, three doctrines of humanity each looking for its own identity, living side by side without ever intermingling.

Patriarchal Religion

First there is the patriarchal type of religion, which is dominant above all in the countryside and continues to be the religious background of the miserable populations who live in the outskirts of the big cities. For this religion, God is the Omnipotent, creator of heaven and earth, who knows everything, understands everything, and is the *immediate cause* of everything that happens. Nobody wonders whether God's action might sometime, in the course of the events, be blocked by the liberty of others. Because God is all-powerful, he does everything he wants; and consequently all things that happen are so many decrees of his will, which one must submit to without complaining. People fall into a kind of fatalism: "God knows what he's doing," is said over the corpse of a baby dead from starvation. Yes, God knows what he's doing; *but he doesn't do everything he wants to.*

To this partiarchal religion corresponds the patriarchal society of the great landed proprietors. This type of society, which was also deeply marked by slavery, still constitutes the base of Brazilian society. In this social formation, only the Father is endowed with a spirit of wisdom and intelligence; there is nothing of the "difference" which the Son and the Spirit bring. In reality these are monolithic societies to which the Son and the Spirit are unknown and where only the Father can make important decisions. The social translation of the Father is the patron, the great feudal lord, possessing thousands of hectares of land; or, later on, the head of industry, or the religious authority (*responsável*). There is no question of a dictatorship, for the Father, even though stern, loves his children. Still democracy is impossible. The children, even when they become adults, continue with the status of minors in a number of domains, particularly in the political domain. To succeed in life one needs a godfather or sponsor who may be, according to circumstances, the patron saint, the municipal councillor, or the vicar. Everything happens through relatives, friends,

---

1. This section owes much to Jean Claude Barreau; see in particular his book *Qui est Dieu?* (Paris: Editions du Seuil, 1971), in his chapter on "God above Us, beside Us and in Us."

influential people—whoever can bring one into touch with an authority that is conceived of in the patriarchal mode. If somebody, even much younger than you, comes to help you, you say to him, "You are a father to me," when in Europe you would say, "You are a brother. . . ." By consequence the woman is slighted, or, rather, plays a subordinate role, because in the distribution of tasks she is not the one who assumes the principal economic role. She is tied down to the material needs of children, and that limits her time and energy to take up the instruments of production. This patriarchal style continues today, even though for different reasons: for equal work the woman receives a smaller salary; and in the household it is always the husband who is in charge. Patriarchal religion is thus highly incomplete and the cause of mutilation of human beings.

The Religion of the Son

Beside this patriarchal religion, but without ever being in communication with it, coexists what one might call the religion of the Son, whose devotees are more sensitive to mutual "fraternity" than to paternity from above. This religion is spread above all in the urban middle class and among the activists. Typical in this respect are the members of Catholic Action and, in a smaller degree, of the base communities. They discover Christ and the gospel, but in a certain way stop with him and don't arrive at the Father or understand the role of the Spirit. They are tempted to reduce the Christian life to an imitation of Jesus Christ. The Christian life, however, is much more than an imitation. Every imitation is "idealistic," and means copying a model; while to be a Christian means participating in the life of God, that is, of the Trinity. The Christian life is an immense surge in which one is carried to the Father by the Son in the force of the Spirit. That is what we call in theological language *theologal* life, life-in-God. If the Christian life is reduced to the imitation of that giant named Jesus, it is not available to anybody, for without the Spirit it is not possible to live like Jesus Christ. Thus the religion of the Son is often the religion of an elite that sacrifices itself—and *in vain*, because its objective is inaccessible, namely, to achieve by a single act of will a gospel ideal.

That is why on the *Left* we come upon the austere religion of the activists who try to translate their gospel ideal into facts—for example, by social action. On the *Right*, the desire for "fraternity" is expressed in quite sentimental groups, like the Cursilhos, where Jesus is "reduced" to the measure of a best friend who offers a helping hand in hard times, and the tenderness that the world is longing for. He is more an all-embracing buddy than the Lord, and these groups are in the end very adolescent, very much like Boy Scouts. In such surroundings, furthermore, the fraternity is superficial and inadequate to the dramas of history. Among them it is necessary only that during the retreat the lawyer should wash dishes beside the street sweeper, to create the conviction that Jesus has resolved the problem of the class struggle.

In these extreme deformations, the religions of the Son deny the Father and the Spirit, and engender Fascist or Stalinist societies red with blood. Totalitarian dictatorships, in fact, kill the father in his role of representing the origin and the past, everything which must be abolished. And they deny the spirit and the interiority that are focuses of subversion; for whoever enjoys a personal thought born from one's own interiority is a dangerous individual who can have unpredictable and nonconformist reactions. That is why totalitarian regimes have always persecuted thinkers and poets, and why official art is so boring. These immense fraternal societies are fatal to the human being; without father, without spirit, nothing remains but brothers bound hand and foot to a Big Brother who becomes the conscience of all and the origin of everything. A monstrous situation, in truth existentially perverse. This was the case with Mussolini, with Hitler, and even with Stalin (although Stalin also had patriarchal elements; he was called "little father Stalin" like the Tsar). These "older brothers" never had themselves called "fathers of the fatherland" but "guide" (*Führer*), "leader" (*Duce*), or "comrade."

Certainly, this is only a hypothesis, but if it can be verified, it will appear how important the great trinitarian equilibria are: these purely horizontal societies, where there is no father representing the origin, no spirit representing interiority, are gravely neurotic, and inevitably destroy the human psychic balance. And in fact what society can live without grave disturbances if it is deprived of the memory of its roots and the liberty of being and speaking?

The Religions of the Spirit

Finally, we also meet the religions of the Spirit, admirably represented in the sects and the thousands of Pentecostal churches in Brazil. The best elements of this tendency have again realized the importance of the interior life and of the human psyche, as well as the specific originality and irreducibility of every person as an individual. Personal inspiration, charisma, again becomes an essential function. Long prayer meetings become important. All this is good. But in their extreme deviations, the Pentecostal churches have a tendency to consider that they are pure emanations of the Spirit. They deny tradition and the past, for they think that previously the gospel was not interpreted in all its purity, and they reject other Christian confessions on the grounds that salvation and truth are impossible there. Their members have a tendency to think that the Spirit invades their thought to such a degree that God speaks to them at every instant: "God told me this or that. He is calling me to perform such-and-such a task." One hears that very often. There is no longer any recognition of the normative value of a father, a master, a brother, an objective rule—that is to say, in the end, of the other, or even of otherness. The door lies open to every fanaticism. In fact, here also, the Trinitarian equilibrium is destroyed: the Father and the Son are in no real way integrated into the Christian life. The vertical and horizontal dimensions disappear. Only the internal dimension of depth remains. But internality by itself is madness. For what is madness but an excess of subjectivity, which separates a human being from reality? To lose one's reason is to shut oneself up in an imaginary world out of touch with reality. So in its turn, the Spirit, when reduced to itself alone, destroys the human being. We need only see what happens in certain sects, or with certain great artists, a Van Gogh, a Nietzsche, a Rimbaud, who lived out their imaginary world with such intensity that their reason could not hold up under the strain; it cracked like an ailing heart that can no longer assure the indispensable circulation of the flux of thought between the real and the imaginary.

To these religions of the Spirit correspond societies that are anarchic or even fanatical. It is true that every authentic social revolution is a privileged movement when the Spirit is manifested. There is always a phase when a true revolution passes through an anarchic moment and becomes a cross between a carnival and a mob scene. We may think of the Paris student revolt of May 1968. During that phase there are usually few violent acts; it seems that a poetic intuition has taken over an entire people, which fills the streets no more to struggle than to celebrate a festival. The Spirit or imagination seizes power. It is not this way at all with counterrevolutions uninterested in novelty and concerned only to reestablish a former regime. They enter immediately upon a more or less bloody repression, as in Argentina or in the Chile of Pinochet, in Nicaragua, and also in Brazil.

But even progressive revolutions cannot prolong their anarchic phase. If anarchy is not restored to equilibrium by the discovery of others with their concrete necessities (brothers and sisters) and by the acceptance of the past (the father) in which the roots of the present are to be found, little by little the revolution begins to deteriorate; it is carried away and ends by devouring its own children. It ends in a kind of crisis of collective madness. Look at Iran after the Shah, where the sinister Ayatollah Khomeini never grasped these great equilibria we speak of, since Islam lacks any counterpart to the doctrine of the Trinity.

Thus in summary. When the Father is not interiorized in the Spirit, he becomes an oppressor God. A Spirit that does not put us in touch with brothers and sisters as well as origins is dangerous madness. The Son who limits himself to himself, who ceases to be the way that leads to that Father from whom the Spirit is received, tends to become a big buddy; or, on the other side, a religious *Führer*, of the sort that has equivalents on earth in the church as well as in society. If society intends to be "trinitarian," it must be neither patriarchal nor Fascist-Stalinist, nor anarchist. It must struggle to become a *communion* where human beings are recognized in their origins (the Father), in the relations as sisters and brothers (the Son), and in their interiority (the Spirit). A human being without origin, without peers, or without an interior life will never be anything but a being in disequilibrium. Perhaps this analysis will be granted at least to the extent that it explains why Fedorov, a Russian thinker with great penetration of spirit, has said that the Trinity, for us Christians, is our true social program. Unfortunately, the churches, above all the Western churches, both Catholic and Protestant, have allowed this central mystery of Christianity to fall into a deep theological darkness. We still have not waked up out of this deep sleep. A more intense contact with the Eastern churches may, in this respect, be indispensable. On this level, the theology of the Trinity and the theology of liberation, in order to meet, must doubtless pass through the necessary mediation of ecumenism. An encounter with the Orthodox church seems to this writer indispensable to restore the balance of the political theologies of Latin America. The theologies of liberation have not yet adequately discovered the Trinity. Liberation, ecumenism, and the doctrine of the Trinity will arrive on the *same road.*

THE TWO DIMENSIONS OF CHRISTIAN SALVATION

A more Trinitarian vision would without doubt allow us better to grasp the nature of the salvation brought by Jesus Christ, and would teach us how to place ourselves more correctly in order to work for this integral liberation of the human being that we all desire. This observation allows us to recognize what in effect are two dimensions of salvation. Their mutual interdependence will easily follow if we have in our head the Trinitarian theology on whose urgency I have been insisting; without it one can hardly see how they fit together.

The Material and Corporal Dimension of Salvation

First, there is a dimension of salvation that is in a real way material and corporal. We have already looked at this in regard to the resurrection. Jesus claims to save everything, including matter, the body, our history of flesh and bone, and not only the spirit. We need only read the gospel to perceive that Jesus sets his face against everything that oppresses the human being: sickness, death, hunger, storms, prejudices, exploitation of human beings by each other, tyrannies of every sort—in a word, *sin*, everything disgraceful and counterfeit. Furthermore, in reading the Bible, we perceive that the Judeo-Christian faith is born in the instant when human beings experience the fact that God acts in history and that *God can be relied upon.* We need to have been in what seemed like a totally dead-end situation, and suddenly to have been liberated from it by some external intervention, to know concretely what the concept of salvation can mean. I was naked, a stranger, penniless, sick, drugged, a prisoner, outcast, at death's door; and suddenly somebody lifted me out of this slough of nothingness where I had been sunk without hope of getting out.

In the Bible the central event from which faith is born is the liberation of the Hebrew people from the land of Egypt, where they had been reduced to slavery. Because Moses knows that God acts in history, Moses also dares to act. Still we have to recognize that Moses needed some impudence to do it! A miserable tribe whose leader is going to come up against the greatest king on earth! Actually, Moses' faith is fairly fragile. We remember the famous debate between God and Moses. What a lot of discussion! So many words from God to persuade Moses, who is doing all he can to get out of the job. "But I don't know how to talk"; "but they won't believe me"; "but they will laugh at me"; and at the end of the argument the famous word of resignation from the future leader of the Hebrews: "Excuse me, Lord, entrust this mission to whomever you want, but not to me." Read chapters 3 and 4 of Exodus once more. Then God was angry, says the Bible, and said to Moses: "Go and I will be with you, I will tell you whatever you must say." Jesus in turn will tell us: "Go, I am with you until the end of the world. . . . The Holy Spirit will tell you what you must say" (Mt. 28:20; 10:19). And the saints, like Seraphin of Sarov or Theresa of the Child Jesus, continue the same tradition: "After our death, speak to us as to the living. . . ." Christianity is one.

The example of Moses is very important, because the foundation event of the faith of Israel is really the *Pascha* (probably from a Hebrew root meaning "to pass over"); for it is the departure from Egypt and the *passage* over the Red Sea, the liberation which allows us to *pass* from slavery to liberty. We need to remember clearly that *this divine liberation has a political dimension*. It's a matter of confronting an oppressor state and of winning another land. "I have seen, I have seen the misery of my people," [says God]. "I have heard the cries that its taskmasters have drawn from it. I know its anguishes. I have come down to deliver it from the hand of Egypt and to bring it from this land into a land . . . flowing with milk and honey" (Exod. 3:7–8). Likewise the signs of the Messianic times are victory over death, sin, and sickness. These plagues can equally well be of a social nature. It is here that we come into touch with the spiritual roots of politics. These spiritual roots are very "material." Faith exists from the moment when one comes to feel that one can count on God. The Hebrews began to speak about the God of Abraham, Isaac, and Jacob from the moment when they came to discover by experience that the God of their fathers was different from the other gods "who never do anything." The God of Abraham is "the living God"; "he who does what he says"; "the one who is faithful and keeps his promises"; "the one on whom a person can count"; "the one who acts with a strong hand and a stretched-out arm"; "the faithful God, the fortress, the shield . . ."—all the titles that serve, in the Bible, to designate God.

The Ecstatic Dimension of Salvation

To understand fully this salvation that God brings us, we need to go beyond a simple liberation of the political, moral, or material type. Certainly salvation in Jesus Christ includes these liberations, but it goes beyond them. Infinitely far beyond. *It is not enough for us to pass out of oppression; we must pass out of ourselves.* That is why we have named salvation in its deepest aspects by the word *ecstatic*, "passing out of oneself" to encounter the Other and the Wholly Other who is the living God. That encounter is love. If things do not come about so, then the social, political, and psychological structures of oppression inevitably rise up again. *Only an encounter with the Other can destroy the tendency to domination.* At the end of the day, liberation comes from the Father only; that is, only through adoration of the one Absolute, which is God. To adore any other form of salvation (that is, to absolutize the means of liberation, even the most valuable) is, when all is said and done, a type of idolatry. Psychiatric healing and social revolution are no strangers to the salvation brought by Jesus Christ, but it is not limited to them. Humanity is something deeper than they know and its ill more grave. Jesus makes that plain in other words: "Humanity (Hebrew *adam*) does not live by bread alone, but by every word that proceeds from the mouth of God" (Deut. 8:3; Mt. 4:4). Two things are necessary for happiness: bread and love. Bread is indispensable for love. Without bread one despairs and dies. Economy is the basis of felicity. But our daily bread, though necessary, is not sufficient.

Thus ecstasy is as necessary for human beings as the air they breathe; and to shatter the frontiers of subjectivity is a question of life or death, if we do not wish to become insane. On this level, love is not one social phenomenon among others, but a constitutive necessity of humanity. Pope Paul VI spoke about a "civilization of love," not as a desirable possibility, but as an indispensable choice if humanity is to survive. On the other hand, we need only open our eyes to see that frustrated ecstasy searches for a thousand ways to satisfy itself. What is the erotic if not an attempt to find in sexuality a brief escape from this boring world? What are drugs but a chemical ecstasy? Drug addicts, when they get under way, use a revealing expression; they say they're going to "take a trip." What is the love of a man and a woman, when it is real, but a man going out of himself to enter his woman and a woman going out of herself to receive a man?

The choice is ours: either counterfeit ecstasies such as numerous sects offer, or the authentic ecstasy announced by the gospel. Certainly the gospel ecstasy is a formidable adventure: in order to go out from oneself and encounter this Wholly Other that is God, one must die. Love is a passion, and the word "passion" has two meanings: we can have a passion for somebody and we can suffer a passion on account of somebody. Both were the destiny of the Lord Jesus, who loved human beings even to folly and suffered passion on their account. But after the passion comes the resurrection, that is, the new life, which springs up if the affair has been well conducted. Scripture says that when the encounter with God really happens "the glory of God covers us with its cloud," and that "we all reflect as in a mirror the glory of the Lord by which we are transformed into his likeness, ever more glorious" (2 Cor. 3:18). In Hebrew "glory" means "weight" (*kabod*). When the "weight of the glory of God" (2 Cor. 4:17) falls on a human being, in the first phase that person is destroyed by it, as Saint Paul says: "the old humanity in us is destroyed, so that the new humanity may be born." To heal human relationships, to take their center out of themselves and put them again on their axis, it is necessary for people to submit themselves to the law of death and resurrection, which imposes its conditions on ecstasy, as the gospel teaches. But is not such an ecstasy, this "superabundance of spirit" as the hymn says, much better than destruction by drugs and the exhaustion of the profligate? Gospel ecstasy, even though it leads us to death, is a death for the purpose of resurrection. That death is calm and "totalizing." Above all, far from separating us from others, it puts us—and this is the sign of its authenticity—in communion with them. It is the opposite of a solitary evasion, whereby other ecstasies isolate their subjects and turn them in toward themselves.

In summary, let us say that Christian churches must be *mystical* and *political*. If they are not mystical, people will go elsewhere to find satisfaction for their need of an "elsewhere" and of a Wholly Other—forgetting that precisely on this earth there arise the cross and the paradox that the kingdom can be built only through many trials. If the churches are not political, their most generous members will decide to respond here and now, outside the church and without God, to all the needs of humanity—forgetting that only openness to the Father cuts at the root of the tendency to domination. The first group are too falsely divine and the second group too falsely human. Only the union of divinity with humanity resolves the question.

Here is where we come back to our theology of the Trinity. The only complete ecstasy is that which is Trinitarian; it alone leads us to God and leads us back to humanity. That is what we shall now see.

THE "EPICLETIC" STRUCTURE OF SALVATION

The *epiclesis* is the prayer by which the Holy Spirit is invoked over the bread and wine of the Mass (and also over the assembly), for them to become the body and blood of Jesus. The "epicletic" structure of salvation displays salvation as seen from the side of the Spirit and not solely from the side of the Son. Salvation in Jesus Christ opens us up to Trinitarian ecstasy. The Christian life is nothing other than a voyage: an ascension to the Father, by the Son, in the Holy Spirit, of every human being and of all humanity. We then need to study more deeply the difficult problem of the relation of Father, Son, and Holy Spirit, their relation internally within the one God, if we wish to avoid falling into grave disequilibria. Our ancestors in the faith had a good reason for their long disputes over the *filioque* clause in the Creed of Nicaea: Does the Spirit proceed "also from the Son" as well as from the Father? For it was a discussion about the place of the third person of the Holy Trinity. It was not a pastime of withdrawn intellectuals in ivory towers; for always behind this debate there remained and remain high stakes, which condition, even today, the daily life of Christians and their mode of actualizing the salvation of Jesus in the world and in history.

TWO THEOLOGIES OF THE TRINITY

There are two theologies by which the Trinity may be confessed. The Western church, in its most usual theology, especially since Saint Augustine, in the first place contemplates the unity of the divine essence to arrive afterward at the diversity of the three persons of the Trinity; while the Eastern church first looks at the person in each case, and through the person encounters the divine nature.

Maura da Conceição Marques, in *Pneumatologia nas relações eclesiais entre Oriente e Ocidente*, writes:

> For the Latins, the personality of each of the persons of the Trinity is seen as a mode of the divine nature. For the Greeks, the divine nature is seen as the content of the person: each *hypostasis* (person) is seen as a personal manner of assuming the divine nature. Hence this consequence for Eastern theology: *each person, in its singular reality, goes beyond the relations of origin, which are not, for the East, a unique foundation of the persons who would constitute them and exhaust their content.* Saint John of Damascus wrote: "Each divine person contains the unity just as much by its relation to the other persons as by its relation to itself." For the West, the relations within the Trinity are seen as relations of opposition (one person is not another) and by themselves, and constitute the divine persons. For the East, these relations are by themselves of diversity, interpenetration, and reciprocity—and they do not constitute the persons, for it is the diversity of the persons that determines the relations, and not vice versa.

If the writer may speak personally: I choose the second theology, the Oriental, to express my faith. In the first place, it seems to me closer to the Bible. Jesus never laid out a systematic theology of the Trinity and never developed the system of one God in three persons; he spoke in a very simple and concrete way of his Father and of the Spirit. That is why it seems to me more biblical to begin with the specific character of each of the persons rather than from the unity of the divine essence. The unity of God in the theology that I have chosen does not rest on a unity of the divine essence, but on the *monarchy* of the Father (in the etymological sense of the Father as the "unique beginning") and on the *consubstantiality* of the divine persons. To say it in simpler language: God is one because the three divine persons share the same substance and because, in God, the Father alone is origin and source. Gregory of Nazianzus states clearly that the idea of *cause* is never applied to the Son: "The Son possesses everything that the Father possesses except the faculty of being cause; the Spirit possesses everything that the Son possesses, except the quality of being the Son." And because the Father is the only one who possesses the faculty of being the cause, for this reason he is the principle of the divine unity. That is what I mean by the divine monarchy. It is well known that Western theology, especially since Thomas Aquinas, was modeled after the concepts of Aristotle. This further reinforced the "essentialist" vision of the Trinity (where the attention is fixed on the unity of the divine "essence" or being at the expense of seeing each of the persons as participating in different ways in the divine substance). The question that I formulate here is this: Is it possible to conceive of the specific character of each of the divine persons, and in consequence to conceive of the fullness of the salvation in Christ, if we start from the "essentialist" vision? My answer is: not with sufficient adequacy. If we lose sight of the specific character of each of the divine persons, we no longer see clearly the relationship of reciprocity and distinction that really exists between the "economy," or role, of the Son and the economy of the Spirit in the dynamics of salvation. Hence all the problems that I raised above.

In particular one tends to fall willy-nilly into the old heresy of subordinationism, according to which the work of the Spirit is subordinated to the work of the Son. Pentecost becomes merely a consequence of the incarnation, and the Spirit becomes merely a function of the Word. But Pentecost has its own proper value in itself: "It is the second act of the Father through which the Spirit in person comes to us," writes Paul Evdokimov in *L'Esprit-Saint dans la Tradition orthodoxe*. Irenaeus said that the Word and the Holy Spirit are the two hands of the Father, spread wide to embrace humanity. There is no inequality in the "economies," or roles, of the Son and the Spirit. The Spirit does not exist solely in relation to the Word; it has a personal value in itself and, therefore, in its "economy." The distinctions of the Council of Chalcedon are the most fruitful here: the work of the Spirit and the work of the Son are at once without separation and without confusion. The Spirit is in full reality the second advocate announced and promised by Jesus: "It is better for you that I should go away; for if I do not go, the Advocate [Greek *parakletos*] will not come to you" (Jn. 16:7). That is the one who carries out the work of salvation to its fullness, who adds nothing to what Jesus does, but makes it possible and universal. Jesus himself, according to John the Evangelist, recognizes these two phases in the work of salvation. In a certain manner he considers himself the precursor of the Spirit: "On the last day, the great day of the feast, Jesus stood and said, 'If any one is thirsty, let that one come to me and drink. . . . As the Scripture says, out of that one's body will flow rivers of living water.' He said that concerning the Spirit which those who believed in him would receive; for the Spirit was not yet, because Jesus had not yet been glorified" (Jn. 7:37–39).

Paul Evdokimov explains that Christian salvation also possesses an "epicletic" dimension and not solely a Christological dimension. What does that mean? The prayer of *epiclesis* in the Mass has as its goal that the *true* "fire from heaven" (Lk. 9:54) should fall. One day Jesus, whose whole life was an epiclesis, let fall this word: "I came to cast fire on earth, and how I wish it were already lit!" (Lk. 12:49). The fire of love is at the same time unbearable and consuming for the evil ones who do not wish to see it, and indescribable happiness for the saints. We should pray the epiclesis on every occasion, and not just at the Mass, so that the fire of love should fall on us and on all human beings. "This central function of the epiclesis shows, with the Scripture and the whole line of tradition, above all the Syrian, that the manifestation of the Trinity cannot be reduced in the economy solely to the sequence Father–Son–Spirit," wrote Olivier Clément, in *Contacts*. We must also give its value to the sequence Father–Spirit–Son, shown with particular clarity in the manifestation

(Greek *theophany*) at the Jordan, where we see the Spirit take the initiative in revealing Jesus on the day of his baptism: ". . . the Holy Spirit descended on him in bodily form like a dove, and a voice came from heaven saying, 'You are my beloved Son, in you I am well pleased' " (Lk. 3:22). We are accustomed to begin our prayer by the sign of the cross: in the name of the Father, and the Son, and the Holy Spirit. But we could also say: in the name of the Father, of the Spirit, and of the Son. Theologically speaking, it is only the Father who cannot leave his present place, the first, because he alone is the source and origin in God, as we said above: he is the origin of the Son whom he begets and of the Spirit, which proceeds from him. All that is not playing with words, but a clumsy effort to fathom the unfathomable mystery of God. To think of the Trinity with the Spirit in second place, without of course excluding the other more Christological formulation of the mystery, helps us to grasp why Pentecost is more than a consequence of the incarnation.

Between the role of the Son and the role of the Spirit there are, then, relations of equality and reciprocity in mutual service. In reality, there is no superiority in the Most Holy Trinity. Our words are powerless to express the mystery. Still, if we should try to represent the Trinity, the most adequate geometric form would doubtless be a circuit, a circuit of love where the Father is at once center and circumference and where the divine persons meet, equal in splendor, power, and majesty, without confusion or separation. The tri-solar fire of the Trinity presupposes the equality, specificity, and total reciprocal communion of each person. To quote from Maura da Conceição Marques:

In each relation of any one of the divine persons, the others are present: the Spirit proceeds from the Father, the unique origin, at the same time as the Son is begotten and in relation with the Son; the Son is begotten by the Father at the same time as the Spirit and in relation with the Spirit who manifests the Son. The unbegotten character ("innascibility") of the Father, the generation of the Son and the procession of the Holy Spirit mutually imply each other to the extent that no one of these properties could ever exist without the others.

How to apply these reflections to our theology of liberation? Dogma underlies practice. Conversely, our practice, which is born from our life with the people of the margins of society, leads us to a dogmatics more faithful to the practice revealed by the gospel. If, as Jesus seems to have taught, one initially confesses the divine persons, then one will not succumb to an exaggerated Christocentrism and, we may hope, will reach the point where one can more easily preserve the two dimensions of salvation that we spoke about earlier. Thanks to our theology of the Trinity we can maintain, without danger of being alienated from the needs of society, that the fundamental attitude of the Christian is contemplation, for salvation on its deepest level is, at the end of the day, ecstasy: human beings must be grasped at the heart of their subjectivity if they are to be saved. To repeat: unless, at whatever cost, we pass beyond the frontiers of the Subject, social and individual life become hell. In other words, the axis of salvation is God-centered ("theologal") and not moral. Salvation, before it is manifested as morally good behavior, is an offering of oneself; it consists in *yielding oneself*, yielding oneself to the great liberating force of the living God. Faith precedes good moral conduct. *Salvation is operative when a human being is situated between two extensions.*

1. At first the attitude must be *adoration*. The person observes the Son, who is the door and the Way. Nobody goes to the Father except by the Son. Through the Son one penetrates into the abyss of the Trinity. The force that lifts one to the Father is the Spirit with which the Son is filled. But as soon as one arrives at the Father, the source and origin of all, and the objective of one's ascent to God, the person is turned back over to the Son again. And the force that draws one to the Son is the same Spirit that proceeds from the Father, the unique origin, in union and in relation with the Son, the unique way.

2. And when the person arrives again back at the Son, the mystical ascent by its very nature places one in the *world* and in *history*, because the Son is also the Incarnate Word who assumes in his flesh human nature, both social and individual, and who brings to the entire cosmos the divinization that it anxiously awaits. The children of God, united to the Word that has become flesh, must then assume concrete tasks of human liberation—social and political, psychological, medical. Those are at the same time tasks of transfiguration of the creation through technique, through science. To be a Christian is to achieve awareness, to wake up, to participate actively in this Trinitarian circuit—this "interpenetration" (*perichoresis*), the fathers of the church would say—which ceaselessly recommences: from the incarnate Son one bursts up to the Father, in the force of the Spirit, and so on. . . . Our life becomes a true festival, a Trinitarian banquet, a sacred dance.

In this scheme there clearly appear the structures of salvation, which are at one and the same time "epicletic" and Christological. The Spirit is not subordinate to the Son; for it is the Spirit that takes the initiative of revealing the Son to the person in adoration, and of rooting one in the world by plunging the person into the incarnate Word through its baptismal function. The Son for his part, as the unique way that leads to the Father, takes the initiative in raising the person, together with the whole cosmos, up to the Father from whom the Spirit proceeds. The Son is not subordinate to the Spirit.

This Trinitarian dialectic makes it evident that salvation in Jesus Christ infinitely surpasses the tasks of human liberation, which are of political, social, or economic character, but at the same time includes them. Faith and politics cannot be in opposition. Christian salvation includes politics and goes beyond it. Liberation from oppression and from all forms of tyranny is the preliminary sign of the advent of the kingdom. If there is no liberty for the wretched one dying of hunger or for the political prisoner, it is a sign that our religious action has betrayed the Spirit. "The Spirit of the Lord is upon me because he has anointed me, he has sent me to announce good news to the poor, to proclaim release for the captives and recovery of sight for the blind, to set at liberty those who are oppressed . . ." (Lk. 4:18-19). So went the great epiclesis over the world pronounced by Jesus in the synagogue of Nazareth. The adventure in God is authentic if it draws a human being at the same time into the depths of the Trinitarian abyss and into the heart of human masses. It should now be clear from this perspective that "engagement" in the world is not sufficient by itself to heal human relations, sick with a mysterious malady; and that in the end this cure must be realized for the kingdom to arrive in its fullness.

In conclusion we may say that the salvation envisaged by the gospel is at once political and poetical. *Political* because it attacks social structures whenever they render love "structurally" impossible; we must resort to politics to create this civilization of love. *Poetical* because to cut off evil at its root and to create what is beautiful—namely, the new world—a wholly special inspiration is needed, inspiration from the Spirit of God. The word "poet" comes from the Greek verb *poiein*, "to create, to make." Poets, by their inspiration, know how to see the hidden side of things, they know how to discern the secret music of being. They render love touchable; and likewise death, beauty, the future. In this sense they exercise an indispensable mediation, because they allow the artisans of the new world to see as realized the blueprint of what is still no more than a dream. Thanks to the poet, the relation of a human being to the world and to others achieves here and there that degree of depth which is salvation itself. Because of this mediating function the poet and the mystic are as indispensable as the politician and the scientist. Woe is us when the world, eliminating the poet, hardens social relations by *reducing* them to their political, economic, or technical aspect. Woe to the world that becomes a machine!

4

Grace and Power

A FRATERNAL QUESTION

This chapter was written at the time of the popular uprising in Nicaragua. It is the result of reflections made at that time by the Serviço Nacional Justiça e Não-Violência in Brazil in respect to events in Nicaragua and Central America. It was impossible for us not to take a position. Nicaragua in point of fact is a beacon of hope for all of Latin America. And its Christians participated and still participate en masse in the popular uprising, as they do also in El Salvador. Among them were a number of priests, in particular two, Miguel d'Escoto and Ernesto Cardenal, who had begun their revolutionary pilgrimage by advocating active nonviolence. Miguel, in an important article, "The Power of the Cross" (published in the *Catholic Worker* in 1979 and based on an interview of December 1978 in Managua), explains clearly, long before the outbreak of fighting, that his appeal for nonviolence had not been heard by the churches of Nicaragua. He said that centuries of religious education that distorted the true meaning of the cross in Christian life had unfortunately for the time being blocked the unleashing of a true nonviolence, a popular nonviolent uprising, in Nicaragua and in Latin America generally. The current position of these brothers of ours calls nonviolence radically into question. Some reflections on our part are all the more important, for we need to know whether the historical choice to which our Nicaraguan comrades were compelled is the most strategic, the most human, and the most effective in the long term (and even in the medium term) to create a different society. Will the blow that they struck against a perverse society help or compromise an authentic struggle for liberation across the Latin American continent? Everybody understands that the events in Nicaragua are not simply local events: they are the concretization of a line that all Christianity in Latin America will be able to take. Is it advantageous to place the peoples of Latin America on a terrain where the ruling class holds a crushing superiority in economic resources and weapons? The adversary, at one moment hesitant and indecisive (like the Carter administration in respect to Nicaragua), the next moment shows how cruel and savage its repression can be when it throws the full weight of its forces into battle, as in Guatemala and El Salvador—even though we do not believe that the Salvadoran guerrillas can be defeated by the military junta without direct intervention by the United States. Might it not be more opportune to develop, while there is still time in Latin America, other modes of envisaging the conflict? To construct other strategies?

Independently of this observation in the strategic or political realm ("What, speaking militarily, is the most efficacious stance?") there is also a question in the ethical realm. Practically, politically, what is meant by the commandment of Jesus "Love your enemies"? What could be the theory and practice of such a conflict—or, to use church vocabulary, its theology and pastoral practice? These questions must be faced. Furthermore, we believe that ethics cannot be separated from politics and strategy. The morality of combat touches the heart of humanity; and the purity of the cause, along with the means employed to assure its triumph, is not without effect on the people's emotion. The support of the people also lies in the ethical realm. In spite of all, we see that very clearly in France, where an old socialist tradition, antedating Marx, has claimed in its own right themes—full biblical themes!—such as sharing, justice, and respect for human rights, whose moral meaning has a strong effect on people. A cold conduct of affairs is not enough to elicit popular support. Technocracy, both in the West and in the East, is in the course of showing its limitations.

A THEOLOGICAL APPROACH TO THE POLITICAL QUESTION

There are many ways to approach the preceding question or questions: political, economic, psychological, military. As for us, we believe that the theological approach, though certainly not exclusive, is nevertheless fundamental, and that no society in the process of overcoming domination (that is, oppression from whatever source) will be correctly formed if the religious dimension is neglected.

Economic or Political Level?

Generally the thinkers who wish to remodel societies focus either on the economic function or the political function. Either: How to reorganize production and the manner of working? or: What kind of state? Marx devoted himself to studying the economic question: his sociology is just a part of his political economy. Hegel, more profound than Marx in our opinion, sees in the political realm the true point of entry for social change—or, speaking even more radically, for nothing more or less than human change. Hegel believed in an Absolute Spirit, hidden in the heart of the world, which like every spiritual reality tends to perfection without limit. According to him, the organized emergence of the Absolute Spirit with all its parts in our epoch would happen on the level of the state: that is, in the specific place where conflicts are conducted and resolved. The political art of *savoir-vivre* in the resolution of conflicts is then for our times the key virtue, the fundamental skill. For that is what allows us to arrive at a higher social synthesis, a new society. If Hegel is right over against Marx—and everything leads us to believe that he is right—the political realm, in our days, would be a privileged place where the Spirit breathes, because it is the place where the Spirit emerges. The crossroads of humanity and divinity simultaneously demand and produce political saints. Can one not say that in the person of Gandhi and Martin Luther King, for example, such have begun to show themselves? Other epochs raised up saints of a different type. It is not absurd to say that today sanctity is concentrated in the political realm in a special and original manner. That realm must then be worthy of the age.

That is why, in this domain, Christianity, especially in Latin America, has a fundamental word to speak. Our fear is that once again it will be courageous but still incomplete; that it will not have reached the final point of its intuition. Is it not the case that at present Christianity in effect has recourse to physical force, to armed violence (even though as in Nicaragua as a last resort and without brutality) to topple the mighty ones from their throne? But, is not force the weapon that the mighty ones of this world use when they have nothing better to propose? Our perception is that the raison d'être of Christianity is something different. It is, rather, to make possible the entry of grace into this world, to graft it into the heart of history. Hence there arises a mysterious dialectic between grace and power, which we wish to study insofar as possible in these few pages. We have chosen this way of posing the question in order to ask our comrades in Nicaragua: What is the force that will lead the Latin American peoples to "socialization" in the true sense of the word, that is, to communal sharing of their human and material resources in the economic, ideological, and political realms?

GRACE AND POWER

We do not think that the force that will lead those peoples to community can be power, even the revolutionary power of the proletariat, because at the end of the day power always exists as something *outside* the human being. *No power in the world can persuade me, in my heart of hearts, to give, to give myself.* At the root of oneself rests an unassailable will to autonomy. And that is as it should be. For this irreducible autonomy over against the other makes one different, "distant," from that other one. And it is nothing else than the difference and distance that permits love. I—speaking personally—could never love somebody who melted or dissolved in me, but I can love somebody who faces me and whom I face. All the attempts to make one's own self abdicate—for example, to submit itself to a discipline imposed by the building of socialism—rebound into bureaucratic, totalitarian, or dictatorial societies where all the best of socialism evaporates.

If any doubt that, we strongly recommend that they submit themselves to some mini-experiences of socialization: for example, possessing in common a car, a house, or a television set. How difficult it is to possess things in common! How low the level of socialist consciousness really is, even among the vanguard of the working class. Only with great difficulty will people submit themselves to a communal discipline freely accepted, will they arrive at consensus on the criteria of usage. That is why, at least in the beginning, groups who live a communal life undergo many crises and setbacks: the car breaks down and nobody, or almost nobody, is willing to take responsibility for repairs; the telephone bill soars to the stratosphere; the cupboards are dirty, the ashes are never emptied. The group tries to react and then it "produces" rules, laws, decrees. Once again *law prevails over grace.* The old story of the Bible begins again: covenant with God, of course, and guarantee of the Promised Land; but so that the people should not fall back into idolatry (for people make their gods after their own manner and live their own lives as they decide), Moses is obliged to decree the law of the Ten Commandments, and a whole code (Leviticus) of community life appears. Once again in the bureaucratization of the revolution, Moses turns back the progress made by Jeremiah and Ezekiel, who announce (Jer. 31; Ezek. 34) the arrival of an epoch where the law will be inscribed by God on the heart of the human being. It will no longer be "exterior" to the human being. For just so far as law is conceived of as superior to the Spirit, bureaucracy and oppression will return to lord it over the Spirit, even in the interior of progressive revolutions.

In spite of these laws and rules of socialist or communal living, each one picks and chooses among them, even those who consider themselves the avant-garde of the proletariat: hence arise dachas, privileges, perquisites. It might even happen that the most advanced militants engage (at a low figure) the services of one of the "Lumpen-proletariat" (perhaps a black house-cleaner) to tidy what they have made dirty: the socialist leaders are no longer there in order to serve.

Afterward, little by little, things get better. What helps in overcoming the initial crisis is the strong friendship that unites the members of the group and immense hope aroused by the project of a new society, a new world to be constructed. What impresses everybody who goes to Nicaragua is the popular joy, joy at being harnessed all together to the task of building a new world. What changed people, at the end of the day, was not any law, any external power, but friendship, a vision intimately lived in common, a love. This revolutionary comradeship is the only true force that can help in dealing with the criticisms, the inevitable failures in an enterprise of this sort, during this concrete apprenticeship of the socialist life. The grandeur of the cause exercises a further attraction, at least on the first revolutionary generation.

At the beginning of the experience, no persons submit themselves to communal disciplines because there has not been born at the root of anybody's being the conviction that one must so submit oneself. In the first place it is a simple lack of experience. But also, it seems to us, there is a lack of generosity. Will the French truly have the civic generosity of their socialism, which has made all the third world vibrate with hope? Probably not! Are the different social categories ready for sacrifice? One must confess that inside the head of each proletarian is a petty bourgeois who is not slow to make its appearance. Marx said correctly that the ruling ideas are the ideas of the ruling class. It has been a long time now that French and American workers have been living in a capitalist society. But we do not think that this sociological explanation is sufficient. The egotism of each one does not come solely from an ideology of the ruling class or system injected into the head of the ruled. In our own mind we judge that the evil is more serious. For until now nobody has succeeded in bringing about a revolutionary organization, truly born from the "base," truly traversed by a creative spirit, strong enough to destroy the social structures of oppression, the mental scaffolding of egotism plain and simple, which lead to the desire of exploiting the other or at least of reclining supinely on the other. No "political" re-education, at least until now, has succeeded in seriously correcting this mysterious deviation of the human race. But, in our opinion, there will be no increase of the revolutionary movement or reinforcement of a communal society until each individual participating in this social change remains convinced in the most intimate heart of his or her subjectivity that it is worth the trouble to subject oneself to the freely accepted demands of a common life and initiative. Here finally we stumble on the existence of a factor, which for want of a better word we call "grace."

What is grace but the free and spontaneous opening of one person to another, that is, to what is different from the self? It is an inspiration, poetic if you will, which convinces the heart of each person to trust the self to a social organism that transcends the self, even though one is an operative part of that social organism, and to assure its functioning. Grace is a gift that persuades one person to trust another. *From trust, unity is born. Unity in turn permits organization.* In this sense grace is opposed to power, for grace neither commands nor organizes, but inspires. Power is not the *cause* of sharing even though in the end it alone can organize sharing. Power is not the source of sharing, but the means put to its service. Grace is the only cause of this immense upsurge that leads people to put things in common; it convinces people in the depths of their heart to give, to give themselves, to collaborate freely in a great social structure, to submit to civic disciplines.

Like power, grace has then a political function that we must rediscover: its effect is to permit, or rather, to help human beings to aspire to communal life in a society of sharing. By touching the heart of each one's subjectivity, it alone can conquer egotism at its root.

We were just speaking of political re-education. Why have there been such monstrous deviations in the re-education camps in the various socialist countries: the psychiatric clinics of the Soviet Union, the gulags, the Cambodian work camps . . . ? Behind these deviations must lie a perversion in theory: entrusting to a psychological or political institution (boring meetings on political reeducation, long hours of criticism and self-criticism) a task that belongs only to grace. In this realm the political philosophy of Hegel, the economic theory of Marx, the science of Freud and Reich are inadequate. Neither the state, nor a transfer of the means of production to all and for all, nor the analysis of the unconscious can open up human beings to the depths of their subjectivity and heal them, so as to become capable of a harmonious social life. Another "instrument" is needed to refashion "souls," that is, the profound psychology of the individual: there is also a psychoanalysis conducted by the Holy Spirit.

Hence we believe that there is a subtle and complex dialectic between grace and power. Both are necessary, but without confusion or separation. It strikes us that there is as yet very little awareness of this dialectic, perhaps because theologies of liberation still lack an approach to human interiority and a more extensive theology of the Trinity. As for European theologies, they do not adequately possess the practice of life with the poor; and in consequence they do not perceive that the marginalization and the exclusion from society of millions of human beings by misery of every sort is also a Trinitarian scandal! Is not the Trinity a society of three persons who are neither confused nor separated? And what is the third world (or what we may call the fourth world—those rejected from advanced industrial societies) but the mass of those human beings who have been either absorbed or exploited (confounded) or isolated and marginalized (separated) by a system gone mad? Apart from the question of a more systematic theology hidden behind this problem, we can look with a more attentive eye at the way Jesus acts in the gospel, and draw from this observation precious teachings for our political activity.

THE POLITICAL STATE OF GRACE

Certain points are clear. Jesus came to proclaim his kingdom, which must be sketched out in the communal societies that we desire. What does he actually say? To create the kingdom, neither power, nor possessions, nor knowledge suffice. Even if the economy is going well and bread is in abundance; even if the kingdoms of the world are able to set on its feet a planetary authority and to organize themselves better; even if science and official ideology make miraculous leaps ahead to the extent of seducing the human masses—all that is inadequate for the birth of a harmonious relation among human beings. The reader has recognized in our description the three temptations of Jesus: to change stones into bread; to receive the homage of all the kingdoms of the earth; to conquer by a miracle the place where the national ideology is formed, the temple of Jerusalem (Mt. 4:1-11). To get on his side the scientist, intellectuals, and priests! Today Marx suggests that the secret of human happiness lies in the rectification of economic relations. Freud reveals to us the abyss of the unconscious and shows that each of us contains a sexual and emotional repression, caused by a distorted image of the father implanted in us by a patriarchal society. Reich makes a synthesis of the two: he abandons Freud's individualism and assumes Marx's socialism; according to him, society as a whole locks around our necks an iron collar of character, which must be broken.

We are far from wishing to reject the substantial scientific (or better, rational) contribution of these great men. Still we have to say that Jesus' good news is something different. It may very well presume this or that scientific truth, but it says something different in its own name. It says, at the end of the day, that in order to be happy the human being must once again enter into relation with its deepest root, which is a divine root. The axis around which the kingdom of God is constructed is an interior and communal act that has consequences in all domains, including the social and the scientific. This act consists in the opening of each one of us, in union with the others, to the Father as Jesus has revealed him. Here we need to repeat some thoughts on the Trinity: since God is not Father alone, but also Brother and Spirit, this opening to him contains nothing oppressive about it. For Christians, only openness to God and God's grace can convince each person to give, and to give self: this is undoubtedly one of the high points of Jesus' preaching, the "hidden treasure" of his thought, which few know how to find. Only the creator can attain the root of the being that the creator has created. No exterior constraint or intervention—neither power, nor organization, nor psychoanalytic cure—can be substituted for the free intervention of grace. And even the knowledge of God does not depend on human strength: "Nobody knows the Father except the Son, and that person to whom the Son wishes to reveal him" (Lk. 10:22). Faith is necessary to receive the gift of grace and with it the strength of individual and social sharing. We must have faith: that is, we must ask the Son that we may *know* the Father and thereby live out the Trinitarian harmony among earthly realities. In biblical language, to "know" means to have a strong and organic vital relationship with the one loved.

That has important political consequences. It means that revolutionaries must proceed, with full awareness, in search of grace so that the revolution will not be aborted—will not fall into reformism, or terror, or bureaucracy. It is impossible for us to restrict ourselves to placing our confidence in any revolutionary organization, however excellent it may be, if we wish to remain open to that grace, since, *by definition, grace escapes from every mold fashioned to retain it.* It is possible and necessary to have an "inspired" political power, but the secret of inspiration is somewhere else.

In this sense the current demands of many Left movements in the world—no less in Poland than in Latin America—are indeed interesting: for them, "autonomy," "self-management" *(autogestão)* completes and balances the socialization of the means of production. Autonomy means that every individual, every entity has a life and creativity of its own, which cannot be expressed solely through a larger grouping. For example, the trade union expresses an aspect of the working class that is not necessarily represented in the Worker's party. Hence it is not proper for the union to be absorbed by the party. So each person is autonomous as an individual; and though each has the duty of remaining united with the other members of the group and submitting to a social discipline, that does not mean that any should abdicate personal creativity or be obliged to obey without the right of protest and refusal. That comes down in the end to saying that communal inspiration is not produced through the organizations that are animated by it.

To return to the great men who inspired the political reflection of the past century and a half, we could summarize in the following manner. Marx was obsessed by the question of economic institutions and did not see correctly the question of the state and of power. Hegel perhaps laid the theoretical foundations of totalitarianism, since he makes of the state a kind of God, the place where the absolute Spirit emerges.

In Christian thought, the Spirit comes from elsewhere, from a *different* place: "the spirit blows where it wishes . . . , you do not know where it comes from nor where it is going" (Jn. 3:8). It is this difference, this "elsewhere" of grace on which nobody can put a hand, that nobody can reduce or possess, and that constitutes the *theoretical* basis of the autonomy and self-management of individuals and of groups. For what they most deeply *are* does not arise from human strength. Therefore we cannot absolutely define or control it. There, it seems to this writer, is an important contribution of theological reflection for current political thought. For at bottom, it is monism, whether of spirit or of matter, that lies at the origin of all totalitarianisms.

GRACE AND EXPLICIT FAITH: POWER AS SERVICE

The gospel shows us that the search for grace does not depend solely on explicit faith: for the love of the poor, of the wretched, the sacrament constituted by a brother or a sister in need, is already a real relationship to Christ and to his grace. "I was naked and you clothed me, I was hungry and you gave me to eat—to me the Christ!" "But when did I do that? I didn't even know you, I didn't believe in you." "Each time that you acted so to one of the least of my brethren, it was to me that you did it" (Mt. 25). It is love that will judge us. Still, implicit faith, like any unconscious state, is an abnormal state. We must become conscious of the divine dimension of being. That is the task of evangelization when it is at its most authentic.

In the end, in a theological perspective, provided we resolutely avoid reductionist tendencies, which limit evangelization to the political realm, provisionally we may say that the new societies are sketches of the kingdom of God. But we must never forget: the kingdom of God is *of God*. Without God these "attempts" cannot even be tried, indispensable as they are to demonstrate by seeing that paradise is possible. Hope is nourished by concrete realizations.

Once we have accepted this fundamental datum of a radically different pole from which grace drops down like the morning dew, without difficulty power becomes situated in its proper place. Jesus in no way rejects political power. The apostle Paul requires that Christians should be subject to it, for authority is an order established by God (Rom. 13:2), an instrument of God (Rom. 13:4) to establish justice and punish the evildoer. Precisely on that account, then, it is necessary that public powers should correspond to the order established by God and should effectively help human beings to do good. Jesus, far from rejecting power as a means for installing the kingdom, on the contrary insists that it should be at the service of the kingdom. The concept of power in the gospel is markedly original. Jesus flees to the mountain when the multitudes wish to seize him to make him a king (Jn. 6:15), for he refuses to be divinized in that manner, in the aspect of political authority as in his third temptation, as if that would constitute the ultimate response to the problem of humanity. But on the other hand, Jesus recognizes and encourages the value of *power as service,* which is not the cause of sharing, but which organizes it. Thus, *after* the multiplication of the loaves, he makes the hungry crowds sit down in groups of fifty or a hundred (Mk. 6:40). He suggests to authorities of every type that they should be inspired by his attitude: "You call me Teacher and Lord, and you speak well, for so I am. If I, then, your Lord and Teacher, have washed your feet, then you also should wash each other's feet" (Jn. 16:13-14). "Let whoever wishes to be first among you become the servant of all" (Mk. 10:44).

THE STRUGGLE OF JESUS, OR THE STRUGGLE OF GRACE

But still this attitude of Jesus was never clearly understood, either by the ordinary people or by his own disciples. *Yesterday, as today, the supremacy of grace over force seems unacceptable.* When Jesus began to explain that in order to live out this mysterious dialectic of the kingdom and to receive what power could not give, namely, grace, people had to be fed by his example, his inspiration, his word, his ideas, and even with his whole being, his body and blood—at this point, the scandal was too great and tripped up even the best. The circle of his friends began to disintegrate. We naturally ask: What happens to an authentic revolutionary when the people abandon him, when the people's ramparts around him crumble? Since his presence is intolerable for those who profit from the privileges of the established order, the mailed fist of the ruling classes seizes him, on the grounds that thereafter they will have nothing to fear. Several times in the gospel we read of attempts at assassination of Jesus, or attempts to get rid of him; but at the beginning he was always surrounded by so many people that they came to nothing (conflict with his family, Mk. 3:20-21, 31-32; with religious leaders, Mk. 11:28-32; attempts at assassination, Mk. 11:18; 14:1-21; Jn. 7:32, 45-48, and especially at Nazareth, Lk. 4:28-29). Finally the attempts succeed at Gethsemane, where Jesus is found alone with a few sleeping apostles around him.

THE "CRITICAL" FUNCTION OF GRACE

This dialectic between grace and power, and this supremacy of grace over power are the reasons why, in an evangelical perspective, it is impossible to idolize the state, to make of it an absolute. Openness to that grace, which alone allows communion and participation and which *comes from elsewhere,* means that, at every instant, power is relativized as a final solution of the problems that arise. But it is not sufficient to hold this fundamental position of not turning power into an absolute. We must also draw its practical consequences for the political life of the societies of sharing, which we are seeking. Here again we take a theological approach. What we need is to create social structures in which power rests solely in rules of service, where the administrator washes the feet of those administered. We must set in place a social disposition such that at every instant power can be brought down from its throne, while at the same time enjoying the respect and authority without which it cannot play its role. We take the word "authority" (Latin *auctoritas*) in its etymological sense, "that which makes something *'increase'* " (Latin *augeo).* Power has as its function to make the living forces of society increase around it.

What is the place where the Spirit of God breathes with greatest intensity? Certainly among its people of the poor, the little ones, the humble of the earth. "Blessed are the poor" as we saw does not mean "Long live poverty, misery, exploitation"; but that those ones are happy who, precisely because of poverty, must share to survive. Among the inhabitants of a *favela,* earth, water, and light are already socialized because each one draws water from the same well or faucet, because the lines for electric lights pass from one hut to another, because the earth is by necessity common property (the land is squatter territory where nobody has property rights). For those crowded together in a prison cell, whoever holds something for exclusive use becomes an intolerable burden on the others and will either be bodily expelled or assassinated. Extreme necessity gives birth to either heaven or hell. Heaven, if each one, going beyond self, arrives at a marvelous equilibrium, due to an immense respect for the neighbor; each halts barefoot before the doorway of the other's intimacy and strives to offer and receive from the other all that one has and all that one is. Hell, if even one person arrogates permission to use, in however slight a degree, force and deception to survive. We said that God is love, and that God moves in love as the birds fly and the fish swim in love. That is why atheism, before being a theoretical problem, is a practical problem. In a place where there is no love or sharing, God cannot be present. The prophet Ezekiel relates that he saw the glory of God (that is, God's presence) leave Jerusalem (Ezek. 10–11). That is what happens in societies of nonsharing and nonlove.

Societies that totalize power within the hands of certain persons and that capitalize wealth are necessarily and by essence atheistic. Or perhaps better, idolatrous. In the place of the true God another absolute is placed: the party, science, wealth. That is why the wretched outskirts of São Paulo, or of other big cities of the world, in spite of the crimes for which they are the theater (murders, thefts, drug use) are more *religious* than the middle-class houses, for in extreme poverty sharing has again become possible. There one cannot avoid seeing the misery of the neighbor, one cannot refuse the other a dish of food if one has it. God has less difficulty in operating here than elsewhere (in truth there are very few places in the world where God feels fully "at ease," so great is human egotism). It is then for this *theological* reason and not for a political one that power must be approached from the base: the mayor, the general, the bishop, the priest, the one responsible for a zone must go to the *favela* and not it to them, for it is in these places that the Spirit of God breathes.

The ancients said: *Vox populi, vox dei.* Strictly speaking, the voice of the poor and the humble is the voice of God; the people may lose their senses and demand the release of Barabbas rather than the release of Jesus. But it is with a sound instinct that the Nicaraguan radio repeats that the voice of the people is the voice of God. Power must at all costs stay in contact with this critical place, which in turn criticizes it. Here the voice of true reason, of the uncreated Wisdom, makes itself heard most plainly, with the fewest parasitical attachments, through the mouth of the poor. Then power will avoid the temptation to escape from the earth that saw its birth and from the people that it must serve; it will avoid the disaster of becoming a god, it will be called back to order, it will be comforted by the tenderness of the poor, it will see the true problems. When one enters into contact with the living God, wherever God is to be found, the idols fall from their thrones.

A "political state of grace" (a phrase used by French journalists during the first months of the Mitterrand government) should truly mean a society where power has not been monopolized by a minority and where social changes are such that the functioning of society comes more from a spirit infusing the people than from laws (in the sense of Montesquieu). Such a political state of grace is born in a society when in principle the people do not delegate power to anybody, but entrust limited tasks to public servants. Hence the importance of these new forms of organization for which people are searching: the factory commission, which takes on the administration together with other social partners; the delegate of the street elected by the inhabitants, the assemblies of the quarter; general assemblies of workers in the factories or in agricultural enterprises; a change in the manner of naming bishops who, until now, come down from on high, are more chosen by the groups who direct the church and from among their own number than indicated by the people (see below, chap. 7); the autonomy of regions delineated by history, the decentralization of power; and finally, the emplacement of vital interests of populations on the world level and acceptance of an international mediating power (which will result inevitably in limitations on national sovereignty).

Why is there so much money in the hands of those who have oil or technology, and so little in the hands of others? The earth is for all human beings, it must be repeated. It does not belong solely to Saudi Arabia or to the industrially advanced countries; there are no exclusive property rights, either over goods or over the products of intelligence.

Evidently, to build these new forms of organization presupposes many sacrifices among all, a very great civic generosity. The living standard of most social categories in the first world must be frozen or perhaps reduced if the powers in place are really to start from the genuine needs of the great majority of human beings on this planet. It is not certain that we are ready for that! The political state of grace is perhaps very far off. In any case, a shift in power of itself does not suffice to create it, as we have said a thousand times.

Now we turn to the Christians who, on the one hand, have been forced into the use of violence because their struggle has remained isolated without adequate external support; and to those, on the other hand, who believe that violence is inevitable, in some sense a necessary evil, the lesser of two evils; and even to those who think that legitimate defense by force of arms is a Christian theology. Have we been too far away to help you create alternatives, you who have taken up arms? Did we help you enough when the time came? The fact of revolutionary violence is simply there, and each of us is involved in it. Mahatma Gandhi said that it is better to be violent than passive if, unfortunately, one does not know how to create in advance, both in oneself and in society, a nonviolent mode of struggle.

But we cannot refrain from asking an even more serious question. When we overcome power by force, are we not allowing power to be what Jesus wished it never to be: the ultimate recourse to escape from a situation devoid of grace? Could there not have been in this attitude a fatal germ of mistrust with regard to grace? That is what leads us to ask ourselves: Can the most profound and original part of Christianity continue to spawn revolutions in the third world if it does not take more seriously the alternative of nonviolence?

Another serious question also comes to mind. To solve a problem, the first condition is to state it correctly. Is it not the case that we can no longer content ourselves with an individual nonviolence solely on the level of little, interpersonal conflicts? In fact, and this is the whole point, we must pass from a nonviolence on the level of persons to a nonviolence on the level of states. It is a question of life and death for all humanity.

As for ourselves, we have made the choice of active nonviolence as a method and mystique of combat. To speak the truth, we do not think that there is currently in Latin America an intellectual or spiritual environment sufficient for the message of nonviolence to be heard adequately by the churches. Miguel d'Escoto has spoken excellently on this subject in the article cited above. But we hope that things are in the process of changing. Perhaps we have not worked out in sufficient depth—above all in practice, but also in theory, in the theology of liberation—what the specific effectiveness of the kingdom of God might be. *There is yet to be found a theology and a pastoral practice of conflict,* and with it an organization of the popular movement on the continental and international level along such lines that civil disobedience would become irresistible. Perhaps our Latin American church has not yet sufficiently perceived that its people already know how to struggle to throw off the yoke of injustice in the manner of the Suffering Servant of whom the prophet Isaiah speaks in his fifty-third chapter.

5

Questions to Marx

Chapter 4 led us to raise themes that have been, and always are, at the heart of Marxist thought. How is industrial society to be made into a human society, a society of sharing, of communion—a society really "communist"? How is the mode of production to be changed so that it will no longer lead to the exploitation of one human being by another? Is it enough for this goal that the proletariat should take over power? And so on. No Christian can remain indifferent in the face of such questions, for they are also at the heart of the gospel message: "Love each other as I have loved you" (Jn. 13:34); "And all those who believed were together and had all things common, and they sold their possessions and goods and distributed them to all, as any had need" (Acts 2:44-45).

The kingdom of God is justice, peace, and joy in the Spirit (Rom. 14:17), and the credibility of this kingdom—surely the key idea of Jesus' preaching—is absent so long as there exist chasms of distrust and misery between human beings. We may read once again the parable of Lazarus and the unjust rich man: "There is between us and you a great chasm fixed such that those who wish to go from us to you cannot, nor those who wish to go from you to us" (Lk. 16:26)—the words of Abraham from the bosom of his blessedness to the rich man in torment. The abyss of hell is exactly proportional to the abyss created by unjust wealth. We should note that for primitive Christianity the "union of souls" is accompanied by an economic union of persons: "And the multitude of those who believed had one heart and one *soul*; and none of them called their own the *things* that they possessed, but they had all things common" (Acts 4:32, italics added). An exclusively "spiritual" union was inconceivable. In ordinary language "spiritual" means immaterial, disincarnate; but in biblical language it means something quite different: the presence of the Holy Spirit in somebody or something. Even matter can become fully spiritual, as in the resurrection of Jesus. The drama or, if we wish, the "fundamental contradiction" of the industrial world in its present capitalist form is that it multiplies loaves to infinity, but has not learned how to share them. But Jesus, symbolically, on the day of the multiplication of loaves, correctly gave us the

74

lesson of sharing: he made the disciples sit down "by hundreds and fifties" (as in base communities), distributed the bread, "and they all ate and were satisfied" (Mk. 6:39, 42).

Karl Marx, using the discoveries of the great philosophers, economists, and socialists of the nineteenth century, was the first thinker to synthesize a coherent response to the absurd situation of the industrial world, which can produce but not distribute. Thus one of the first to think seriously about the socialization of industrial wealth, and really to seek a society of sharing and communion, was not a Christian! Marx was an atheist and a ferocious atheist; he said that he "hated all the gods." According to him a human being, like Prometheus of the ancient legend, must win the fire of one's own liberty by one's own efforts and must not await salvation from any savior or God.

Hence the dramatic character of the confrontation between Marxism and Christianity. The Christians, the "specialists" in charity (at least they put charity at the heart of their message), were checkmated on their own territory. "After two thousand years of Christianity," they were told, "your charity has been amply shown up as ineffective; it is an atheist who comes bringing a clear scientific answer to human misery, to the question of the sharing of bread"— the two questions (bread and love) most necessary for life.

That is why Christians and also, in a more general way, Western humanists have had for so long a bad conscience over the Marxists. It seemed that to contradict Marxists or even to state reservations about their position meant putting oneself in opposition to reason, to love, to justice—not to mention compassion for the poor and oppressed. This bad conscience has had positive aspects. It woke up the churches. But also to some degree it blocked them from thinking. It damaged clarity of thought. It blocked the formulation of serious questions, which must be asked of Marxism if we wish to advance the debate— which means, if we wish to promote the union of human beings of good will who want to change the world and work for universal fraternity.

First we must remark—and it is being remarked much more clearly today than yesterday, especially in France—that all types of socialism and Marxism are not to be instantly identified. It would be absurd to forget the nobility of the struggle of the English economists and the French socialists of the nineteenth century who were not Marxists at all. The names of Christian thinkers with a socialist orientation of this era should not be passed over in silence: Lamennais (1782–1854) and Lacordaire (1802–1861) knew on which side the gospel stood, and that it constantly in the course of the centuries fed revolutionary social projects. In 1848 the church was on the side of the *misérables* described by Victor Hugo; Archbishop Affre of Paris (1793–1848) died by assassination on the barricades when he tried to stop the massacre of the people by interposing his body between the combatants.

Unfortunately this movement did not continue. The church and its hierarchy as a whole did not know how to launch the prophetic cry necessary to condemn the martyrdom of the working class, in the act of being born and being delivered defenseless to the violence of the new industrial society in full expansion, when children of seven to eleven years old worked in the factories twelve or more hours a day, tubercular and starved—we should reread Dickens's *Oliver Twist*. Nearly twenty-five years after the Revolution of 1848 another archbishop of Paris, Darboy, was in turn shot to death (1871), but this time by the hand of the workers, during the (non-Marxist) Paris Commune.

What a terrible tragedy this Commune was! Nobody must be allowed to forget that 15,000 workers—men, women, and children—were murdered in one week in the streets of Paris by General Marquis de Galliffet. In all there were 400,000 written denunciations, probably more than 20,000 persons shot, 40,000 taken prisoner, 10,000 condemned. The troops of the bourgeoisie were gathered at Versailles, and with the shameful safe-conduct of the Prussians encircling Paris, enemies of France, they ended history's first attempt at a "communist" society. A communism that was clearly not Marxist! Thiers was the instigator of this repression of the poor, and went on from his victory to become prime minister of the new regime. And the Christian church in France, frightened by the "violence" of necessary social changes and their radical character, for long supported the triumphant bourgeoisie of Napoleon III. (His regime in many ways resembled the military dictatorships of Latin America, in particular the Brazilian dictatorship of 1964–84 in its phase of liberal imperialism.) After the "victory" over the Communards, that bourgeoisie crowned its work by allowing their allies the *bien-pensants* to build the basilica of Sacre Coeur on the heights of Montmartre, the great dedication of the triumph carried off by the forces of law and order. Thus the people's blood served once again to mortar a sanctuary. We are not ignorant of that in Latin America.

So one part of the socialist movement that had been born in the interior of the church was simultaneously persecuted by the Christians themselves and by a part of their leaders. That movement simply did not receive from the hierarchy and from church people the support that would have allowed it to become a viable social alternative. No doubt this partially explains why Marxism in the end was to have such importance in revolutionary socialist thought and practice: it alone, because of the failure or disappearance of Christians, occupied the ground. But this state of affairs is in the process of changing everywhere in the world, beginning in the Far East, and especially in Latin America, even though that is also where Marxism—or rather, types of Marxism—is showing evidence of originality and creativity and retains a power of attraction. But surely this is because on the Latin American continent the Christian presence is most vigorous and most reinvigorates socialist thought—including that of our communist comrades.

However it may be in the future, we cannot wait much longer before insisting on an agreement among the forces committed to building a new social order. The energies unleashed by the Industrial Revolution are such that if they are not rapidly controlled and socialized—that is, put at the service of the human community—we run the risk of seeing them destroy humanity in an ever nearer future. We need only imagine what at this very moment a minority in its folly could do with the energy of the atom; we need only review the crimes committed by the small number of those who have gathered together the world's wealth into their hands, while two-thirds of the planet live in a precarious, not to say miserable situation—think only of Guatemala and El Salvador.

Our conviction is that by denying the religious dimension of reality, Marxism cuts itself off from the most powerful energy in the human being. If it perseveres in this attitude it will be frustrated in its hope of changing, in a decisive manner, the social condition. Every Marxist revolution, even when it is successful, even when it represents "objective" progress with respect to the previous situation, will always end by permitting the reappearance of oppressive structures unless it consents to recognize the importance of the religious factor—of mysticism—in the historical process.

Conversely, we believe that Christianity, without instruments of a social analysis that are scientific, or at least rational, will cut itself off from one of its most legitimate hopes: acquiring political tools to change the world. We have said it a hundred times: the kingdom of God is not merely a message to proclaim, it is also a task to accomplish: to transform collectivity into community under the inspiration of grace.

Marx, like Jesus, was a Jew. It is unfortunate that Marx was born in an age where he was unable, through the screen of Christians and established churches, to catch a glimpse of the unique God whom, perhaps, he might have been able to accept: the God of the carpenter of Nazareth. Jesus the Jew "knew" God, and thereby the true nature of humanity, thus acquiring a deeper and more exact vision of the human person than Marx the Jew did.

Thus it is incumbent on us, on us Christians, in spite of our immense historical faults, to formulate some fundamental "anthropological" questions to Marx and his successors. Perhaps in that way we can contribute a little toward breaking down the barriers that now hold back two worlds, born out of the same stock, from a mutual encounter. In our opinion, only by beginning with human beings and their concrete problems, carefully observing their daily conduct both practical and philosophical, not confusing our vision with a prefabricated ideology, can we correctly formulate the question about the relationship between Marxism and Christianity. The bridge that already joins the two worlds is the will to serve human beings. That is what leads Christianity as well as Marxism to want to change the society that surrounds them both. Witness what the theology of liberation is currently doing in Latin America. This is why our method of working is to begin with an observation of human reality, in order afterward to formulate a question concerning theory that will permit a more penetrating understanding of the hidden mechanisms of history. Why, for example, should we deny or reduce the determinative character of the religious phenomenon, when in fact it constantly recurs in the history of civilizations, through all social collapses?

This then is our proposal: to criticize Marx, but in order to see better how to move ahead. Rightly or wrongly we believe that the political culture of the twentieth century is still too unsophisticated. Decidedly, now is the time to drop once and for all our bad conscience in the presence of Marxists, because it blocks us from thinking. We judge also that a theological approach to the political phenomenon is indispensable.

The critiques that we would make to Marx are in five areas.

THE ALMOST EXCLUSIVELY CRITICAL STANCE OF MARX

Here I have been helped by unpublished manuscripts of Jacques Lefur. Marx shows the faults of industrial society in its capitalist form with an incomparable clarity, and it would be wholly unreasonable to deny the value of his criticism. But it is not enough to analyze the functioning of a given society. We must also lay out the means to arrive at another social structure. It is not enough to criticize; we must also say what is to be put in the place of the thing criticized. "If you are a poet, I am a critic," Marx wrote to a friend in 1860. All Marx's books are critiques; and from 1850 on, solely critiques of political economy. The French proverb has it, "Criticism is easy, art is difficult." Nietzsche let slip the admission at the age of eighteen, in 1862: "I have tried to deny everything; it is easy to destroy, but to rebuild. . . ."

THE POLITICAL REFLECTION OF MARX

The means by which Marx in his youth thought of building another society are astonishingly weak, especially the political means of organizing and directing the new society. Behind this lack lies a very difficult theoretical problem, which has not been properly treated by Marxism up to this day: the problem of the state. Marx reflected much more on the economic realm than on the political realm. He thought it was possible to give a solution to the problems of industrial society while remaining, at least in principle, on the economic level. But in doing so he gravely relativized the purely political level. Did he not prophesy the disappearance of the state? With Marx the political realm always tends to lose its autonomy and its specific character. The different types of power blend together.

This tendency is very plain in the Soviet Union and other socialist-Marxist countries where trade unions, the executive, the legislature, and the judiciary tend to become identified and have no real independent life. The danger that they should become mere transmission-belts for decisions made elsewhere is not small. It accounts for the revolt of the trade union Solidarity in Poland. But should not the true function of politics be as the place where conflicts can be "administered," that is, resolved? Conflicts arise constantly among human beings, especially in the economic domain, where interests are diverse and often opposed, even in the socialist countries. The present evolution in China, including the trial of the "gang of four," is, among other things, the dramatic expression of a violent shock between different conceptions of the economic future and technology of that country.

The fact that Marx's reflection was so much more economic than political explains no doubt why he reflected so little on the nature of political *authority* in its etymological sense of "that which makes something increase." What is the power that makes a revolution grow and provokes very different human beings to band together in the project of a new society? Marx either never thought out, or never had the time to write, the second volume, which his position logically demands: *Der Sozialismus.* He limited himself to the first volume, *Das Kapital,* his critique of capitalism. This is a serious lack, because, when Marxists take power, they do not understand very clearly what to do with it, how to create a socialist society. And thus in the most serious domains they have recourse to the most traditional means of political authority when it lacks original or scientific solutions: they reward, they punish, they legislate, they exercise surveillance—they even bureaucratize.

This does not deny that the Marxist attempts at building socialism contain positive elements. They have built up an instructive body of experience in spite of their improvisations. This simply means that the solutions that have been devised are precarious because political culture is still impoverished. In the East as in the West nobody knows what tune to play in order to reorganize industrial society so that it will be at once creative, dynamic, and more nearly just. For a long time capitalism showed its contradictions and injustices. It seems that only the model of the Marxist hope remained.

But in our opinion this model is in crisis, because international communism is currently in a difficult situation. Many feel deceived by it and are searching elsewhere, sometimes in a most frightening manner as in the Iran of Khomeini. In order to build a revolution, hope is necessary; this was a correct insight of Roger Garaudy, who elaborated a Project Hope proposing concrete solutions for a new society in his celebrated work, *The Alternative Future: A Vision of Christian Marxism* (trans. L. Mayhew, New York: Simon and Schuster, 1974). Marx limited himself much too strictly when he said, or let others conclude, that a communitarian society would come about through the dictatorship of the proletariat—as if the seizure of power by the oppressed class were of itself an event sufficient to release a talented social inventiveness leading to a human industrial society.

It is true that a joyful and successful popular revolution releases a wave of enthusiasm and lets loose the creativity of masses finally freed from oppression. The most impressive feature of the new Nicaragua even before the struggle was the people's joy in finally taking up their destiny. But it remains necessary, so as not to deceive the people, that *political* solutions should be found so as to reorganize society, and that theoretical errors giving birth to dogmatisms should not too greatly hinder the discovery of these solutions. To say, "The party is the avant-garde of the proletariat, and as such it expresses clearly what the people desire," may be true only in part. For an avant-garde of militants may well seize on certain aspects of social change to carry out and ignore others. We must always be attentive to intermediate groups and to persons as individuals.

Certainly Marx often insists that nothing is automatic in the historical process after the seizure of power by the proletariat. Thus things will not necessarily go well without extreme human vigilance. We must be ready for great sacrifices, for a ceaseless struggle, for a constant analysis of reality in order to bring the new society to birth. Still it seems to us that, in practice, many historical Marxisms behave as if the seizure of power by the proletariat by itself released a creative development of history, which step by step with its unfolding would give the answers to all questions of praxis. While this assumption is not in principle wholly false, the course of events in Russia, in China, in Cambodia, and in many other socialist countries shows how chaotic and often bloody these historical developments can be. And if so many types of Marxism behave in this precarious manner, it strikes us that the cause is the theoretical inadequacy of Marx himself, who envisages the primary change on the economic level and has great difficulty in getting his thought to move on the specifically political level. Hence, in our opinion, arise the difficulties of historic Marxism in fully working out social projects or pedagogies for change, and also in deepening its reflection on the nature and specific function of political authority in the new society. Hence our third question to Marx.

THE QUESTION OF THE STATE IN MARX

What a difficult question! Let us have the audacity to approach it. Although it is already a complex task, it is not impossible to transform a technologically backward society, such as Cuba or Tanzania, into a socialist society. When technology is not too complex and the division of tasks is not excessively detailed, it is possible to rotate functions; and the collective control of each one's work is within the scope of the group, because enough of the producers are in command of current techniques. But when technology becomes more sophisticated, we come up against a double complexity: the complexity of *technique* as such (well analyzed by Jacques Ellul), which implies the appearance of specialists, technocrats who are the sole possessors of knowledge in their area; and the complexity of the *management* of society, that is, the organization and administration of the legal-industrial complex that makes production possible.

This administrative complexity brings in a much more rigorous division of tasks. Another technocrat appears on the scene: the administrator of enterprises, the manager of industrial societies. This division of labor, if we think in normal Marxist fashion, inevitably causes the appearance of different social categories and a new caste division of society, even in the socialist countries. So once again a special level of structure must be envisaged to resolve the conflicts among groups—that is, a political power, a state. What would be the nature of this power and its function in an advanced industrial society of socialist type? Is it really possible to arrive at a disappearance, even little by little, of the state, if an inevitable division of labor continues to exist? Who will resolve the conflicts? How can the state of a socialist society be kept securely in contact with the base so as not to become an oppressive structure? Difficult questions—whose answers, to our mind, have both political aspects and theological aspects.

Political Aspects

Marx announces the disappearance of the state. Lenin perceives that the question is more complex; unquestionably he sees that the state is not solely a reflex of the ruling class, but that it exercises specific management functions. A disciple of Louis Althusser in Brazil insists that underlying the tragic divisions of international communism or the factional disputes internal to a country are at least two theoretical problems.

1. The Problem of the State: How shall we think about the state of the proletarian revolution, which, as it travels toward its own extinction, must conciliate two opposing demands: the greatest possible degree of democracy with respect to the masses of the people, and the dictatorship of the proletariat against its class enemies? How are we to avoid the bureaucratization of the avant-garde of the proletariat—namely, the segment of conscious militants—when it is a necessary practical concern to attain these two objectives?

2. The Nature of the Power Needed to Direct the World Revolution: How is the class struggle to be organized and directed on the international level? Historically there have always been two deviations. First, the nationalist deviation, of Soviet type, claims that socialism as realized in a single country must be the locomotive of the world revolution and must direct the class struggle in all the other countries of the world. In fact, this position has always led to catastrophic setbacks for the countries or parties so directed: their socialism and their struggle do not succeed in being really indigenous, adapted to their own needs. Second, the "Trotskyite" deviation—not so much in the sense of Trotsky's own position but of its abuses. It consists in rejecting the hegemony of any party or nation as the leader of the forces directing the worldwide or national revolution, and instead in encouraging a permanent revolution. The revolution is seen as the work of the masses *before* being the work of their organizations. Strategy consists above all in arousing people to revolt, in throwing them massively into action, without making the organization of a party into a dogmatic principle. Pushed to its extreme, this tendency ends up in assassination, in political genocide.

These matters are constantly debated in Marxist circles, but never with fully clear answers. Thus the impoverishment of our political culture is brought into full daylight; for the response called "capitalist" is much more brief.

In capitalist circles, these difficult but essential theoretical questions are never brought up at all. The only concern is to manage industrial society in the short term: that is, to assure the future of existing industries during the next three or four years. For instance, what is Ford or Volkswagen to be in a strictly limited future? Nobody, however, puts any gray matter to work thinking about ways to forge an economy that will be more human, both for the long run and for the whole planet. This failure was explicitly confirmed to us—with great loyalty to his system—by a brilliant Yale economist, as well as by other influential technocrats in the United States and Europe.

We are far from the dreams of Father Lebret (carried on today by Father Vincent Cosmao), who by reflecting correctly along these lines founded the movement Economy and Humanism for third-world development, inspired by the encyclicals of John XXIII and Paul VI. Just the name says much for the ambitious scope of his work. The humanization of the economy presupposes very complex responses in all realms. For example, moderation in the use of raw materials; care for the environment; the quality of work in all industries: how to produce, manage, and share so that the human-being-at-work will work in the most human way possible, in the spirit of John Paul II's *Laborem Exercens*; economic choices so that the industries created will really answer the needs of the poor: Brazil needs tractors more than cars, and intelligent agrarian reform more than a massive concentration of population in the cities; a more logical financial politics: everybody knows that money sticks to money and that loans are made only to the rich. These are only samples of the many necessary decisions, which are all, in the end, of political nature, which have a revolutionary character, and which presuppose a broad local and international civic generosity. Without sobriety and a spirit of sharing, both among those endowed by nature with unimaginable material resources (such as Arabs with their oil), and among those endowed by history with scientific and technological capital (the first world and in particular the United States), there is no reform for the world economy possible, and we are galloping toward catastrophe.

Thus, to repeat, we have thought much on the economic level and very little on the political level. This is as true of Marxism as of capitalism. Hegel, more profound than Marx, concerned himself much more with the political question and his philosophy retains much more consistency on that level. His political philosophy allows us to go further than Marxism, but it does not allow us to dispel the shadow of totalitarianism. We must then turn to those political struggles, especially in Latin America, which are of original character and have brought about progress in political thought and action.

The Brazilian Left, with its concepts of autonomy and self-management *(autogestão)*, has gone a step beyond both the collectivization of the means of production and the previous level of reflection; and thus it separates itself willy-nilly from a far-too-Leninist concept of revolution. The party has been relativized. What in fact does "autonomy" mean? It means that each individual and each entity has its own characteristic life and creativity, which cannot be fully expressed in the life of the whole. For example, the trade union expresses an aspect of the working class that is not to be found in the Workers' party. Hence the trade union must not be absorbed by the party. So the person as an individual, the community as a group, the family, and so on, are all autonomous; each expresses something original. Certainly they must remain united to all the other social bodies and submit themselves to a collective discipline. But that does not mean that they must abdicate their proper creativity, or be obliged to obey without the liberty to protest or even to refuse. Hence the question arises: How is it possible to concretize in socialist strucures, and in particular on the level of the state, this autonomy of intermediate groups and of individuals? This is the whole point. We are very far from a reasoned answer. That is why when revolutionary groups seize power they mostly improvise solutions, which look more like the result of a large intuitive group-dynamics than a thought-out answer. "What will happen when the proletariat assumes power?" "We shall find out! We must trust the people's creativity." A naïve and perhaps tragically irresponsible answer!

Theological Aspects

We do not think that the political approach alone is adequate to deal with the question of power and the state in a socialist society. In the end, who will lead the masses of Latin America into a common sharing of their human and material resources in the economic, political, and ideological realms? Who will convince them to sacrifice themselves to that goal and freely submit to a revolutionary discipline? We repeat: we do not think that this force can be power alone, even the power of the proletariat. Another factor is necessary: grace. Grace to share and work in common with self-sacrifice and love. The base communities of Salvadoran refugees in the camps of Honduras have today a living experience of this reality.

One further observation. Our conviction is that the roots of great civilizations, before being economic, are political, and even prior to that, mystical. A realizable utopia must shine out from the eyes of a very large number before the world receives the energy necessary to make a change. By "realizable utopia" we mean a change in society that is not totally beyond reach; a social "place" that is different but not wholly inaccessible. Our broad options are simple; what is complex is how to reach them, the "know-how." For example: we desire an industrial society of sharing and sobriety, where the problems of food and water are resolved (e.g., through agrarian reform), where the contact of human beings with nature is not destructive (through a renewed sense of the environment). Our desire has consequences. We wish to be able to make democratic decisions about what is to be produced; we do not wish any longer to be chained to the production of cars and electrical appliances that do not correspond to our current fundamental needs here in Latin America. We wish factories where self-management is possible, and this requires the simultaneous presence of several factors: the scale of the factory and its shops must be modest; tasks must be rotated among the workers to avoid infinite specialization; and so on. We also wish decentralized cities small enough to be governed by their inhabitants, even though small scale is just one of the factors in self-management.

To speak of all those things, however, is to dream, in the good sense of the word: that is, to believe in the existence of a poetic and utopian function in every human being. To concretize these dreams, to render them viable, already means engaging in politics—and in politics on the grand scale, in the most fundamental sense. It is remarkable that in one sense the true curve of affairs is as follows. For economics to be human, it must be related to politics; that is, it must rest on intelligent political choices, which are abandoned neither to the whim of the marketplace nor to the stifling rigor of planning. But in its turn, politics must be attached to mysticism; that is, to people's capacity to dream of a new world. Mental representations of justice and fraternity, implicit moral codes, are indispensable to the functioning of societies.

Those who "dream" best and who best know how to make the great moral and religious choices are the "poor"—those to whom it is said that the kingdom of God belongs. In fact, at the end of the day, who possesses the political strength to make decisive and revolutionary changes? Not the technocrats, but the immense mass of the poor who suffer in their flesh the harmful consequences of the present industrial world, who actually operate the machines. Although we recognize the function of the intellectual as fundamental, our confidence rests with the people. That is why we dedicate ourselves with all our strength, and as our top priority, to working with the base communities of the church.

MARX'S RATIONALISM AND SCIENTISM

Is reality rational or not? Hegel declared in a famous phrase, "Whatever is real is rational and whatever is rational is real." This notion, which is not confined to Hegel, reflects the scientism of the nineteenth century, which believed it had found a stunning confirmation of its theses in the triumph of the exact sciences, physics and chemistry, and of technology.

Hence arises the exaggerated optimism of Marxism. In this view of the world, reason, along with its child, scientific analysis, is thought capable of resolving all problems. This optimism as regards the power of reason coincides with the industrial development that infinitely multiplies the productive resources and wealth of humanity. It seemed that everything was possible. Now industry is the child of technology, which in turn is the child of science. The same rationalism and optimism breathe through both capitalism and its most virulent critic—Marxism. Today we discover to our sorrow that reason does not solve all human problems. On the contrary: the fantastic development of wealth, due to industrial, technical, and scientific growth and to the increasing control of reason over matter, far from eliminating misery, has multiplied it. Multiplied also are the contradictions and the forces of destruction.

The Marxist science of history—for Marxists say that there is a science of history—has not yet reached the point of organizing the class struggle and directing history, either within the third-world countries or on the international level. The communist countries, depositories of the "science of history," are engaged in ferocious fighting. In Brazil the factions within Marxist groups are so numerous that the tensions joining and separating them are often inextricable and certainly hold back the proletarian struggle. It is impossible today to work out a common strategy.

Correspondingly, the capitalist countries, who imagine themselves to be more empirical, less ideological, and in the end more "rational," more capable of managing industrial society, do not know how to halt the catastrophic hemorrhage of global resources consumed by their monstrous organism that itself is powerless to call a halt. They do not know how to resolve the problem of world hunger.

There are just two alternatives: either there is, properly speaking, no science of history; or this science is still very precarious, and we should hasten to perfect it. In our opinion, one cannot in fact speak of a science of history. It would be more correct to say that there can be found rational aspects and scientific elements among the historical data. Unquestionably the merit of Marxism lay in submitting to a rational analysis the effects of the mode of production on the conduct of societies. This granted, we have to admit that, after many attempts, reality as a whole—including historical reality—cannot be interpreted or known by the power of reason alone. The philosophers speak of "epistemological breaks," that is, gaps, abrupt jumps, between different forms of knowledge. There are dimensions of reality that are supra-rational, which reason alone is powerless to explain or direct. For example, the love between a man and a woman; or the blend of will and hope that leads one to risk all in order to become a revolutionary. One can heap up more-than-correct analyses and criticisms of a given society and never budge an inch oneself; one can continue to accept the situation as it is, even though profoundly unjust, and persist in being politically inactive, at a point of immobility that is, in effect, on the side of the existing regime. At bottom all indignation is ethical, not political!

This supra-rational aspect of reality explains why religions survive political regimes: Christianity survived the decadent Roman empire, feudalism, monarchy, capitalism; it is alive in Marxist regimes, in the "atheocracy" of a Poland, in the bloody plutocracy of El Salvador, of all Latin America. Political "science" simply does not take everything into account. There is another dimension of reality: the ultimate finality of things and beings, which is the proper realm of the religious. To reduce our knowledge of reality to the rational and scientific is to condemn ourselves, necessarily, to being incapable of living with reality and, frequently, to being destroyed by it. So our industrial societies are menaced by nuclear holocaust. Pure rationalism, which works in science, works less well in politics.

Philosophical perversions determine perversions in other realms and particularly in politics. If whatever is real is rational, we must submit ourselves without complaint to the proprietors of knowledge: either to the science of the party, the enlightened vanguard of the proletariat, which knows where things are going; or to the orders of the capitalist technocrats, who know what they are talking about when they manage industrial society.

This is the "theoretical" base of totalitarianism and of the exploitation of the poor by the rich. Certainly political human beings and those in charge of the economy have their own actual competence. What we criticize here is the ideology of scientism that leads us to place a blind confidence in such persons, or that authorizes them to use every form of constraint when we fail to agree with them. If they believe that they truly know, it is normal for them to conclude that they have a right to be obeyed under all circumstances. We condemn a philosophical error, not transient errors in behavior. Philosophy is not a neutral exercise. It has consequences; sometimes these are tragic. It is necessary to oppose Hegel, Marx, and bourgeois-industrial scientism to the extent that they reduce the real to the rational.

RELIGION AND MARX

Marx was right in underlining the importance of the class struggle in the history of the industrial societies. He was right in seeing in that struggle a factor of progress, one that the history of the century following Marx has not ceased to confirm. It is in and through the class struggle that these societies, in many places, have been improved; that injustice has been pushed back; that the condition of the workers is no longer what it was in the beginning. But Marx was in error, we suggest, when he made the class struggle into the sole motive force behind history. History does not progress solely through the class struggle; besides the dialectic of antagonism there is a fruitful dialectic of *differences*. For example, the difference between man and woman, parent and child, family and base community, trade union and party. And on the level of ideas, between science and religion, reason and poetry, and so on.

Marx introduced into the class struggle an almost Messianic hope, as if the end of capitalist society would coincide with the end of social conflicts and mark the beginning of a truly human society, where each would be respected and recognized by all. This is to expect from the class struggle far more than it can give. Even if we do away with social classes as we know them, even if there are no more monopolists of the means of production, why on account of that should conflicts come to an end? We have seen that the management of advanced industrial societies, even under a socialist regime, is very complex. By introducing this concept of an end of conflicts, Marx invested the class struggle with a metaphysical hope, which contradicts his intention of doing away with all illusions, and in particular with religious illusions.

Certainly, human beings, together, build their future. Certainly, God does not intervene in history as a magician or as a historical force comparable to others. We are accustomed to say that God "inspires" history but respects the autonomy of the divine creation. The correct question is this: What are the conditions under which the future of humanity will be more human? Will it be sufficient to that goal if we are delivered from capitalism and from religion by the "critique of earth and the critique of heaven"? Is it true that "man is the Supreme Being for man" (Marx, 1843), a formula that its author never retracted? As critical as Marx is in other realms, here he is insufficiently critical or, rather, imprudently noncritical. He falls into the old temptation of secular humanism and anthropomorphic religions: making the human being into the center of the universe.

Nietzsche showed clearly that nothing proves humanity to be this center. For him, nothingness is the center of the universe, and people must be courageous in face of this nothingness, rolling up their sleeves and conducting themselves with dignity. Only superpeople will achieve this. Modern science, so much admired by Marx, shows, rather, that the human being is only a tiny animal lost in the immensity of the cosmos—a view that Nietzsche saw long before by his philosophical reasoning. As for Christians, they have always said that not humanity, but divinity, is at the center. At the heart of reality, at the source of the universe, there is a personal Being, full of light and life, ready to illuminate all things as soon as the door is opened for it. But it is already there, in the center; the human being is not.

Pierre Teilhard de Chardin has described the process in superb pages: the little planet Earth—and the whole universe—in the control of a process of "amorization" is softly lighted by the fire of this love; this light is in the act of increasing and of invading all the universe. The earth becomes translucent with beauty and reason. In spite of the dramas and resistance of humanity, beauty and goodness are invading the world—precisely because the human being, since it is not the center, is able to open itself to a divine energy that does not proceed from it.

What is this center? Who is this center? An answer is mandatory. If it is only the human being, Marx is right. But no decisive proof of such a thesis is possible. And in any case what Marx says is an affirmation that is in no sense scientific but, rather, noncritical and (as we have said) naïve. It confounds desire and reality. Nietzsche is more "reasonable" than Marx. Who is this center? If we do not answer this question, we are condemned to never correctly interpreting reality, and to being wiped out—each of us, and all others with us—by blind historical forces, which will arrive galloping from the depths of the horizon, and which will fall, like the four horsemen of the Apocalypse, on those unfortunates who could not discern where the harmonizing force of the universe lies. That is why the question about God is a human question from which nobody can escape.

It is interesting to observe that Marx was no innovator in the matter of a critique of religion. For the most part he only repeated the theses of Feuerbach. He criticized the "closed religion" rejected by the great French philosopher Henri Bergson, but never over the whole course of history glimpsed the existence of the "open religion" defined so marvelously by the same philosopher. It is true that he and Engels recognized the positive role of early Christianity, but, obsessed by their initial antireligious hypotheses, they could not draw from that recognition the appropriate conclusions for a more embracing and objective assessment of the religious phenomenon. So they passed by a great truth unawares. (See chap. 1, above, journal entry of Dec. 19, 1980.)

These are some of the questions that we would like to present naïvely to Marx and his current disciples—precisely because we recognize all the positive contributions of Marxism, and because we feel it urgent to arrive at a union of all sincerely democratic and proletarian forces.

6

Church Base Communities

THE CONCEPT OF CHURCH BASE COMMUNITY

Although church base communities exist on other continents, it is in Latin America that they have acquired their key status in the contemporary church. These communities are defined by the three parts of the name.

As *communities,* church base communities are groups of human size, that is, of a size wherein one can learn the name and the history of each member (generally numbering between 20 and 150 persons). In the countryside, the communities average more members than in the city. In the city, the poor, over and above their economic poverty, are uprooted persons, from every corner of the country, who do not know each other. Furthermore, in the city the working schedules are so inhuman that the time available for meeting is much less. In the countryside often, though not always, the misery is greater, but more *time* is available; the church is the sole place for meeting.

The life of a base community is intense. In it the members jointly take on the essential struggles for survival or for the improvement of living—the struggle for water, for clinics, for sewers. Above all is the struggle for land, in the city as well as in the countryside; for in the city, land on which to build a house or squatters' land on which to establish a *barraco* are the objects of ceaseless fighting. There are struggles for job training, for day-care centers, in opposition to police violence, for the rehabilitation of young people on drugs or in armed gangs, on behalf of families who arrive destitute from the interior of the country, for the defense of local traditions and popular festivals, against the increase of the cost of living in support of strikes. The list goes on and on. It should be understood that these base communities are not "communes": they hardly ever reach the point of a full sharing of goods or of common meals.

Still there exists a minimum of community structures: a coordination team *(equipe coordenadora)* elected or chosen, usually renewable; a common fund; a yearly and monthly program; regular general assemblies; several gatherings each week. The intra-church tasks (assisting at the sacraments, liturgical celebrations, catechesis, biblical groups) and the extra-church tasks (people's struggles in the *bairro* or factories) are taken by laypeople. The same persons may take responsibility both for tasks called "religious" and for tasks designated as human or political betterment; the same one who gives the Bible instruction or who preaches at the Mass may also be the chief union activist. Theologically, we call these "charisma" or "ministries": a particular gift from God to one of God's children (a charisma) corresponds to a task (a ministry), which is taken on for the good of the collectivity. There is no "division of tasks" properly speaking, even though much time is spent in organizational meetings. It is practice that reveals the gifts of each one, and there is no delegation of power as such from the community. Whoever is able to do so takes responsibility for the community meeting by taking account of each one's competence and putting order into the gifts. If certain ones are not in the right place, they leave their jobs under pressure of events: people, without saying anything about it, no longer come to the meeting, the liturgy, the activity that no longer is able to attract their interest. In general there is no official recognition of these ministries except in more difficult situations where it is necessary to reinforce the authority of somebody who has taken on a task with competence.

Finally, the base community is a community and not a group, because all the generations are represented in it: children, young people, adults, old people. There are families; the unmarried; and frequently, visiting guests.

As *church-oriented,* the principle motivation of base communities is religious. Practically speaking, all are built around the urban parish in the poor quarters or around the country chapel. They are strongly connected with the bishop; whereas in Europe the base communities, often having a different social origin and being communes rather than communities, are mistrusted by the hierarchy, and vice versa. These are communities of faith, hope, and charity, which are gathered together around the word of God and the Eucharist, and receive the energy to change the world through the celebration of their faith. They represent a church revolution to the extent that they correspond to a gigantic *restructuring* of the Catholic community on the Latin American continent. It is estimated that in Brazil there are 80,000 base communities of this type, meeting in the local parish churches.

As *base communities,* these communities are overwhelmingly made up of people who work with their hands: mothers of families, domestic servants, workers in industry, the unemployed, those who have retired from work (often at a young age, because of sickness), peasants occupying the land without title for generations, agricultural laborers, small farmers, bricklayers, workers on big public projects or with urban contractors building the homes of the rich, migrant laborers, and so forth. The community members are mostly people with three to four times the legal minimum monthly income. They live in rented buildings on the outskirts of the big cities, or in places they themselves have built during weekends on sites that they are buying through long-term mortgages in the face of rampant real-estate speculation, or in shantytowns *(favelas)* on land that does not belong to them and on which they have simply squatted.

In the countryside they live either in little villlages or on the outskirts of small towns where they are picked up each morning in trucks to be employed as agricultural laborers by the day or week. Such are called *boia-fria* ("cold dish"), for they have no way of heating food at the workplace. Whether in the city or in the country, they are illiterate or only marginally literate; some can recognize the alphabet letter by letter, but cannot grasp the sense of something they have just read. Some can read, but without retaining much of what is written, and can only write with the greatest difficulty.

Carlos Mesters, a Dutch Carmelite who has lived and worked in Brazil for many years, has learned how to study the Bible with the people and make it accessible to them. He says that the base communities have received a triple mission from Jesus (Mk. 3:14): to be with Jesus; to proclaim the good news; and to have authority to cast out the numerous demons that fill our society. Correspondingly, Mesters says, these communities must remain faithful (Acts 2:42): to the teaching of the apostles (through the biblical circles); to fraternal communion (through mutual aid and sharing); and to the breaking of bread (in the Eucharist).

There is no doubt that the guiding model in the Spirit for these communities, once again, has been the community of the Acts of the Apostles (Acts 2:42–47; 4:32–35), as it always has been in the ages of church renewal.

THE CHURCH BASE COMMUNITY IN BRAZIL

Let me here recount my personal experience, which unfolded in a big city, the megalopolis Osasco, itself a suburb of São Paulo, during the years since 1968, when I began to work in Latin America. I came there from Aubervilliers in Paris, where for seven years a group of us had tried to build what we then called a *communauté de quartier.* Our original team was composed of Georges Joulin, Gilles Renaudin, and me; later additions were Olivier Fradin, Bernard Fèvre, Jean-François Girette, and Jean Kodische. In vain. That was not the pastoral orientation of the French church. I had heard that in Brazil the bishops spoke of base communities. The first such appeared either around 1960 in Nísia Floresta near Natal, or in 1964 in the diocese of Volta Redonda. I arrived in Brazil in January 1968, shortly after the reappearance of repression and the expansion of an extremely brutal military dictatorship. In December of that year a "law of exception," Act 13, overshadowed the country by suspending nearly all citizens' guarantees over against an all-powerful state obssssed with an anticommunist psychosis. At that time, while remaining a secular priest on assignment *(fidei donum)* from the diocese of Saint-Denis in Paris, I was part of the team of the workers' mission São Pedro e São Paulo founded by Father Jacques Loew, which had been in the field for some years. We had no parish. We picked a *bairro* and made our living working in the factory. There were six of us: Paulo Xardel, Pierre Wauthier, Manuel Retumba, Gaspar Neerinck, Jean Mazeran, and me.

The repression that fell on the country had a lot to do, in my opinion, with the efflorescence of church base communities. There was a confluence of several factors.

The Lay Character of Brazilian Christianity

Brazil has always had very few priests—at present, 11,000 for 120 million inhabitants, and almost half of them foreign. Hence there has always been a layperson, even though illiterate, able to gather the people together to say the Rosary, for example. The Brazilian church in its historical formation has not at all been a clerical one. The best elements of the clergy have always been persecuted by a power jealous of its authority and insistent on finding no limit to its thirst for exploiting the fabulous riches of the country—a thirst to which indigenous Indians or blacks imported from the African colonies of Portugal (or elsewhere, e.g., Dahomey-Benin, Nigeria), especially if organized by the church, might create some obstacle. It must never be forgotten that some hundreds of Jesuits were expelled in 1759 by the Marquis de Pombal, first minister of the king of Portugal; and that one of these Jesuits, Gabriel Malagrida, was in fact burned alive in a public square in Lisbon because, "deaf to the terror which cowed the nation, he dared raise his voice when Silence was the law" (J. Lúcio de Azevedo, cited by Eduardo Hoornaert in his book *Formacão do catolicismo brasileiro, 1550-1800: ensaio del interpretacão a partir dos oprimidos* [Petropolis: Vozes, 1974]). Why such a wave of terror? Very simply because, after numerous tentative efforts, the Jesuits had really succeeded in "evangelizing," at least among the Indians. (The blacks, for reasons too long to go into here, to all intents and purposes have never been defended by the church.) The result was the formation of "reserves," actual republics, among them the republic of the Guaranis, which extended in the north as far as Maranhão in Amazonia, scene today of violent land conflicts; and in the south as far as Paraguay.

In these base communities of that age, even though somewhat patriarchal and paternalistic, the Indians learned how to escape from the steam roller of colonization and to achieve awareness of their human rights—namely, their rights to the land. That represented potentially a great danger to the Portuguese, few in number, while the Indians were nearly 5 million; hence the expulsion of the Jesuits by the Marquis de Pombal. The colonial government always mistrusted the religious orders, which, by their international organization, their direct dependence on Rome, and the higher level of training of their members over against the secular clergy, represented a counterforce on which the government could not lay a finger. But under the empire, when Brazil became independent of Portugal, the novitiates of the religious orders were closed for fifty years.

Today things are nearly the same. The church, whose secular clergy and bishops have considerably improved, thanks to, successively, the Benedictines, Catholic Action, and Vatican Council II, naturally makes up the great focus of opposition to the regime—for the federal government in Brasilia cannot remove a bishop from his seat, whereas between one day and the next it can shut down Congress, arrest recalcitrant generals, dismiss the state governors, and close down the trade unions.

The historical reminders will help us understand that the Brazilian people— these descendants of Indians, blacks, and European immigrants—have very often had to pull their own chestnuts out of the fire without the help of priests. Catholicism has been transmitted mostly through the family, or (in a style something short of evangelical) by the colonial lord: a great landed proprietor, or the owner of a sugar mill, processing the crop of thousands of hectares of sugarcane through hard labor. A lesser role has been played by an inadequate clergy, often poorly trained, whose return in force—and at that with a very Italianate style—did not begin to make itself felt until the beginning of the twentieth century.

Repression

A second element that helped to generate the base communities was the special type of repression that has fallen on Brazilian society. The base communities were really born in 1968 (in this writer's opinion). By Christmas of 1968, after the toughening of the regime in December of that year, the priests and religious—the "agents of pastoral ministry"—had to make a choice: either join the guerrilla forces and the clandestine subversion, as urged by certain Marxist and even Christian elements of the middle class, or attach themselves, more seriously than before, to a pastoral labor at the base, in order to get close to the worker militants and peasants and form communities with them. Those options were never laid out with the clarity just used here, but they were real. Many factors entered into the decision.

The Distancing of the Church from the Military

A further factor was the gradual growth of mistrust for the church among the military, and vice versa. It must not be forgotten, as we have just said, that the church is the sole area of life that extends its branches into the remotest corners of the Brazilian territory, with the state unable to change its personnel. In the beginning, the clergy supported the military coup d'état of 1964 out of fear of communism. Then a conflict of interests arose. Since the people had no other vehicle to express their sentiments than the church, it saw swelling toward itself a wave of complaints from those who had been subjected to the exactions of a very brutal capitalist revolution, as by eviction and assassination. Then the Christian militants of Catholic Action, their chaplains, and certain bishops were themselves subjected to police persecution, prison, and torture. A conscientious position was established. The church responded as a single body, especially in face of the ever increasing use of torture. Some diocesan newsletters and religious magazines were confiscated by the public authorities or censored; bishops were threatened with trial, while the number of political prisoners rose to 10,000.

The Character of the Bishops

Another historic stroke of good fortune for the Brazilian church was and remains the courage and greatness of its episcopate. From the point of view of both intelligence and apostolic courage it is of the first order. Certainly, leaders are not everything. Without the people they are nothing. But if the leaders turn traitor at the hour of the decisive battle, the troops do not advance as a solid body and they are picked off like rabbits. The Brazilian bishops never acted the traitor when they were in a difficult situation. It is not everywhere thus. At the time of World War II the European bishops could not bring themselves to face Nazism in the same manner, with a few brilliant exceptions—in Poland for example, here and there in France and elsewhere. A number of episcopates in Latin America today, apart from the Brazilian and Chilean and some others, are behind the times or frankly reactionary.

The Brazilian bishops had a double measure of courage. On the one hand, they displayed a *civic courage* in refusing to accept the unacceptable: torture, assassination, the breakdown of law, crying social injustice, lack of sharing. On the other hand, they showed an *apostolic courage,* whose effects will be felt for a longer period. They said to themselves: "If Christians are accustomed to gather around a layperson to say the Rosary, why not have them read the Bible also?" Here the renewal of Vatican II was fully operative. "If Christians are the people of God, let us give them knowledge of their origins through the knowledge of the Scriptures." Thousands of biblical circles were created. Priests and religious, nearer the base because of the repression, wasted the least amount of time in dutiful consultation with the authorities traditionally allied to the church, but by then suspect. Instead they became the advisers of their flocks and gave training in Bible-reading to the lay people, who from time immemorial have brought their sisters and brothers together. The reading of Scripture describes situations and lays down truths both of which are subversive. We have already mentioned the words of Genesis, "God created heaven and earth"; then the earth and everything built on it (factories, for example) belong to all. The first Christians had everything in common; why not we also? I repeat, our revolutionary discourse is a *religious* discourse, not initially or in the first place a political discourse. And that deeply disconcerts the classical Marxists as well as the ruling classes!

Furthermore, the men and women of extreme simplicity who have a tendency to consider themselves less than nothing *(Nós, não somos gente,* "But we, we aren't anybody"), when they began to read Scripture recognized themselves in the woman taken in adultery, the tax collector, the sick man, the thief crucified with Jesus, the apostles. And they took heart again, for these humble ones of the gospel are people like themselves. But for Jesus those people are the *agents* of the kingdom of God, the new world, the new society where the new creation that God wills is sketched. The reading of Scripture in a group plays the role of a true psychodrama. This group dynamic modifies the cultural climate. A very simple woman said, "Before, I went to Mass because I had the faith. Now I go because I understand."

The Spontaneous Appearance of Sacramental Cadres

This new understanding through Scripture generated something that nobody expected, the gospel extra, of which Jesus speaks: "But seek first his kingdom . . . and all these things will be give you *in addition"* (Mt. 6:33, italics added). Out of these base communities has arisen a cadre of thousands, those whom, in our theological language, we call "ministers," that is, servants of the common interest. And so it came about that this church, which was so lacking in priests, the classical agents of the traditional pastorate, that it had to bring them in from outside; this church sees rising up thousands of responsible ones, laypeople, poor and humble, generally young, who take care of every kind of service, including religious, ecclesiastical, and sacramental services, that the community needed. And also it came about that we, who had never thought of making it a high priortity to set up a pastorate generating priestly vocations, saw rising up a generation of young men who put themselves at the service of the church and took their place in the channels of the sacrament of holy orders. That is not to say that we ever denied the specific value of the sacerdotal order on the grounds of the flowering of lay ministries. But it is important to note that a pastorate to create priestly vocations is empty and even unhealthy unless it is preceded by a pastorate building the mission of the Christian people, taken in its entirety, with respect to the modern world. A living church always raises up cadres, draws in "vocations" (although, as we shall see, the expression is misleading), whether or not there is a vocational pastorate.

PEDAGOGY OF THE CHURCH BASE COMMUNITY: ONE WAY TO GO ABOUT IT

We shall speak here about our personal experience with a base community in a big city, more exactly in the miserable outskirts of the big Latin American cities. We are aware that roads different from those that we have followed are possible.

May we start by making a general observation. Church base communities, like Catholic Action earlier, nearly always have at their beginnings a priest or a sister. These are movements of clerical origin, even though their evolution right from the beginning leads to a state of affairs where the clergy no longer concentrate all the power in their own person. This is not the case for all such movements. Active nonviolence in Latin America, much more than the base communities, is a movement born out of lay experience and under lay guidance. In Brazil it was a lawyer and family man who initiated it; afterward, some time afterward, the church picked up the torch. In Argentina it was an architect, a husband and father. In Columbia and Chile, likewise, young laypeople are in the front lines of active nonviolence of the Gandhian type.

It was on the whole normal that the church base communities should have been the responsibility of pastors; for in the end, what was going on if not the *restructuring of the Catholic community*? And this is properly the bishops' task: to supervise the growth of love within communities and the good order of Christian assemblies, as well as their multiplication and their mutual relations. That is why it is such a great shame that in Europe the bishops do not perceive the role that they could play with respect to this flowering of communal experiments, which still linger on in the catacombs of history because those chief pastors do not know how to extricate them. After 1968, what are they waiting for?

Here is the method that we have followed in the creation of church based communities. It falls into six stages: living together; prayer; restoring a voice to the people; restoring action to the people; the expansion of ministries; toward collective action.

Living Together

A beautiful Portuguese word defines this stage: *convivência,* living together. Friendship takes time. Jesus lived thirty years at Nazareth before acting and speaking. The "wretched of the earth"—those who from their ancestors onward suffer oppression, descendants of black slaves, of Indians who have been the objects of veritable acts of genocide, of those poor European immigrants—are very suspicious: they have been deceived so many times! Much politeness, little friendship! Politeness is not merely the expression of a happy nature. We often forget that it is also a weapon of combat; people do all they can to avoid conflict when they are in a situation of inferiority. Hence infinite rules of manners, an amiability that can seem false if we overlook its motive. But those who are really integrated into the community do not misunderstand. As time goes by we can make a clear distinction between true friendship and the politeness that carries a two-edged sword. An advocate of nonviolence, who in truth risked everything in a workers' struggle that lasted ten years, spent the first three years in winning the confidence of the principal activist. During those three years he was constantly spied on.

So there is no shortcut, no recipe. One must embrace the cause of the oppressed, break with one's position in the ruling class, "live with" even in material circumstances if in any way possible as regards one's quarters, daily work, and so on.

Prayer

Always start from people's traditions, above all their religious traditions. For my own part I always began my base communities with prayer, even with reciting the Rosary! There are two reasons for that.

First, these migrants who come to live in the big city do not know each other. They are uprooted people who come from all states of Brazil, especially from the northeast and Minas Gerais. Only a slender thread still holds them together: popular devotions. If the padre calls a novena, a Rosary, a *casa em casa* (a progressive novena from house to house in the neighborhood), everybody comes, and it is a chance for the neighbors in the same street to meet each other or to deepen a passing acquaintance.

Second, prayer or, rather, the activities of prayer create the anticipation of a new world within societies in the process of change, which must not be underestimated. In my *bairro* of 40,000 inhabitants where I am the only priest, at a conservative estimate there are twenty cult centers of which only six are Catholic; activities of mystical type outstrip *futebol* and *pinga* (fermented sugarcane) in their power to bring people together. There are all kinds of mysticism and cults: Afro-Indian religions; voodoo (called *candomblé*); Pentecostal sects of Protestant origin, which commit everything to the Holy Spirit; the spirit-centers of Alan Kardec and others; the "Brazilian Catholic Church" separated from Rome. Furthermore, animism is immediately present. In short, an intense religious vegetation; and the seers and seeresses, the healers, astrologers, Jehovah's Witnesses, and so on have not been mentioned. All this is not to be laughed at: when people live in an unhappy world, they celebrate in a thousand ways the new world that they wish to have. This religion of miracle, of the supernatural bordering on magic, does not spring from alienation alone. In fact, what do we know of the invisible world? The West has become strangely insensitive to religious reality; it has grown cold. African and indigenous religions have retained in this realm a wisdom, an art of living that defies classification. Many centers of *candomblé* exercise a genuine group therapy through dance and the "incorporation of spirits," good or evil, which free the personality from its traumas better than any psychoanalyst. The "fathers and mothers of the saints" (the priests and priestesses) have received in the areas of insight, psychological intuition, and mental healing an inheritance of experience and understanding on which this writer carefully avoids passing a hasty judgment.

There are undeniable perils: one of the great dangers of animism, this religion of spirits, is that one gets in the habit of mistrusting everybody. Nothing that happens to one, whether for good or bad, is natural, but the fruit of a "work" (what is in effect a magical operation) done by somebody for or against one. So one begins to live in fear. Still very often the "mothers of the saints" are full of tenderness; you should see them wiping off the sweat-covered faces of the initiated who enter into trance under the impulse of the spirits, watching to make sure that "ecstasy" does not get out of hand. A truly charismatic group!

Christian prayer is all the more important in this setting. That is why all our base communities begin their gatherings with prayer and liturgy, which we strive to render as beautiful and intelligible as possible.

Restoring a Voice to the People

Another essential stage, which can begin very early, is that of bringing down *(devolução)* the word to those without their own voice. Everybody knows that before taking the Bastille, it is necessary to take the word. What does that mean?

It arises from the situation where, as the Bible says, the word of the poor has no worth. The person speaks and nobody listens; "they say, who is this fellow?" (Sir. 13:22–23). Among themselves the poor have got into the habit of self-depreciation. What a laborer says has no weight besides the word of an engineer or a priest. "At least they have studied. You are like us, you know nothing." How can the world be changed through a people as discouraged as this? That is why each base community is founded through a gentle and gradual pedagogy, which teaches the humble once again to listen to each other and speak to each other *in community*; to *give worth* to what they have to say as they express themselves to each other. It is really the miracle of the healing of the deaf-mute once again. Later in this stage we begin to read the Scripture together.

Telling What Happened Today: It is evening at a gathering of the base community, or a study day. Each one describes his or her day from morning till evening. Very often at the beginning we hear something like this: "Who, me? Nothing interesting. As usual. Washing the laundry. Cooking. . . ." She has let the word slip out: nothing interesting. It is important for a mother of a family to be able to tell what time she got up; how many times she got up during the night or at dawn to give the bottle to the baby, to heat the coffee for her husband who is going off to the factory, to fix the lunch-box for her oldest son who leaves later, to get the children ready for school. We go around the table and each one is able to describe the day that has just finished.

Introducing Family or Friends: In the course of the gathering each one presents the family: how many children they have, their names, where they work. It must be done with discretion and some brevity; it should not sound like a police interrogation. Sometimes we use the old method of the Catholic Worker Youth, the *"diagram of relations,"* to present one's most basic relations to the participants in the community gathering. It is a piece of paper with the name of the one speaking in the center; that person writes down the names of the people that he or she *regularly* meets at work, at the bus stop, in the street, at the church, at home, or elsewhere. Very often in this way the participants discover mutual friends or acquaintances.

Telling One's Story, the Past: In the end, during these gatherings, the fundamental needs of every human being are reached. After family, the past; origins. Where do you come from? These are very emotional meetings; friendship and mutual confidence are presupposed, because in the end each one is describing his or her misfortunes. What a way of the cross has been traveled by these lives that come from the very depths of the country's interior and that, from misery to misery, end up in the big city! We must listen to the young mother of a family tell how at the age of thirteen she was placed as a domestic in the city, in a household where her patron took advantage of her, and how she did not dare tell her mother, because she was the family's source of income. Or the young man who has become a specialized worker tells how, when he was a child traveling to São Paulo with his family, they all had to interrupt their train trip because they did not have enough money left to buy a loaf of bread: "And my father and I would not look at each other, because he knew that I was hungry, and I knew that he didn't have any money."

Mao Zedong, as it turns out, did the same thing in China. When the Red Army, before it took power, passed through the villages of inner China, not only (as it is said) did it behave well, respecting persons and property, and paying for its food; but also it held gatherings of this sort. A whole village would be gathered and Mao would ask to hear from all the inhabitants what he called "exposing of bitterness": each told of one's life and misfortunes.

Certainly these exercises of recalling the past and the communal discovery of each one's history can be used differently. The best can be lifted up along with the worst. In it a Christian can see the narrative of each one's sacred history: like that of the people of God, it is made of weal and woe, of horrors and beauties. Also constantly present for whoever can see through appearances and read the signs of the times is grace: that is, the presence of the good that triumphs over evil; the faith that helps overcome every wish to abandon the struggle; the intervention of friends who, like the prophets, come in to condemn evil, to warn of dangers, to console; the "miracles." It is a religious reading of each one's history, done in a setting of prayer, during these gatherings.

There can also be a scientific reading of the past (an idea of Brother Betto's): the important events in each one's history are written down in a column. In a parallel column are noted important events in the life of the country or of the world, which happened at the same time. Thus the very poor learn to find their place in general history; historical memory is amplified.

Evoking the Future: After the past, the future: "If you had the chance, what would you want to get before everything else for yourself and your children?" In one column is written down the wishes, the "Project Hope" of each one. In the second column, the obstacles in the way of this "dream." In a third column, there can be proposed the first embryonic solutions. That is action. Note that here we are using the old method: see, judge, act. In a fourth column could be evoked the eschatological dimension of the kingdom, that is, citations of scriptural texts, parables, words of Jesus or of the prophets, which show how the kingdom is to be realized. It is good to have a political reading of the hoped-for future, but also a theological reading.

Additional topics that work well in getting people to talk are the following (always based on fundamental human needs):

The Bairro: *Its greatest needs:* We proceed in the same way as before, by a system of parallel columns: "If you could, how would you change the *bairro*?"

The Factory and Workplace: Narrate a day at the factory from beginning to end. On the blackboard draw a plan of your work area and of the other parts of the factory. Explain how it operates. "If you could, how would you reorganize your work area, the whole factory . . . ?

Clearly this is a simple method. For people to be able to recover their power of speech, they must be able once again to express themselves about time and space: their personal time (their own story, past and future) and their personal space (family, friends, workplace, home).

During this stage, as we noted, we begin to read the gospel, to read about the things that happened to Jesus and his friends. Generally each meeting has a substantial time reserved for reading and explaining the word of God. We have already stressed the fact that the biblical text is in a certain sense the ideal mediation: it allows all those who live in oppressive situations to find themselves in a character of the Bible who lives the same reality, and thereupon to see how grace operates its salvation in them and in us—a true liberation of the whole being, individual and social. ("Zaccheus, that's me!" "I am Magdalen!" Etc.)

The meeting of the base community can proceed in many other ways. The following is typical: (1) song or initial prayer, after the usual greeting; (2) reading a text from the Bible; (3) storytelling by the participants on one of the general themes listed above (obviously not all the themes or all the participants can be included in a single meeting); (4) discussion of problems that have been discovered during the meeting, or an effort to solve an urgent question that has come up in the *bairro*; (5) prayer and final song.

It will be seen that all this is flexible and that not all the items need to be covered each time: perhaps the group will concentrate on just one. The essential thing is that life should never be separated from faith, acting from seeing.

Restoring Action to the People

Now we arrive at the decisive moment in the birth of a church base community. Everything we have said until now is preliminary. A group does not become a community until the day it decides to *act together*, to pass to action. Mission creates unity. Action permits a verification of whether or not the word has truly taken on flesh. We must leave Egypt in order to journey toward the Promised Land; the exodus of action is always necessary.

As for us, our community took form the day when the group, which had been talking together and studying the Bible, decided to reconstruct the *barraco* of a widow with ten children and expecting the eleventh. Her husband had been killed some days earlier on the highway that passes not far from us. So it was decided that one Sunday morning all the volunteers would show up with saws, hammer and nails, and axes at seven in the morning to work on the widow's house. What happened was what has been happening since human beings appeared on earth.

Initially there was laziness or fatigue. A person who has worked hard all week long, on an impossible schedule, never wants to lose Sunday rest. And so a certain number of the biblical circle were not there at the hour agreed on. The rest waited for them, in vain, all day long. No doubt each one had a valid excuse.

And throughout there was the usual difficulty that people have working together. Nobody wants to be ordered around by somebody else, especially when the task is one of benevolence. "I know how to build a *barraco* at least as well as you do." "I don't need to take orders from you." Each one has a different idea how to proceed. And a third part of the volunteer army disappears into the woods on one pretext or another. It looks very much like the story of Gideon's army: the force that was to confront Midian shrank from 20,000 to 300! It was with 300 courageous men, chosen by God, that Gideon confronted the enemies of his people—a remnant fighting against a much more powerful enemy (Judg. 7:1–8). It is the same way with base communities. In the case we describe, those who stuck it out to the end at the widow's house, who overcame the obstacles to action, still today, after six years, make up the cadre of the community!

Surprises were not lacking all during this little event. Inspectors from the town council came to tear down the hut, which although only partially built was already being lived in, and the widow had to pretend to go into labor—she was so frightened that she almost lost the baby. The next week we had to employ a ruse. The walls of the hut were to be constructed separately, at a distance, and then assembled in an instant the next Sunday. We had barely finished when the officials appeared again on the horizon. The widow barely had time to install herself in her new lodging, still unfinished, with a bundle of clothes; for a municipal decree provides that no dwelling whatever may be demolished if it is actually occupied by the person who takes shelter there. So that was a victory.

Still today, as in the age of Gideon, we have to destroy the altars of false gods where human energies are destroyed under Satan's sun: namely, the unjust laws and social structures that turn the human being into a machine for production, instead of being a creature in the image of God made to love and be loved. It is certain that prayer, the celebration of the faith, biblical and theological study, and nourishment by the sacraments are indispensable to gospel energy, as we have insisted. But we must never forget that only action can verify whether or not prayer is authentic: "Not those who say 'Lord, Lord' . . ." (Mt. 7:21). People can pray together for twenty years side by side in the same church and never have a disagreement. But on the day when they begin to act together, everything starts to change. That is when we see whether the charity that "bears all things, hopes all things, believes all things, endures all things" (1 Cor. 13:7) will win out over our egotism and allow us to work together.

That is the decisive moment when a base community is born. Afterward we need simply continue in the same direction: in the name of the love of human beings that animates us, because God by the Holy Spirit has poured divine love into us, that we may throw ourselves into action in order to rescue our brothers and sisters, to love them. Let me set down a parable told me by Jean-Claude Barreau. Every Christian life, every human life, is like an airplane flight in which each passenger enjoys the usual comforts but also has a parachute on his or her back. At a certain moment during the flight, the captain's voice is heard: "Ladies and gentlemen, those who wish are invited to present themselves at the rear of the craft to make a parachute jump!" Only the minority take the risk; the others prefer to continue their flight carried by the plane's wings, and arrive uneventfully at the airport, perhaps joyfully. But for those who jump, it is an extraordinary experience; they enter another dimension of reality. Plunged into the void, with the impression of hurtling toward an earth suddenly become hostile, they put their trust in their parachutes and in the word of the men and women that have already passed that way. For, an extraordinary surprise: the bags on their backs open, expand; and they discover a power that holds them up, sustains them, allows them to slide gently toward the earth they must rejoin.

So with the power of God. If, in the name of faith in Jesus' word, we throw ourselves into actions that are apparently impossible, out of love for our brothers and sisters and toward the construction of the kingdom, God in divine omnipotence will be with us and sustain us. We shall not destroy ourselves, we shall not be destroyed, even if the event leads us to the sacrifice of the cross. It is not an affair of throwing oneself from a pinnacle of the temple to astonish the crowds; it is an affair of doing what is commanded by love, of discerning together whether or not it is love that is speaking—and then of going at it. Only those who take a risk in the name of the faith will experience the faith, that is, the presence of the living God in their lives. The others are not bad people, but their uneventful flight will leave them nearly insensible of the divine. They will be cold.

The Expansion of Ministries

Ministries appear and are differentiated at the heart of action. That is easy to understand: gifts are revealed when one is put to the test during a struggle. Those gifts are charismata—gifts of the Holy Spirit, grace accorded, in view of service to brothers and sisters for the common good of the collectivity. In struggle one person reveals gifts as head, as organizer; another is shown able to speak, express things clearly; a third discovers qualities as a strategist. Also there appears the person to handle money and plan the budget. Certain men or women reveal awareness of the theological aspects of the struggle, others of the political aspects. Also required are wise ones who can keep in balance different aspects of the struggle of the people of God—family life, the life of activism.

We would like to underline that the ministries in church base communities in Brazil are as much secular as religious. These two words are not felicitous, for nothing is secular in itself; it is we who secularize it. We simply wish to make ourselves clear by using the common distinction. The base communities, as we said, mostly begin out of a religious motivation: there are not many priests, and there is a pressing need to guarantee the services that a church generally provides to its parishioners—worship, sacraments (e.g., baptism), biblical study, the catechism, the organization of the community and its finances, help for the sick, prayer for the dead, the creation of other community centers. There is a real danger of turning the base community into a mini-parish, and the layperson who takes on some ministry into a mini-curé. This danger has not always been avoided. What makes all the difference is the orientation to mission right from the beginning. As we found in chapter 2, above, authentic mission is not worship or catechesis, but the transformation of the world so that love is possible.

This vision of our work brings about the evolution of ministries, even those apparently the most clerical, toward an all-embracing service of humanity. (As a matter of fact, church base communities in Latin America simply do not feel that gap between faith and life, which is so prevalent in Europe and is constantly being attacked by, for example, the French movement of Catholic Action.) A brother may be led to preach on Sunday at the time of the regular liturgy; a sister may be led to introduce the prayer of intercession for people's needs and the world after the sermon. By so doing, cultivating this charisma that the community recognizes in them, they acquire the gift of public speech. And these same people, in the course of the week, may be those who will take up the word in the name of their *bairro* at a meeting with public authorities; or who will be the "animators" of their comrades during the massive strikes that have broken out in recent years. During these strikes, nobody steps forward as head, spokesperson, or delegate, so as not to be singled out for repression. "We are all the head of the strike" is the classic answer. Still, the role of the one who can explain things clearly is fundamental.

Following Pedro A. Ribeiro de Oliveira, we may distinguish three types of ministries in the base community.

First, the coordinator *(coordenador)*. This title covers all the ministries that deal with the coordination, organization, and unity of the community. The coordinators exercise in fact a gift of command in the group and are recognized as such by the others. They are called "leaders" *(líderes)*, "directors" *(dirigentes)*, "animators" (*animadores*), or "presidents of the community council" when such exists. They may be elected for a limited period, perhaps two years, or just implicitly recognized. They need not be men. My community always had four: a man, a woman, a boy, and a girl. Their role is not to exercise an autocratic or clerical control. They are, rather, available to the group to divide tasks according to the desire of all or of the majority, and help create unanimity on the most important decisions. They bring about order and unity, but they are not "heads" *(chefes)* in the classical sense of the word, on whom everything depends. The community assembly remains sovereign. We are in a regime of direct democracy. Their function is very close to that of Indian chieftains. In the Mato Grasso there is the Indian tribe of the Nhambiquara; the *cacique,* or chief of the tribe, is called *Ulikande,* which (according to Lévi-Strauss) means "he who unites, who binds one to another."

The coordinator "animates" meetings, organizes discussions, sets times and agendas, asks for an accounting of tasks undertaken by members of the community, exhorts, encourages, reproves. The coordinator, or the coordination (for there may be a team with a principal *responsável*), is in charge of the general conduct of the community, no less its internal church life (catechism, Mass, liturgy, study days, finances, etc.) than its social life. In the latter area, people turn to the coordinator for the most varied tasks possible: a corps of volunteers to help a sick comrade who cannot work, construction of a *barraco* for a needy family, collective petitions to the mayor, struggles against police violence, deciding whether or not to make community facilities available to an outside group that is requesting them.

It is important to note that this charisma, which is put at the service of the *unity* of the group, is exercised along two main tendencies. It may be a *royal* charisma: like King David, certain ones march at the head of the people to lead it with authority. This is the role of the coordinator in the precise sense: the servant-king at the call of one's subjects. Or it may be a *sacrificial* charisma. Certain ones, like the prophet Jeremiah (himself a priest), like Jesus, like the Suffering Servant of whom Isaiah 53 speaks, do not "command" but sacrifice themselves by going from one to another, whatever the criticism, to assure the unity of the group and to "gather the children of God dispersed" by sin (Jn. 11:52)—and God knows how the danger of division lies in wait for a community! Here it is more the presbyteral charisma than that of coordination. But it also serves unity in its way, and in a fundamental way, as we shall see when we discuss eucharistic ministry in the base community.

Second, the minister of the word. This name covers the varied ministries, mostly lay, that have to do with the word of God; they have multiplied by thousands in base communities. Ministers of the word need a knowledge of the Bible more than the ordinary, indeed a passion for it. We know some who study it for hours on end. They know how to explain the word of God to the others, that is their specialty, their gift, recognized by all. They are listened to with pleasure. They know how to organize new groups for Bible study; they do not remain with the same group of the faithful, but move around, recruit others. They know how to be silent. Their questions are relevant; they do something more than just "preaching" and "teaching." Their questions make people reflect and help them make clear the relationship between the word of God as lived in the Bible and the word of God as lived today.

We can distinguish different types among the ministers of the word: The evangelizer, the preacher, and the catechist. The evangelizer, in the strict sense, corresponds to the missionary dimension of the church: "Go and make disciples of all peoples . . . teach" (Mt. 28:19), "explain." There are three marks of the true evangelizers. (1) They must help people meet people, help little ones have confidence in little ones. We know that usually it is the opposite: illiterates, manual workers doubt that their like can help them. The evangelizer tells them: "In fact the gospel is for *you*. God has promised the Holy Spirit to the meek. You and your colleagues are going to understand the word of God and apply it; no need of a college degree for that." (2) The authentic evangelizer raises up other groups, multiplies. (3) The evangelizer evokes a liberating action, makes concrete the proclamation of the word through an action that, in fact, changes people's lives.

The preacher takes up the word in public, before a Christian assembly; for example, by speaking the homily. The catechist has one of the gifts of the Holy Spirit, the gift of knowledge. This gift can be exercised with all the apparatus of exegesis and theology, which is very useful; there is the university theologian, but also the catechist. The two have in common a power to organize the essential data of the faith in a more systematic and synthetic manner.

Third, the celebrant. A large number of laypersons in the base communities fall into this category: all those who preside in the absence of the priest at religious celebrations, including the Sunday worship (celebration of the word, distribution of communion); baptism (preparation and actual celebration); novenas, Rosaries; spiritual help for the sick and dying; burials; and prayer vigils.

Besides these ministries properly so called, there are what we may call *diaconias,* "services." Actually both words imply the act of "serving." The types of *diaconia* touch the internal life of the church less directly; they express the charity of Christ "outside." Following are three examples.

The diaconia *of money:* Everything that deals with the finances of the church and the base community comes under this heading. We do not charge for any Mass or sacrament; the church lives by the Sunday collection and by the "tithe," a biblical notion if there is any such; we set it at two hours' worth of salary per month or about 1 percent, a tenth of the biblical tithe. Two treasurers are elected for a period of two years and give account regularly of their management. Important expenses are decided by a general assembly, as is also the budget.

The treasurer's business also includes whatever has to do with help for the poor and unfortunate. Relief in money or kind is designated, with the approval of the coordination or the general assembly, by case according to need. The diocesan district receives monthly an accounting of income and expenses along with 10 percent of the receipts.

The diaconia *of the poor, sick, migrants:* This is far from being limited to the treasurers. The whole community feels itself responsible for this service. It is carried out in particular by the *clube de mães,* the "club of mothers," which meets once a week; and also by the groups of young people from twelve to fifteen years old who are preparing for confirmation. How often the end of Mass is devoted to an announcement about a particularly urgent case, and everybody digs in for their mite; a team of women is sent to visit the unfortunate family.

The political diaconias: The base communities generate a large number of people's activists for political action, but by themselves cannot provide all the training needed for a person aroused for this type of action—in the trade unions, the workers' movement, political parties. Hence other structures have been created, specialized pastorates: the workers' pastorate, agricultural pastorates *(pastoral da terra),* the Indian pastorate. These bodies do not aspire to direct the people's movement, the workers' movement, or the political movement; but only to provide a double training, at once theological and (in the broad sense) political, so that members of the base communities who arrive at this level of struggle will have religious and political standards for their action. The double goal is to provide instruments of analysis, on the one hand, and on the other, to show the possibility of constantly comparing one's struggle with that of Jesus.

Toward Collective Action

In fact our discussion has already moved onto this level. A base community evolves very slowly. In our opinion, it takes ten years for it to arrive at maturity. Does it not take about the same time to train a priest, a doctor, an engineer? Priests have at least six years of seminary, not counting periods of review and supplementary studies. It is at least as difficult to shape a Christian community as to train its members—at least if we really want it to hold together.

At the end of five or six years, certain ones discover that creating a civilization of love is not all that easy. Structures must be thought about. The spontaneous mutual assistance of the *bairro* is no longer adequate.

THE PHASES OF A BASE COMMUNITY

In general, a base community passes through four phases regarding its social and political involvements.

First, a base community is in search of itself as a community: it is centered on the religious activities for which it was originally founded. It is looking in the gospel for answers to its everyday problems.

Second, a base community participates in broader movements, where it meets not only Catholics but non-Catholics, not only believers but also nonbelievers. These are called "popular movements" because they are oriented toward the most numerous strata of the population, those that are trying to organize themselves in the *bairros,* or on a nationwide level, to improve their existence. To strive for a clinic, sewers, a day-care center by uniting several *bairros* is to create a popular movement.

Third, a base community, so to speak, passes from the *bairro* to the factory. The people's base little by little is woven into a web of small organizations—of the *bairro,* of the factory, of farm workers who have learned to act together. From these have emerged the activists *(militantes)* who are working to regain control of their trade unions. Currently the Brazilian trade unions are not autonomous over against the government; they are dependent on the Ministry of Labor. Further, they are organized according to a "corporative" system, in which each professional grouping has its own trade-union structure forbidden to unite with the others: chemists must be united only with chemists, metal-factory workers *(métallos)* with their kind, and so on. Fascist Italy under Mussolini invented this type of trade-union organization. There is not yet any unified central organization of workers corresponding to the AFL/CIO in the United States. Finally, the officers of the unions are generally in the pocket of the state; they are called *pelegos.* (This word originally designated the blanket that a rider put between the saddle and the horse's back to cushion the animal against the person's weight; by analogy, a *pelego* is a man who is at the right hand of the state, and who softens the shocks between authorities and workers.) It is from the church base communities and their people's organizations that there have emerged the members of the trade-union opposition and of the authentic trade unions—namely, those who wish to give the union back to the workers. Thus there has reappeared an autonomous workers' movement, in the city and in the countryside, in industry and in the fields, whose strands are composed for the most part of members of the church base communities.

Fourth, a base community raises the political question (the phase we are now in, in Brazil). It becomes necessary to build political parties in order to gain access to the political bodies that govern the nation: the Senate, the Chamber of Deputies, the state governors, the mayors *(prefeitos),* the municipal councils *(vereadores),* and so on. This step is much debated. The church base communities as such do not endorse any political party. But many of their members, including those who make up specialized pastorates (workers' pastorate, agricultural pastorate, and so on), frequently support the Workers' party of the great trade-union leader Lula. That raises questions.

But all this is *consequence,* however inevitable. The *essence* of the church base community is not in the political but in the religious realm. (However, what we have previously said about the relation between those two realms must not be forgotten.) The church base community, like the workers' pastorate and the agricultural pastorate, is not a political body but a body for the celebration of the faith and the overall education of the human being. It is the place where those gospel energies are awakened and strengthened that aim to transform the world so that charity may be possible in it and God may reveal the divine Name. If political instruments are created to get a firmer grip on reality, that is a consequence, one that should not be confused with the normative activity of the communities. That is why the communities, like the pastorates, are distinguished without separation from the trade union and the party. They are not separated, because many of their members belong to a union or a party, as we have noted. But union and party must forge themselves in an autonomous manner, "outside" the community, so to speak, not identifying themselves with it, which would be a catastrophe no less theological than political: the community would lose the religious character that constitutes its energy and raison-d'être, and the trade union or party would become an instrument of a new Christendom.

7

The Eucharistic Ministry
in Church Base Communities:
An Ecclesiology

THE EUCHARIST IN THE BASE COMMUNITY

The eucharistic life of the base community is a central issue. The whole Christian tradition proves it, and our theological analysis here reinforces that conclusion. The Eucharist is at the center of the church, "the source and the summit of mission" according to a statement from Vatican II. Christians have a vital need to nourish themselves on the body and blood of Jesus so as to participate in the fruits of his sacrifice. In the first place that means being liberated from sin, that mysterious deviation of each human being that prevents one from entering wholeheartedly and truly into a relation with one's neighbor and with God. Sin is manifested in the forms of egotism, pride, intemperance, anger, lust, envy, and laziness. We have already stated that there can be no remedies for this deviation that are confined to the political, economic, or psychological realms. In the second place, such participation means being united one to another and receiving strength to be sacrificed in turn, in the world, so as to make it the permanent habitation of God and God's children. The Eurcharist constitutes the church.

In what sense does the Eucharist constitute the church? There we touch on a difficult question. When and under what circumstances does a Christian community exist? It can be said that a cell of the church exists whenever, in the midst of an assembly of men and women, Jesus is really present and *they are aware as Christians of Jesus' presence.* Without explicit faith, conscious awareness of Jesus' presence, we cannot yet speak of the church as such. One must be baptized in the name of Jesus to be a Christian. When two or three are gathered together in the name of the Lord, Jesus is present. Of course, it is not enough for people to be physically present together in one place; they must also

107

be united in heart, by love and faith; that is, with the formal wish to continue the work of Christ, to construct God's kingdom. Another real presence of Christ comes into being, recognized or unrecognized, whenever people put themselves at the service of the poor, prisoners, the unfortunate: "what you did to the least of these my own, it was to me that you did it." When those serving are baptized persons working in explicit faith we may again speak of the existence of the church.

In general, then, we may say that a Christian community exists when the assembly of disciples of Jesus, those who have been baptized in his name, do his will by loving each other and by gathering together to continue his work in the world, principally with respect to the marginalized of our society. Therefore, the cell of Christian community is *baptismal* before being eucharistic. "Church base communities" come into real being, even without the Eucharist, when these minimal conditions are met. Thousands of base communities can be born without the sign of the Eucharist being manifest.

What then is the ecclesial role of the Eucharist? It is also the real presence of Christ but, like all the sacraments, it has an "intentional" character in the philosophical sense of that word. That is, this real presence of Christ in the sacramental sign—the presence of Christ sacrificed and raised from the dead—is an invitation to the Christians who are participating in it to make real in their lives the thing that the sign stands for. And the thing that the sign stands for is this: the sacrifice of these participants for a new world, namely, sharing and love in all that they have and in all that they are, so that a sketch may be drawn, among human beings, on this earth, of the kingdom that will unfold into perfection in the age to come.

Traditionally in the church the safekeeping of the Eucharist has been entrusted to the bishop and his "particular church," the diocese (in the language of Vatican II); while baptism falls more directly under the responsibility of lay people. The eucharistic nature of the church according to this thinking would then be more the specific mark of the particular church than of the base community. Nevertheless this observation does not render invalid what we have to say in this chapter. It is evident that the church base community, being Christian and "ecclesial," that is, of the nature of the church, has also a eucharistic dimension in its makeup. We shall go on to say that the emergence of a specifically eucharistic ministry is *starting to happen* in the base community, and that this fact must be recognized so that the base communities may arrive at their ecclesial maturity.

A new type of presbyters could arise—perhaps already potentially exists—in the base community. These presbyters could very well be integrated in the Pastoral councils that are starting to make their appearance in Brazilian dioceses, expecially in São Paulo. These Pastoral councils, composed in great part of laypersons exercising specific ministries, decide together with the bishop the main pastoral orientations of their "particular church," the diocese. A new type of collegiality could be born in the Catholic church thanks to church base communities, rendering it a more *synodical* church.

The base communities must be allowed to arrive at their ecclesial maturity, which to a large extent can be measured only by the level of their eucharistic life. But now, if the base communities do not achieve the possibility of developing the eucharistic ministry *within themselves*, just as they do for the other ministries, it will be as if the mission, which brought them into being, had halted halfway along the road. Something will have interrupted a normal evolution. There will have been an actual abortion. A life begins and does not proceed to term.

It can easily be seen that placing an obstacle to the eucharistic life of a base community is to damage its mission in the world. In fact there exists a profound relation between the "sacrament of the altar" and the "sacrament of the person." We mean by that, that if the Eucharist is the efficacious sign of the real presence of Christ, a brother or a sister is also the real presence of Jesus, above all when such a one is offered in the person of the poor, the unlucky, the abandoned, the prisoner. "I was hungry and you gave me to eat." "But Lord, when did I do that? I don't even know you." "Each time that you did it for the least of my own, it was to me that you did it." Each time that people make their communion, they receive the strength of sharing: by sharing the bread of life, the body of Christ, the sharing of physical bread becomes possible. That is the very sentiment Pope John Paul II expressed at the National Eucharistic Congress of Fortaleza in 1981. Participation in the eucharistic sacrifice of Jesus is, as we know, an act that has its own efficacy; it leads the disciple of Jesus onto the road of sacrifice—self-sacrifice to renew the world.

Christians engaged in the struggles of the present world, when they are gathered together in the name of Jesus to renew his memory and thus to have strength to continue their way, have the right to approach the Eucharist in a more natural manner than is today the custom: that is, they should not always depend on a priest who comes from somewhere else than the base community itself to celebrate the Lord's Supper. At this writing there are 80,000 base communities in Brazil. How can it be expected that the priests on active duty could be available to them on a regular basis when there are only 12,000 priests to serve the whole country? It would therefore be only logical, in view of the dynamic that led to the creation of so many base communities in the first place, that they should be granted the right and option of choosing from among themselves the one to preside over the Eucharist, the minister, the "elder" in experience of life, who would have the duty of manifesting through ministry the eucharistic maturity of the community, that is, its ecclesial fullness.

For that last is the whole point! If we insist (as we do) that we wish the eucharistic minister to be chosen from the interior of the base community, it is not primarily or fundamentally to fill up a gap, to implement a policy providing for available clergy, to make up for a lack of priests. Absolutely not! The basic reason is not along those lines. It is, rather, for a theological, ecclesiological reason: we repeat, the base community must walk to its end the path of its ecclesial nature, which is at root eucharistic. If it is really an authentic assembly of the followers of Jesus, it is evident that it has within it the natural aptitude to celebrate the Holy Supper. Certainly that will not and cannot happen except in agreement with the universal church. We shall return to this point in an instant. For now we wish to insist on one truth that our experience and practice has revealed to us. All of us, we outsiders who work in the *favelas* of the third world, in the poor quarters or primitive villages lost in the interior of the country, we bear witness that constantly there appears in the communities a person who has a special gift, a charisma, to preside over the unity of the brothers and sisters who make up the base community. This minister of unity in the service of the collective becomes apparent in daily life: visiting those who are quarreling, making dialogue easier, agreeing to be mediator or even scapegoat, taking on the sin of the community. This minister provides the means by which unity is maintained.

We have spoken about the sacrificial will of the priest; that is what is here under discussion. Such a one makes the community holy by sacrificing (*sacrum-faciens*) self for unity; that is the specific sacerdotal role that exists in each baptized person, but more specially in the presbyter. If this labor for unity is exercised in daily pastoral life in the person of the presbyter, it is appropriate that it should likewise be expressed on the level of the *celebration* of the liturgy. It is normal that the elder should preside at the sacrament of unity: the Eucharist. The "elder" is one who has been granted a gift for realizing (*a*) a community that is one: the elder is alert that the brothers and sisters of the same community should remain united and open to each other; (*b*) a community that is holy: the elder is alert that the community should remain united and open to the Father "from whom comes every good and perfect gift" (Jas. 1:16–17); (*c*) a community that is catholic: the elder is alert that the local community should remain united and open to the other communities of the region, and to that center of communion constituted by the Church of Rome and its bishop; (*d*) a community that is apostolic: the elder is alert that the community should remain united and open to the genuine tradition of the apostles, without an overlay of conventional or foreign customs that do not fit in with the Spirit of Jesus, of the prophets, and of the saints, and that the transmission of this genuine apostolic tradition should continue, for this is the true sense of mission in which the missionary dimension of the church and the presbyter is realized.

Certainly it is the community as a whole that must be attentive and active to guard and strengthen those four fundamental marks by which the true church of Jesus Christ is recognized. If a community is disunited, without the spirit of prayer, closed to other communities, shriveled up in a particular tradition, whether new or old, that is not specifically evangelical, *it is not of Jesus*. The community as a whole watches over that, but certain ones have as their particular function what is the duty of all. These are Christian priests. Their task is so difficult to carry out that the church, since its beginning, has recognized the need of carrying out a special and very solemn prayer over this class of ministers: hands are laid on them and they enter a special order; for they are the guardians of unity, of fraternal love, of openness to God and to others, that is, of all the dimensions we recalled above—oneness, holiness, catholicity, apostolicity.

The basic texts that underlie the theology of the Christian priesthood as such are much more the Acts of the Apostles and the pastoral epistles of Paul, which speak to us about the organization of the Christian community, than the epistle to the Hebrews. The latter speaks much more about the priesthood of Jesus Christ, sole mediator between God and human beings, who alone entered into that temple not made by hands—the true presence of the Living God. The Christian priest represents Christ as priest; but all Christians, by their own baptism, participate in the priesthood of Christ. The Christian priest does not substitute self for the priesthood of Christ. In the liturgy (and in particular in the eucharistic liturgy) and also in daily community life, the Christian priest is "set apart" in a certain way to render visible the presence of Christ, the Head and source of unity for his mystical body, so called because it is an association of the baptized united to his person by vital and organic links.

But it is not the fact of being set apart that constitutes the priest as an *alter Christus*, another Christ, however, but baptism! To call the priest "another Christ" is a characteristic distortion of Tertullian's original formula according to which the Christian is "another Christ." All Christians by their baptism are separated from the world in every respect in which it is evil, in order to reproduce in their personal existence the image of Christ: all are called to make themselves into another Christ, "It is no longer I that live, but Christ who lives in me" (Gal. 2:20). Let us not confuse the presbyteral ministry and Christian *sacerdotium*: the first is specific to a particular type of service exercised by certain ones in the church, the other is common to all the baptized.

That said, it nonetheless remains the case that the ministry of the one who watches over unity in the fellowship, in all the senses of the word (unity with respect to God, the neighbor, other communities, and the tradition of the apostles), is so essential that *that person alone* in the church can preside over the Eucharist, the sacrament of unity. One deviation would be to underestimate the role of the ordained minister. In fact there seems no evidence, however far we go back into the history of primitive Christianity, that the Mass was ever celebrated without the presence of an ordained minister. And the reason no doubt is that the importance and the weight of the bishop in the Christian church was determinative right from the beginning. "The bishop is in the church and the church is in the bishop," wrote Clement of Rome in the first century. The Catholic and Orthodox traditions, both of "episcopal" churches, are unanimous on this point. The bishop, as the name (*epi-skopos*) implies, is the one who "watches over" unity; this task is so important that in the beginning the Eucharist seems normally only to have been celebrated when presided over by the bishop in person. Today the priest represents the bishop in the liturgy, since in fact the priest exercises a ministry of episcopal type and there is only a difference of degree, not of nature, between priest and bishop. Nevertheless *one single* bishop presides at the communion in a diocese.

Another deviation also must be avoided: we cannot say that it is ordained ministers who consecrate the bread and wine by themselves. All the baptized, by virtue of their own baptism, participate actively in the Holy Supper; all say the *epiclesis* by which the Holy Spirit is invoked as sanctifier to come on the assembly and on the symbols that are to become the body and blood of Christ. Both parties are concelebrants or, according to a Trappist monk of the twelfth century, *co-consecrators*. (The writer is indebted here and throughout this chapter to Hervé Legrand, O.P.)

If things are indeed so, why not choose, from within the base community itself, its full complement of ministers of the Eucharist? That is, true presbyters emerging from the community, who could, in the context of the sacrament of order, preside both over the charity of brothers and sisters and over the Sunday sacred assembly, the Mass. We saw in the last chapter that the ministry of coordination and the presbyteral ministry very often in practice do not fall together. One can imagine base communities with their priest, on the one hand, and their lay "president," on the other.

Here is a strange and contradictory state of affairs. On the one hand, we are demanding autonomy for civil society, "self-management," democracy, collectivization of power and of the economy; on the other, we are unwilling to let the base communities "manage themselves" as regards the Eucharist. (With respect to this formula we shall go on to explain that the church is neither a monarchy nor a democracy, and that bishop and priest are never consecrated by the community they serve.) If the base communities do not reach this eucharistic maturity, it is probable that little by little they will degenerate, for something essential of their nature as church will have been refused them. A living organism cannot be mutilated if it wishes to maintain its identity. At bottom, it cannot be denied that still in the body of the church there exists a fear: a fear of base communities, of people organizing themselves without asking the central structure of the church for its opinion. It is feared that the base communities will keep apart and become separated from the diocesan administration, from the Roman Curia. Let us admit it, there also exists an ecclesial "sovietism"!

Certainly it is fundamental that communion between the communities of a diocese and the "particular churches," the dioceses of the whole world, should be maintained; that is the essential task of the bishop and the pope. Furthermore, it cannot be denied that base communities, if entrusted *exclusively* to the forces that spring from the base, run different risks: the temptation to reduce their ecclesial reality to a simple political dimension, or the danger of becoming sectarian, a "chapel" closed to the great universal church.

Nevertheless, the various efforts that have been made to avoid these risks are certainly not along the correct lines either: the clericalism that tries to keep everything under the control of the clergy; the centralism that keeps within a few hands certain important powers, in particular the nomination of bishops and of key diocesan officials; and the attempts at "stifling" (*abafamento*) new ministries perceptible in the "corrections" made from Rome in the texts of the Puebla Conference after the fact.

ECCLESIOLOGY OF THE BASE COMMUNITY

Christian Equality and Unanimity

We know very well that the church does not correspond to the concept of democracy; but neither is it a monarchy. The exact theological notion that defines it is the idea of communion, or *koinonia* in the language of the Greek theologians of the first centuries. It means that the church is a communion of brothers and sisters, a body of baptized people where the Spirit of God is in all, in each member, from the least up to the pope. In the end there is a fundamental equality among Christians. And when we look at the matter carefully, the church is not of a hierarchical nature: there are no degrees of possession of the Holy Spirit among the faithful. Now the Spirit of God alone is authority, not people. That is why the true rule for decision-making among Christians can only be unanimity, consensus. Herein lies a great truth to be rediscovered, of which traces still remain in canon law: since the Spirit is in all, it is necessary to reach universal agreement, or quasi-universal, in the church, when important decisions are at stake, for the Spirit cannot speak against the Spirit. If therefore Christians resist a decision of the "hierarchy," if they have difficulty *receiving* a new order of things, a new definition of dogma, a censure, then that may, on the one hand, be a rebellion of certain ones, or a fossilization in archaic attitudes; but it may also be a feeling diffused among the people of God that something outside the apostolic tradition is being invented and that something is being distorted. Let us never forget the resistance of Christian people against the bishops in the age of the heretic Arius! The people turned out to be right.

That is why at the councils it was required that decisions be reached by a two-thirds majority. This rule is the practical translation of an attitude that was theological and not at all political. The intention was to seek unanimity, for the decisions of Christians are most fully authentic when the Spirit of God, which passes through each one, succeeds in bringing all into agreement. In base communities there is this constant striving for unanimity, for general or nearly general consensus; otherwise they would not be able to live, they would break into factions, into many segments. We institutionalize this search for consensus in the holding of regular general assemblies of all the people or of the persons most concerned.

So if the eucharistic ministry were entrusted to presbyters emerging from the church base communities, the true way of avoiding the dangers that we have recognized and condemned would not be a return to centralism and clericalism, but an exacting search for unanimity. The function of the bishops and the pope here is irreplaceable: in order for this unanimity to appear, to be orchestrated as a harmonious symphony, to be directed and governed, their intervention is necessary. We know very well that this ministry of governance is a special charism, which is specific to them and which confers unique powers on them.

This charisma does not come from the people, but from God, and *that is why the church is not a democracy.* But on the other hand, unanimity does not reside solely in the bishops and the pope, but in the whole people of God. In practice, not to take into consideration the desires of the people, as manifested in those ministries that are born from the people, and in particular the presbyteral ministry, is to disregard the special nature of the church and to clericalize it. For the church is born from the people.

The Choice of Bishops and Priests: Vocation

As long as there is lacking such an ecclesial fullness, through which the people of God can make its voice heard, in an explicit manner, at the moment when important decisions are to be made, just so long will there continue to be a kind of contradiction between the church of base communities, which is born from the people, and the church that *names* priests, bishops, and nuncios from on high and *sends* them to communities. That was not the custom of the primitive church. Its equilibrium was more complex. On the one hand, communities, whether local as in the form of a parish or a diocese, were recognized as having the right of nominating their candidate to join the presbyterate or the episcopacy. There did not exist the concept of the sending by religious authority of a pastor, whether priest or bishop, who was in some sense external to the community. Generally the priest was chosen from inside the local church. Sometimes there was even a requirement that the priest should have been baptized there. But on the other hand, the local bishop had to come and confirm or reject this choice, and only the bishop could ordain the one proposed by the people. For it was recognized that no community ever formed a separate whole, closed in on itself, without any possibility of intervention by other churches and the religious authority.

The same procedure held as regards the episcopate; the people had an active voice. It will be remembered that many bishops were elevated to their office, sometimes against their will, by popular acclamation: by the cry, "Ambrose, bishop!" "Augustine, bishop!" This was the way Ambrose was elected bishop of Milan; Augustine, of Hippo. These cases illustrate very clearly the genuinely conciliar and synodical character of the primitive church and the participation of the people in this conciliarity.

Cyprian, a key figure in the early church and patriarch of the churches of Africa, said, "From the very beginning of my episcopate I made it a rule never to decide anything alone, following my personal opinion, without bringing in the counsel of all you priests and deacons, as well as the *suffragium* of my people." This "suffrage" probably means the vote of the Christian people. Certainly that rule covered the choice of the bishops dependent on Cyprian. Along the same lines Father Yves Congar appropriately recalls a legal maxim of the Middle Ages, *Quod omnibus tangit, ab omnibus tractari et approbari debet* ("What touches all must be discussed and approved by all"). Pope Celestine declared, "Let a bishop not be imposed on a community who has not explicitly been requested by it through a clear statement of its intention." And Leo, a highly authoritarian pope of the fourth century, declared no less clearly, "He who is to preside over all must be elected by all. Let no bishop be consecrated against the will of Christians and unless he has been explicitly requested by them."

On the other hand—and herein lies the extent of the primitive equilibrium—*never* was a bishop (or a priest) consecrated or ordained by the person's own community. The bishops of the three neighboring cities came to verify whether or not the bishop-elect held the catholic and apostolic faith, and possessed the qualities of a pastor. They had in their hands the power of refusing a candidate. There remains a liturgical relic of this procedure. Still today the new pastor of a diocese is consecrated by three other bishops; this and this alone remains of the primitive custom. To repeat: the community was never an isolated whole closed in on itself; it always had open a window for intervention and control by its sister churches. Thus communion was assured; and the twin dangers of bureaucratic centralism and of sectarianism were avoided.

Thus there was a clear functional differentiation in earlier days, which may be summarized as follows: (*a*) Vocation is vested in the local community, which is entrusted with calling the candidate. At first vocation was not a subjective phenomenon, as it is today when someone "feels" called to be a priest. (We may add here, parenthetically, that since in our days the sacerdotal vocation is above all subjective—"*I* feel myself called"—it should be no surprise that priestly resignations are also subjective: "*I* am no longer made for that, whatever the community may say.") (*b*) The neighboring communities, represented by their bishops, have the function of attesting the apostolic faith of the one elected and of installing the person in the new order. In the case of the priest, this function of witness and ordination is undertaken by the local bishop. (*c*) The one elected receives the pastoral charisma, presbyteral or episcopal as the case may be, from God and not from the superior authority (as in the monarchical deviation) or from the community (as in the democratic deviation). The superior authority and the community are, on the one hand, necessary agents of mediation: God gives but not directly, for there is a logic of the incarnation. But their proper role is only one of discerning whether or not a gift truly exists, which does not come from them but from God.

Today matters are exactly opposite: the religious authority names and sends, the one elected "feels" the vocation, the community has hardly anything to say at all. Some may reply: "But today a diocese may set up criteria, design the robot-portrait of the ideal bishop!" The answer is easy: "We do not choose criteria, but persons."

In any case, it seems to us that church base communities, where in fact the practice and style of operation is to decide *together* on important decisions and choices, would fit most naturally into this understanding of the church. In point of fact there is a discrepancy: a certain practice in the base community is contradicted by a different practice on the level of the universal church in the West. This contradiction, in our opinion, accounts for the uneasy reaction from the structure each time an attempt is made to improve the status of the base community, as happened at the Puebla Conference.

The Status of Missionary Work

"What happens when in a certain territory or environment there are no existing churches?" is often asked. That is the case when we can think of a legitimate sending of priests, bishops, and missionary Christians in general by the religious authority. It is good to remember, however, that since the origins two networks have always existed in the church: a fixed network of communities already formed with their ministers; and an itinerant missionary network commissioned with the planting of new churches. Thus in the first century, for the churches that had already been formed there were the presbyters in the Jewish-Christian communities, and the bishops and deacons in the Gentile-Christian communities; on the other hand, there were the "apostles," "prophets," and *didaskaloi* (catechists) mostly dedicated to missionary service. Thus one could easily imagine in the future of contemporary Christianity two types of presbyteral ministry. One type would be missionary, itinerant, composed of priests who were for the most part celibate, sent to create new churches. The other would ordinarily be composed of married men, ordained to the priesthood, originating from already existing church base communities, charged to remain in their place. These latter would have a pastoral task much less burdensome than that of the missionary priest, and would therefore be able to carry out family responsibilities; but they would be no less endowed with this charisma of unity that equips one to be ordained and to preside at the celebration of the Eucharist.

Rome and Its Bishop

The Christian church is not a mere collection of sects, because each community, each local church is subject to the right of control by other communities, which attest whether or not the tradition of the apostles is faithfully lived out in it. The ultimate center of reference as regards the apostolic character of the faith lived out by a particular church, or a group of churches, is the community of Rome and its bishop, the pope.

The most ancient tradition recognizes that the bishop of Rome has a right of intervention in other churches, a right that can be extended, above all if the Christian faith is in danger or when a pastor is in error. "Simon, Simon, lo, Satan has asked for all of you to sift you like wheat; but I have prayed for you in particular that your faith should not fail; and when the time comes that you are converted, strengthen your brothers" (Lk. 22:32). The fact is that the Church of Rome, where Peter and Paul together confessed the faith by martyrdom, this church, perhaps founded by Christians from Jerusalem fleeing the persecution, that is, by men and women from the community founded by Jesus in person, is the mother church of all the others, and the cornerstone on which the Christian world rests: "You are Peter and on this rock I will build my church" (Mt. 16:18).

This does not mean that the Church of Rome must necessarily be, as it is in fact today, the administrative center of the Western church. At the hour when a planetary conscience and awareness is being born, it is certainly of extreme importance that a universal voice be heard. To be the center of communion and arbiter of the catholic and apostolic faith is one thing. To be the center of government is also conceivable, if its nature is clearly recognized. But to be the central bureaucracy of the church is a very different thing. Once upon a time bishops and patriarchs simply notified Rome of their election to their sees and exchanged letters of communion with the mother church. But to name and send bishops to their sees; to legislate; to exercise a direct and immediate ordinary jurisdiction over the faithful of the whole world, passing over the heads of the local pastors—these are modes of procedure that must be reviewed in the years to come if the ecumenical unity of the whole church is to be realized in a way corresponding to the doctrine of the church implicit in the church base communities, where the ecclesiology of the undivided church is being reborn, it seems, in our own days.

We have spoken several times of the fraternal control that churches exercise over each other and of the special role of the Church of Rome in this area. It seems to us that a Christian church that gave more respect to its Trinitarian nature, which in a manner of speaking was less "Christocentric," would succeed better in maintaining a happy equilibrium in the reciprocal relation of ministries and communities. If in fact the fullness of the gifts of the Holy Spirit is not of human origin, but comes from God, who is the unique origin, then both the "monarchic" and the "democratic" deviations are avoided; in the Christian church, the gifts of God come neither from the heads nor from the people. If, furthermore, these gifts are in fact distributed among all the members of the body of Christ, which is the church, and are not concentrated on the head of a single person (the clerical deviation) or on the community (the sectarian deviation), the possibility that ministries and communities could be turned in on themselves disappears. There is a mutual *inclusion* of ministries; each person has need of the other who also has received a parcel of the divine splendor. Neither a person such as a priest or a bishop, nor a particular church, even though it should be the Church of Rome, nor a base community can pretend to the fullness of the gifts of the Holy Spirit. On every level self-sufficiency becomes impossible.

Finally, the church is also the temple of the Holy Spirit. In a true sense it is the Spirit that "specifies" its gifts to each person and each community; and that means that the ministry of each is irreplaceable. The ministries are not "interchangeable." Each individual is responsible for the shining of a spark of the Glory of God, which in its nature is wholly unique. The grace given to the church of São Paulo in Brazil and to its bishop is a special one, uniquely appropriate to it, and it plays an irreplaceable role in the symphony of churches. In the same way, nobody can claim to alter or to limit the role of the

Church of Rome and its bishop in the concert of churches. It alone and the bishop alone are qualified for this function.

We can testify that the church base communities are precious stones, each one different and marvelous, in which is worked out day by day an apprenticeship of communion in the diversity of gifts, whereby the liberty of each one is submitted to the unity of all.

This is the understanding of the church, the "ecclesiology," that must be made explicit in the years to come if the Christian mission is to continue in the world. How can we ask for liberty and justice in society if the churches are not able simultaneously to live out autonomy and communion? Furthermore, without ecumenism, the base communities will not arrive at maturity: the rediscovery of the Trinity, liberation, ecumenism, and a true ecclesiology must all come by the same road.

8

The Pastoral Strategy
of the Archdiocese of São Paulo

DEFINING "PASTORAL STRATEGY"

There is no mission without strategy. Strategy is the art of disposing one's forces to obtain essential objectives; tactics is the art of surmounting secondary obstacles. One can lose a tactical battle, but it is catastrophic to lose a strategic battle. Above all we must not lose sight of the forest for the trees. The church is preoccupied with liturgical quarrels of small importance and forgets the principal goal of the Christian presence in the world: to make charity possible.

The pastorate—the work of the Good Shepherd organized by the church—is more an art of applying wisdom than of applying prophecy. The pastor is the one who knows how to guide the people of God through the concrete and changing circumstances of this world so that they can live in it and fulfill their mission. Thus there is a pastoral theology for each place and time. According to the place in which we find ourselves and the history that we are living through, we must know how to determine the main missionary objectives of a community and of a church, and the means to reach them. That is what is meant by "pastoral strategy."

THE PASTORATE: MYSTICISM AND THEOLOGY

The pastorate cannot dispense with either mysticism or theology. Mysticism is one's personal experience of the living God, one's "feeling" of God's presence and grace. But mysticism needs to rest on a sound theology, that is, on a sound organization of the rational data of the faith. The phrase "rational organization" may strike some people wrong. But theology, the knowledge of God, is also an experience of the living God through the senses: "See how the Lord is good. . . ." The true mystics, even when illiterate, are the true "theologians," those who "know" God. Still we should not downgrade the rational aspect of the faith. We are heart *and* intelligence. The reason that each age strives to organize its religious thought is because it is indispensable to establish communication with another; well-organized discourse permits us to explain to the other what we mean. We have already spoken of this in chapter 2; since the problems of each age are specific, Christian discourse must constantly be reconstructed. Thus it is supremely important to have a theology that is truly synthetic and balanced, that does not give any particular aspect of the faith either less or more importance than it deserves. Otherwise pastoral practice and mysticism will suffer by becoming bogged down in the charismatic, in militancy, or in the liturgical. There are a thousand ways of going wrong. We believe (for example) that a Christology which had got out of hand was the cause of the present lack of faith of former Christian activists. It is impossible to "imitate" Jesus, for he is an inaccessible giant; it is possible to live in him, carried along by him and his Spirit in a Trinitarian life. But that presumes more than a Christology! Thus every Christian (even a child learning a catechism) is called to make this effort of "logic"; all are called on to have a coherent account to give so as to be understood by those around them. The first condition of evangelization is to make oneself understood.

Mysticism, the pastorate, and theology are in a permanent reciprocal relation. Philosophers would call it a dialectical relation. Constantly we observe ourselves going through the following sequence: I see my faith from day to day and I try to transmit it; that is, I carry out my own little pastorate. This daily practice leads me to reflect on theoretical questions. Questions about God, evil, life, death, the Gospels, faith, politics were asked me and I was not able to answer them. So without having intended it I set myself to carrying out some parts of systematic theology. I try to answer by an organized discourse a religious question that has been asked me. But my response comes from my love of God. I feel God in my life and I frequently speak to God. Then all this missionary, pastoral, and theological struggle also takes place on the level of my personal intimacy with God, of my mysticism.

PRACTICE—THEORY—PRACTICE

Philosophers have always asked how truth may be attained. If theory alone can attain truth, then practice is nothing but an application of theory. But in fact the theologians who hammer out theological theories in their study are incapable of pastoral work: they apply these to reality, and reality rebels. Thus in Brazil at first the Jesuits wanted to teach the catechism of the Council of Trent to young Indians in the schools, and it did not work. It can even be said further that such theologians are incapable of reaching a sound theology because they have not perceived how truth is grasped.

In reality, the true theory is that which comes from practice and brings us back to practice. One has an experience; one studies it in a more detached way and draws some general insights from it; one returns to one's field of action. This is always the way we proceed, whatever the realm of our activity, whether in science, commerce, politics, or religion—at least if we proceed in sanity, with the desire to achieve a result that has some actual grasp on reality. Thus it is practice leading to theory leading to practice that is the vehicle of truth, as Gustavo Gutiérrez constantly insists.

PASTORAL ACTION IN THE ARCHDIOCESE OF SÃO PAULO

In São Paulo we find no exception to the general rule of the relationship between practice and theory. The Christians immersed in this enormous city are trying to be good theologians and good pastors; they wish to render the charity of Christ possible in their city. They have begun to *act* to reach this objective. This concrete action has taught them that they must simultaneously organize their action and their thought to get there—and to do it in a very precise manner. Thus there has appeared a specific pastoral strategy for the archdiocese of São Paulo.

The Context of Pastoral Action

The context is São Paulo, an immense metropolis of more than 11 million inhabitants in 1982, surpassed in number on the Latin American continent only by Mexico City. Brazil has a population of 120 million, of whom 25 million are in the one state of São Paulo. The municipality of São Paulo increased from 6 million in 1970 to 9 million in 1980. Greater São Paulo, with its thirty-eight municipalities, had 13 million inhabitants in 1982, and the projection for the end of the century is 26 million. If this estimate is realized, São Paulo will one day be one of the largest cities in the world.

Already it is the largest industrial city of Latin America. It has more than 200,000 metalworkers in the city proper, many more if we include the neighboring municipalities that form part of Greater São Paulo and (for the most part) of its archdiocese. The inhabitants are in large part poor migrants, illiterate or marginally literate, almost all of recent rural origin, recently evicted from their land, which they left with almost no possessions; each day interstate buses and trains disgorge entire families with countless children carrying on their backs bundles of all their possessions. More than half of São Paulo's 11 million inhabitants were not born in the city. This may give some idea of the torrential character of this migration.

The structure of the great third-world cities is as follows. They are all alike.

1. In the center are banks and businesses, and also some residential buildings. Behind these substantial buildings, in their back courtyards, are rabbit warrens *(curtiços)* inhabited by large numbers.

2. Around the center are the middle-class quarters.

3. Around the middle-class area are the industrial zones. In São Paulo industry fills a whole section of the heart of the city, representing the oldest stratum of industrialization.

4. At the circumference are more people's quarters, which look like temporary encampments, as if an innumerable population had for a time set up its

shacks and huts, made out of bricks or concrete blocks or wood. They stand on the red hills of the city so as not to be too far from the factory, the hospital, and the school. (Lack of these three in rural areas, along with evictions from the land, is the main reason for the ceaseless swelling of the urban centers.) Here they live precariously with minimal infrastructure—often lacking running water, paved streets, sewers, or electricity—attached to prefectures unable to keep up with the city's growth.

5. On the steepest hillsides, on the banks of polluted streams, beside railroad tracks, wherever there is a bit of uninhabited land, the *favelas* infiltrate. They are not very obvious. The hut of the *favelado* looks like a doll's house; the *favelas* occupy the cracks in industrial society. In ten years the population of these shantytowns in São Paulo rose from a few hundred thousand to more than 1.5 million. Nearly 4 million human beings in 1982 comprised the population of the city living in unrelieved misery. The archdiocese estimated in 1975 that there were 26,000 unregistered streets, 5,000 clandestine subdivisions, about 1 million persons in the shantytowns lacking sanitary facilities, and 2 million more with inadequate housing. Believe it or not, 95 percent of the families had television!

6. Finally, where the furthest edges of the city meet the country, close to crowded quarters and often part of them, are the rubbish and garbage dumps, where clouds of women, children, the unemployed, even the sick wait for the trucks that dump the city's refuse, including food; part is consumed on the spot, the rest taken back "home."

Thus, to sum up: here is a very poor industrial population, very young (the median age is under twenty years), very close to its rural origins, uprooted here from its native land and its culture, coming from all twenty-two states of the Federation, but above all from the northeast and from Minas Gerais in the center. The evictions were no accident but, rather, the fruit of a conscious two-part policy: on the one hand, to industrialize the city, starting with simple technology, the manufacture of cars and of electrical appliances; on the other, to pay off the country's external debt by selling soybeans, meat, coffee, and raw materials. To produce meat and practice large-scale cattle-rearing it was necessary to expel the peasants from their lands, which then were sold to big financial groups.

A veritable sociological deluge! Just as the tropical streams, swollen by heavy downpours, wash off the fragile layer of fertile soil from the deforested hills of our great city, so the torrent of indiscriminate industrialization has fallen on a farming population with fragile equilibrium at best and transported it suddenly into a mindless urban universe. No wonder, under these conditions, that violence is one of the most characteristic marks of the city. The generation born during the military dictatorship arising from the coup of 1964, which opened its eyes on the world during the dizzying increase of evictions from the countryside to the city, is not surprisingly a most violent one. Boys aged fifteen to seventeen smoke *maconha* and swagger through the streets with gun in hand. In many of the people's quarters nobody dares walk outdoors after dark.

Hundreds of young men are shot down each year by the police or in gang warfare—unless the population, tired of so many assaults, proceeds itself to undertake more and more frequent lynchings. The poor execute the poor! The increasing unemployment and the economic crisis of these last few years have made their effects cruelly felt among us. No wonder that attacks by armed gangs have so much increased! São Paulo is one of the most dangerous cities in the world.

General Principles of Pastoral Action

What is to be done under these conditions? How is the gospel to be proclaimed? How shall we actually *bring it about* (and not just merely find a way to say) that the church is good news for the city? Clearly, the whole body of sufferings of this innumerable population, their problems, must be firmly grasped, and an effort made to find a solution. Every risk must be taken in such an enterprise—criticism, persecution, death, even ambiguities of action.

Whether a right step or a wrong step has been taken, is not yet clear even from the moral and religious point of view, so great are the ambiguities involved in this task of innovation. But our faith promised that the omnipotence of God would be with us if we dared to act, to reenact a new exodus from Egypt. At the beginning we received clear pastoral indications from outside, which reinforced our own priorities. All the bishops of the Latin American continent, represented by some from among their number, had already decided at the Puebla Conference in 1979 to make a preferential option for the poor and the young. In point of fact, the continent is a continent of the poor and the young. How, in the archdiocese of São Paulo, were we to make concrete these two preferential options?

Furthermore, for a number of years the church in Brazil had laid out its principal lines of pastorate on a national level. They were six:

1. *Visible unity of the church and its training:* This line of action in essence looked toward forming and training the cadres (priests, sisters, laity) of the church, and also of community movements and structures, so that they would visibly manifest the unity of the church in actions for the common good of the people. Too often pastoral care had been fragmented and the people of God fragmented because the training of key leaders and groups had become attached to particular schools and theologies. One was of Paul, one of Apollos: that is, one group was attached to the Dominicans, another to the confraternities of Italian background, and so on. In short, a mosaic of disparate influences existed. Hence a necessary effort of unification and training was needed. There were countless study seminars and encounters—and finally an original and unifying theological reflection: the theology of liberation (see chaps. 2 and 3, above).

2. *Evangelization:* This line had for its goal to assist the church in effectively being good news for its people. The church base communities are a concrete realization of this effort at evangelization, for they consist in restructuring the

Catholic community so that it can effectively become a place of human dimensions. Within it one poor person can go to the help of another, thanks to the power of Jesus, in a real way "felt" and shared among brothers and sisters, in an assembly where people know each other.

3. *Catechesis:* This line always consists in preparing Christians for better knowledge of the word of God, for ability to explain it, for power to witness to it by their lives. The poor are given a simple theological synthesis.

4. *Liturgy:* The celebration of the faith is as essential for its transmission as is its practice in daily life. Beauty will save the world, said Dostoevsky. How are we to set beauty at the heart of the church, to express in liturgical celebration what grace allows to be felt in the depths of the heart, both in personal life and in great collective actions? How, in the end, shall we together renew the memory of Jesus each time that an event shakes the life of the local community, either on an individual or on a collective level? How, finally, is this to be done in a way consistent with our predominantly Afro-Indian temperament?

5. *Ecumenism:* This line was chosen because of the significant Protestant presence in Brazil. How can Catholics be helped to stop being *anti:* anti-Protestant, anti-this, anti-that? How, in action, are we to be joined to the Christians of other confessions to practice the charity of Christ? How, beginning from this "practice," are we to resolve divergences in theory? How are we to pray together? We found, once again, that mission creates unity.

6. *Social promotion:* This line of work consisted in concrete help for the poor, abandoned children, workers, families broken down by social mutation, peasants and Indians evicted from their lands. Social justice, education, housing, health, political and trade-union freedoms—all formed part of this sector of activities.

Such were the main pastoral lines chosen by the church in Brazil as a whole over a number of years. We call the totality of these lines the "Integrated Program." Within the context of this structure, and following the indications of the Puebla Conference and the needs of the city, the church of São Paulo went about choosing its priorities.

The Priorities of the Archdiocese of São Paulo

Four priorities were defined to render more effective the integrated program and the preferential options of the Puebla Conference. From bottom to top, the whole archdiocese was put to work. The smallest communities were consulted: schools, parishes, base communities. Nobody was forgotten. A sequence of slides shown in all the church buildings helped to make the discussions more real. The eight episcopal regions of the city held general assemblies, and at the end of five months of work, more than 250 delegates (four laypersons for each priest) were convened as the general assembly of the church in São Paulo. In that synod, meeting every two years, the four pastoral priorities have been affirmed and reaffirmed. They inspire our apostolic labor.

It is revealing to observe that these priorities do not concern instruction, the sacraments, or vocations, but *human service* (not in the first place the service of the church). And that is right in line with the understanding of evangelism that we laid out in chapter 2, above. To repeat once again: What should we do so that human beings can be effectively children of one God, so that nothing, not even social structures concretizing sinful situations, can create an obstacle to that goal? The goal of mission is charity; and charity, lifted up by grace and remaining under its inspiration, is necessarily human service.

First Priority: A Pastorate of Human Rights and of the Marginalized

The primary work of the archdiocese is the defense and promotion of human rights. By the "marginalized" we mean all those who are pushed to the margin of economic progress and participation in social life precisely because of the economic mechanisms that spring from chosen policies. There is much more at stake here than a humanistic demand! There is at stake a theological insistence: How can we raise up the children of God to live without degradation, either physical (as regards health, food, security) or moral (over against violence, drugs, sexuality, consumerism, sectarianism, occultism)? How are people to be defended against the steamroller of industrial colonization and the political and police repression that accompany it? How shall we prevent the image of God from being destroyed? "And God created humanity [*adam*] in God's own image, male and female created he them." We find there all the theology of humanity as image or "icon" of God so correctly emphasized by the fathers of the church.

The archbishop of São Paulo expressed this very clearly at the assembly of the archdiocese in December 1980: "Never before in the history of humanity has it been so clear as today that the poor are the indication of a nation's health, its thermometer. If the poor are trampled under foot and abandoned, the whole nation is trampled under foot and abandoned. If the poor begin to hope and create, the whole nation begins to hope and create."

This priority was concretized by the formation of a Pastorate of Human Rights (Pastoral dos Direitos Humanos) in each episcopal region of the city, so as to have a structure around which to build people's cadres, emerging from the base communities, which would have the necessary level of competence to guide the struggle in a manner representing the gospel and to be effective through the techniques of law and politics. Thus were multiplied the regional centers for the defense of human rights, community organizations of the inhabitants of a region, with their goal to set at the people's service the law, which is not badly designed but hardly ever applied. At bottom these are organs for popular pressure. On the one hand, they rest on the support of the base communities that can in time of need go out into the streets and mobilize the people like Solidarity in Poland; on the other hand, they use the services of lawyers on call to ensure that the law is applied, and the support of the media to insist on justice being done. The Center for the Defense of Human Rights (Centro de Defesa dos Direitos Humanos) is an organizing center for all the people of the region, to facilitate their struggles to get water, a clinic, sewers, a day-care center, and so forth. It is oriented more toward the quarter than the factory, and uses the methods and "mystique" of active nonviolence. The struggles carried out in the civil-rights movement led in the United States by Martin Luther King, Jr., strongly resemble, in another context, the struggles carried out by the centers for the defense of human rights in São Paulo and throughout Brazil.

Second Priority: A Pastorate for the World of Labor

Human beings at work is second only to human beings in their quarter and in their residence. Since São Paulo is the biggest industrial city of Latin America, this priority is fundamental. It takes the form of a Pastoral Operária, a Workers' Pastorate.

This pastorate stands as far as possible from a claim to be *directing* the workers' movement. But it is a level of structure making possible a double education, at once theological and political. Certainly the base communities have raised up thousands of people's activists during the 1970s and on. But the base community is still only a first step, a place of awakening to action, to a more evangelical faith. It is not equipped to train worker-activists in the precise sense of the term, that is, men and women capable of directing a collective action, of carrying out a political action, of acting on the very structures of society. This type of action presupposes special political and theological preparation.

A political preparation: To be an active member of a trade union one must know the laws that govern it. That is not ordinarily taught in the base community, which is dedicated to more elementary work. In Brazil the trade unions are linked to the Ministry of Labor and hence controlled by the government. How is a trade-union opposition to be formed that can reconquer the union and turn it back to the workers? That question inevitably leads to confrontation with public authorities—a very complex political question. There are many ways to analyze the contradictions of the industrial world. The Marxist analysis is one among many, and there are a number of possible Marxist analyses. There is not *one* Marxism, but many—in Brazil perhaps twenty-seven different factions. Every activist is by necessity led to confront this type of interpretation. Here, then, is another political question—a question of political economy, of political philosophy. The Workers' Pastorate does its best to answer such questions and, to some degree, transmit a political culture that will not be simplistic, that will not be just "anti" or negative, but will show the difficulties and limits in each possible answer.

Further, the Workers' Pastorate will do its best to provide instruments to analyze society and its interconnections so that activists will not be operating in the dark. What policy decisions unleashed the gigantic migration from the countryside to the cities? What are the primary facts of the nation's political economy? What is the reality of the process of *abertura* ("opening up"—the gradual movement from military government to democracy) in Brazil, begun in 1978? What will happen to political parties in the future, to the Partido dos

Trabalhadores (Workers' party) founded by Lula? How will the authorities most likely react to the extension of this party's power? These are some of the questions that inevitably arise when Christians decide to "go into politics." An institution for training is thus indispensable. We have sexual education; why not political education? That is one of the tasks of this pastorate of the world of labor. The necessities of action have led to the posing of these questions, which are practical when seen from the point of departure, but theoretical when we come to the point of actual reflection. Lenin said that without revolutionary theory there can be no revolutionary practice. We must never underestimate the difficulty of the questions that spring up as soon as we undertake to change society and turn love into a possibility. It is no favor to set up cut-rate political training that downplays or ignores the specific difficulties of politics.

A theological preparation: Is the seizure of power all that is needed for inspired human beings, or an inspired social class, or an enlightened vanguard of the proletariat to create a happy society? Christians think not. We have already treated this problem in chapter 4, above. To repeat: power alone, even the power of the people, is unable to persuade human beings to share or to submit themselves to a communal discipline of socializing the means of production. In addition, grace is necessary, a communal inspiration that persuades each one, in the intimacy of oneself, to abide by the required changes.

Christian thought believes that the deviations preventing love and sharing, and therefore the birth of a communal society, are much more serious than a merely economic and social disorder. To cut the evil at its root requires more than merely changing the relations of production. The contradictions that tear human society apart come from a defective relation between the human being and the divine, which by ricochet brings about false "egotistical" relations among all the members of the society. Christians call this mysterious deviation "sin" and affirm that only God can cure us of it. They establish a distinction between a mistake and sin. Mistake or error is an incorrect interpretation of reality springing from a lack of *knowledge*; sin is a lack of *goodness* due to these false interpersonal relations. We are responsible for our sin ("It was my fault"); while we may well be excused for our mistakes ("It was ignorance, the fault of my training"). These two ideas represent very different situations in real life.

The matters that we are surveying so rapidly here are no longer political matters but philosophical or theological. Christians judge that Jesus' interpretation of the evil that chokes the world and the solution that he recommends for the birth of a new society are the only ones that go far enough—and are therefore *the only realistic ones*! They believe with Jesus that we may sketch out the kingdom of God on earth, that is, struggle for a different and better society, and that we may start today. But for that we must adopt Jesus' mode of struggle. According to them, without this religious awareness it is inevitable that revolutions, instead of becoming new Pentecosts with all people in communication, will become new towers of Babel. The grace of a love that has not achieved awareness of the source from which it springs, the living God, remains ever fragile. A passage from implicit to explicit awareness is necessary. That is the role of evangelization. That is why Christians constantly compare their manner of struggle with that of Jesus to find out whether they are "in his line." Therefore they renew his memory, and they go on to review their lives.

Evidently numerous common points in the understanding of how humanity and society can be transformed were held by Christ, the prophets, and the saints—and by the other great religions. These questions define the theological role of the Workers' Pastorate: to provide a space for contemplation and reflection, which prepares for militant action, and helps it to be constantly inspired by the militant action of Jesus. Training takes place in and through action. By and large, we may distinguish three "pedagogies," all resting on a single fundamental conviction—that it is necessary to act, to do something. Thus in one of the episcopal regions of São Paulo each activist in the Workers' Pastorate, each minimal team or "nucleus" of this pastorate (ordinarily attached to one of the more active base communities), looks for a main objective of struggle. This might be, taking examples at random, *(a)* to build a chapter of the construction-workers' union in a region that does not have one; *(b)* to take the first steps toward forming an association of domestic employees in a given quarter; *(c)* to put pressure on the management of the metalworkers' union to engage a physician who will verify whether or not the law has been followed in cases involving accidents on the job (which are very frequent in Brazil) and who will insist on minimal conditions of health and safety; or *(d)* to reinforce the opposition trade-union movement.

Each activist submits the action chosen to regular control by the nucleus at set meetings. (It has been hard for this process to work systematically.) Hence there arise the three pedagogies.

First pedagogy: life review: We have taken up again the tried and true method of Catholic Action. In our case, this life review begins with an analysis of the action taken on as priority by activists or by the nucleus to which the activists belong. But inevitably a review of the action seriously undertaken leads to a review of the personal life of the one who is conducting it. It has become a complex matter, which cannot be fully laid out here. Basic questions in four areas should always be asked: How is it with your activist life, your main struggle? How is it with your professional life—have you an adequate professional level to retain your job or to find another if you are fired from this one? How is it with your family life—are your wife or husband, your children standing behind you, and do you save enough time for them? How is it with your church life—do you take part in the prayer of your base community and its life?

Second pedagogy: a specialized course of theology: We have worked out for the militants of our region a course of theology with a double goal: to show the struggle that Jesus was engaged in and in what historical context it took place, and to organize in a sufficiently rational and systematic manner the principal data of the faith. Our conviction is that we can catch sight of Jesus' "secret," the secret of his kingdom (Mk. 4:11), only if we watch him escape from the temptations by which his adversaries, and the Adversary, tried and still try to derail his action.[1] For that, it is indispensable to relocate Jesus in his social setting, in his time, in the middle of the groups that opposed him or that tried to attract his sympathy. That leads to a re-reading of the gospel from Jesus' point of view in order to see the nature of his struggle. In addition, as we explained at the beginning of this chapter, it is indispensable to acquire an intellectual structure, so as to be able to give an account of one's own faith and understanding of struggle. Life review by itself is insufficient.

Third pedagogy: prayer: The prophets constantly warned the people of God against the danger of idolatry. Every political conflict arouses the most violent human passions. The oppressors elevate power to the status of their god, and the oppressed are tempted to make the seizure of power into their idol. When we look carefully at the matter, it may turn out that there is no atheism at all, only idolatries: everybody turns some limited good into their own god; the false god expels the true God from the heart. The best way to avoid the worship of idols is to worship the true God. Hence an incessant effort of the Workers' Pastorate to become a center of prayer: a monthly celebration of the Eucharist, which brings together the activists of the whole region; an annual retreat; daily meditation on Scripture—these objectives are presented to all.

The pastorate is directed by the activists themselves. In the episcopal region of São Paulo there are about a dozen nuclei of the Workers' Pastorate, with about one hundred people trained or in training, coming from different communities, against a total population of 1.5 million. An executive committee of fifteen members coordinates the activities. But for an action to be effective, we appeal to "assessors," who need not be workers. Three in particular play an important role. *The legal expert* shows the strongest legal lines for the priority action of each nucleus to move ahead. This person may, for example, explain how to form an association of domestic employees. Activists without exact information discourage the comrades whom they invite to a meeting. *The political expert* analyzes the political situation and helps in anticipating the possible evolution of events. Such a person is constantly on call. *The theological expert* raises communities out of passivity and moves them to action; and provides the necessary information and adequate clarification so that the style of action will remain that of Jesus and the apostles, and so that the community is freed from false understandings that block action.

Third Priority: The Pastorate of the Periphery

This is a pastorate for the poor quarters of the city. A proverb has arisen: "How can the city of São Paulo raise its head proudly if it is crowned with thorns?" The Pastorate of the Periphery (Pastoral da Periferia) had as its original idea, today partly realized, to put at the service of the poor quarters the

---

1. This course has been published. See Domingos Barbé, *Teologia da Pastoral Operária* (Petropolis: Vozes, 1983).

communities and associations of the center, who are better supplied with human and material resources. Thus a parish from the center or a middle-class quarter, with more resources, may take responsibility for a network of poorer base communities—not to take over from their leaders, but to provide them financial or legal support. Likewise physicians and lawyers of the residential quarters are invited to donate some hours of their week to the inhabitants on the periphery. It is evident that here also we have a priority envisaging human service. It has the great advantage of setting up an exchange among the communities of greater São Paulo and making it into a more unified whole. Rigid partitions begin to fall.

Fourth Priority: The Church Base Communities

It is in the logical order of Christian mission that this priority should come last. But that does not mean that it is the least important. Quite the opposite. We serve humanity in love. We show our love by coming concretely to help humanity in its quarter, at work, in its poverty. We try to make charity prevail in society. But because this work is very hard, we find the need to be joined in community to restore our strength, to renew our courage, to exchange the joys of our mission.

Let us recall what we said in chapter 2 on the two theologies and in chapter 6 on the base communities. Three types of bread restore our strength: the bread of the Eucharist, the bread of the word, the bread of friendship. The minutes before and after Mass are as important as those of the celebration itself. That is when everybody hears each other's news and rejoices or grieves over the fortunes of the other. That is the time when people ready themselves to continue the struggle. The celebration of our faith is as essential for our believers' struggles in the factory, at home, in the union, or on the street as the air we breathe. These celebrations are great moments of joy: the sharing of these three types of bread that we find in the church gives us the strength to continue to struggle to share the fourth, physical bread: struggling for a civilization of sharing and participation. The mystical event represented by each community meeting, in spite of sin and sadness, is what makes the base communities the cement of the unity of believers, the guarantee that we are in a Christian church, and the place where mission can be expressed and take flight for another week. Above all, the Eucharist is essential: among the Christians of the base communities, it amounts to much more than a popular devotion or obedience to a rule. It amounts to the will to hear God speaking and to feel the presence of the risen Christ, along with the presence of our brothers and sisters, to reactualize the sacrifice of the cross in order to have, in our turn, the courage to sacrifice ourselves for the kingdom of God—the world.

THE ORGANIZATION OF THE ARCHDIOCESE OF SÃO PAULO

The archbishop explains: "Planning presupposes broad-based consultations as regards objectives, material and human resources, and action on several different levels. Because we are a people of God, we have to share responsibilities to realize God's project at any given time. *The Community of Faith and Love cannot dispense with organization"* (diocesan journal of Sept. 12–18, 1980).

In São Paulo there are 1,200 priests to serve more than 10 million of the faithful. A breakdown of that total number must partly be extrapolated from figures for the state of São Paulo as a whole, but is probably reliable. Of these, then, 70 percent are between thirty-five and sixty-four years old; 67 percent are Brazilian and 33 percent are foreign; 43 percent are diocesan clergy and 57 percent are in religious orders. The archdiocese is divided into eight episcopal regions, each under an auxiliary bishop. The regions are to a high degree autonomous; but the episcopal college of eight meets once a week with the cardinal, who is the sole titular bishop of the city, and in fact the pastorate does form an organic whole. These eight regions contain forty-two "sectors," each composed of five or six parishes. The priorities are as stated. Thus many parishes strive to create base communities within their parochial bounds; but the great majority of the base communities remain in the poor neighborhoods.

At the head of each episcopal region, at the side of the auxiliary bishop, are two councils. The Presbyteral Council deals with matters concerning priests; the Pastoral Council has a majority of laypeople coming from the five to seven sectors of the region. The latter directs the Pastorate of the Local Church. Thus the direction of the pastorate is collegial, a "college" of laypeople and priests, with the laity in the majority, gathered together by the bishop. But the status of the priest remains very important; and the bishop retains the powers of decision-making, although normally in the role of conductor of an orchestra. The *responsáveis* of the base communities are attached directly to the bishop without having necessarily to go through the priest in charge of the parish or quarter. Thus to the old vertical structure

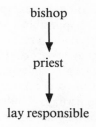

bishop

↓

priest

↓

lay responsible

has succeeded the triangular structure

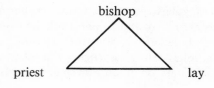

bishop

priest   lay

In the General Assembly of the archdiocese in December 1980 the forty-two sectors of the city each sent five delegates, the majority of them, as we noted, laypeople.

There has never been a campaign as such to elicit vocations to the priesthood in the archdiocese. Still, more than twenty candidates presented themselves in 1981 at the doors of the diocesan seminary to enter the first year. The number of candidates for the priesthood is increasing in a significant manner. Clearly here is the proof that a living church recruits its own cadre. The pastorate of the church need not be at the service of the church, much less of priestly vocations. It should be at the service of humanity: "Seek first God's kingdom and justice and all these things will be added to you" (Mt. 6:33).

A survey in February 1981 (reported in the diocesan journal of Feb. 20–26) confirmed the satisfaction of the clergy and the good health of the church. Seventy percent of the priests of the state of São Paulo were in charge of a parish or community and therefore in touch with the people of God. There are few priests in administration or commissions. Some 86.5 percent declared themselves very satisfied with their pastoral work, and 88.4 percent said that "they would do it over again." Although we have no statistics on hand, we know that the groups, the pastoral agents, and the lay responsibles number in the thousands. It seems, then, that the pastoral strategy that has been adopted has been well received, corresponds with the needs of the people of God, and is bearing good fruits.

SHADOWS IN THE PICTURE

Nevertheless, there are shadows in the picture. Religious practice is very weak, from 10 to 20 percent among those who call themselves Catholics. The sects are multiplying. The catechetical training of most of those who do practice is still very deficient. To say nothing of those who do not practice! And the creation of the church base communities, the place of formation for true Christians, mission-oriented and responsible, has met with much resistance, on the part both of the people who wish to remain with a simple popular Christianity, and of a by no means negligible part of the clergy. The government, the ruling classes, and sectors of the local or universal church are frankly hostile to them and do everything they can to check their advance. The 80,000 base communities in Brazil comprise perhaps 3 million persons, at once an enormous but small figure, in face of the total population of 120 million. They do form a respectable part, at least 10 percent, of the total of practicing Catholics in the big cities. Still they are a small minority attacked on all sides.

In the *bairro* within Osasco, which we know best, out of 40,000 inhabitants, there are less than 400 irregularly practicing Catholics, but more than twenty halls open for Pentecostal or Afro-Indian non-Catholic worship. This means that "practicing" non-Catholics are certainly twice or three times more numerous than practicing Catholics. Those practicing Catholics who are not connected with a base community or union movement are also very unstable:

today Catholic, tomorrow Assembly of God, day after tomorrow *umbandista* (voodoo). It all depends on the "grace" that they did or did not receive. If things don't feel right with the Catholics, you go to a different church, or vice versa. Certainly the Roman liturgy—cold, intellectual, formal—is far from corresponding to the temperament of these children of Indians or blacks, in spite of our best efforts. The *candomblé,* at least in its liturgical expression, could be the form of celebration best adapted to them, if its forms were adapted with intelligence. Many traditional Catholics are ashamed of the African forms of religion, even though they practice them in secret. The question is often asked whether Catholicism is not in fact a superficial religion in Brazil. Underneath, in its underground strata, the people exist and are searching for something different. The Black movement, which was born out of the church base communities and the most progressive sectors of the church, does not wish to be a pastorate of the church even while it remains in contact with it. So many centuries of oppression rest on the blacks and the Indians! And the church, especially as regards the blacks, has much with which to reproach itself.

There are also difficulties as regards the training of the militants at the point when they discover politics and the various ideologies. Many matters remain to be set right in the realm of the specialized pastorates (human rights, the world of labor, of the countryside, of the indigenous). But our subject was not to speak at length on the progress that needs to be made in São Paulo. We are all quite aware of it.

CONCLUSION

We have simply wished to demonstrate that a pastoral strategy can be elaborated for a megalopolis like São Paulo; and that the fruits that it bears are, by all the evidence, so fair that one would have to be blind not to admire them. The demonstration has been made that a great city can be put to work to give a response out of the gospel to the problems of those who live there. *An urban pastorate as a totality is possible.* Why should there not also be a pastoral strategy, arising from the particular context, for Paris, London, New York? A challenge has been thrown down.

9

Why Active Nonviolence in Brazil?

The word "nonviolence" is unpleasant to the ear, because it seems to denote disincarnate idealism, passivity, or low-grade pacifism. Those who have studied the matter know that it is none of these. Nonviolence is an original mode of struggle, of dealing with conflict. It is realistic because it recognizes that conflict exists, that human history is woven out of it. It is creative because it dares to claim that inflicting death is not necessarily a genuine mode of combat at all. One can be "human" in battle even against human beings who have become wild beasts. Nonviolence is not a discovery of yesterday. It is found at all ages, in almost all civilizations, among many peoples. In our age it was popularized by Mahatma Gandhi and Martin Luther King, Jr. We approach this matter from three different viewpoints, the psychological, the socio-political, and the theological.

THE PSYCHOLOGICAL APPROACH

The psychology of conflict has its own rules; and understanding them is of the highest importance in designing and implementing adequate training, and thus in preparing the strategy of victory. The reactions felt and aroused by an armed person or a group are very different from when persons are unarmed. The aggression present in both cases is not expressed in the same way. Four examples follow.

The Peasants of Alagamar

The state of Paraíba is in northeastern Brazil. Its capital is João Pessoa, its bishop at this writing Dom Jose-Maria Pires. There, farm workers and guards hired by a great landed proprietor have been in conflict for a long time. One day the guards tried to evict by force 300 workers—men, women, and children—who were planting beans. These peasants had already been introduced, superficially, to nonviolence; for in this diocese for some time there has been a network of church base communities and a Center for the Defense of Human Rights. The guards arrived with their usual threats; there were ten of them, all armed to the teeth. The peasants, without saying a word, surrounded the guards; and some of the peasants, the oldest men, took the weapons out of the guards' hands and went off to give them to the police (even though the police were in cahoots with the landowner). This action of 300 unarmed peasants, in silence approaching ten armed guards and encircling them created an amazing psychological effect, the effect of numbers, despite the fact that the guards were heavily armed. Certainly one must be prepared for an action like this and, above all, not be afraid. But the tone must not be provocative or humiliating, and events must take place rapidly in order to use the factor of surprise.

Now imagine a different scenario. Suppose the same number of guards confront the same number of peasants, but with the difference that some of the peasants have brought their weapons "just in case," and that as tempers rise they take their weapons out. Anybody can see that the combat will change its nature, for the psychological mechanisms are no longer the same. The guards will be afraid, for they thought they were confronting unarmed persons and here are guns pointed at them. Then they will attack so as to defend themselves, or at least be prepared to fire, even though afterward the crowd will overwhelm them. Here fear is in charge.

Again, the psychological conditions that permit nonviolent struggle disappear when one or two members of the nonviolent group run away. The cowardice of a few will lead the soldiers to conclude that they have before them people who will give in at the first shot. Neither arrogance nor cowardice, if nonviolence is to be effective.

Again, suppose the peasants are now only thirty in number and the guards remain at ten. Thirty peasants cannot easily encircle ten firm, armed men; whereas 300 peasants determined to advance, even though without weapons, cannot all be neutralized; there is not time to kill them all if they maintain a genuine element of surprise. Thus conflict has its psychological rules, which constantly change according to the scenario.

It is plain that the driving forces of this nonviolent confrontation are the *wisdom* to evaluate the forces that one is confronting, and the *courage* to make a calculated risk of one's life, since nonviolence is not suicide. And above all the internal disposition of wishing *neither the death nor the humiliation* of the adversary; the guards feel that neither their life nor their honor is being threatened, while at the same time they recognize that this people's force is irresistible, because it is in large number and will never retreat. We always say, *"Podemos morrer mas não vamos correr"* ("We may die but we won't run"). Active nonviolence comes from the association of two principles, force and gentleness. Starting from these psychological mechanisms, one can image a whole style of combat and, hence, a strategy.

The Strike of the Metalworkers of São Bernardo

In April and May 1980 there was a long strike of forty days among the metalworkers of Greater São Paulo, in particular those of the Volkswagen plant, under the leadership of the union of São Bernardo municipality, a union headed by Lula. The whole city was mobilized to support the strikers and their families. The dioceses of Santo André (under Bishop Claudio Humes) and of São Paulo were in the front lines, since the cause was just and the methods peaceful. It will be recalled that in Brazil the unions are not autonomous but subordinate to the government, as in Poland. There is no one national central workers' union as there is in France or in the United States: that is, there is no liberty of association among the different professional categories, so that a metalworker cannot belong to the same union as a bricklayer or a domestic employee. That obviously weakens the working class very much. Furthermore, there are no collective contracts. In most countries, contracts are collective: the business signs the labor contract with the totality of the professional category, and in case of a dispute it is the *representatives* of the workers who do the negotiating. In Brazil it is the court system that sits in judgment when the working contract is broken, which very much impedes the legal process. In Brazil a single worker signs an individual contract with what may be an enormous enterprise. Always there is the disproportion between an isolated worker with nothing but one person's skills in face of the enterprise that recruits the worker and has elsewhere to turn.

Add to all this that the living standard of half the population is about 10 percent that of the same group in the United States. The workers in big multinational corporations are in general better paid than most of the population. Fifty percent of Brazilian workers are at the legal minimum or less, in 1985 values $40 per month. Still it must be recognized that the workers in big corporations are the drive-wheel of the economy and that the fate of all other labor disputes hangs on the outcome of theirs.

In the strike of the municipality of São Bernardo, the churches made their parish halls available for meetings and for collection and storage of food for the families of the strikers. When the police first blocked off the stadium, then the public square, for general assemblies of tens of thousands of strikers, Bishop Humes opened up his cathedral, which became in an new way the house of the people. The church base communities were mobilized throughout the city to gather food in all the quarters, even the poorest. Aid from outside also was significant; international solidarity from trade unions and other sources played its role.

This strike was without violence but not in the strict sense nonviolent. By that we mean that the great majority made no conscious, principled choice of nonviolence, and that the nonviolent activists played only a minor role. But they participated by safeguarding the movement of food trucks each night toward the regions that had been blocked off. This role won them the confidence of the strikers and allowed them to propose an idea for the celebration of the First of May. For that day the mass of workers determined, at whatever cost, to win back the stadium of São Bernardo where the general assemblies had been held until the police closed it. A Mass was scheduled for the first thing in the morning. At the planning meeting a typical nonviolent proposal was made. An activist from the nonviolent group of São Paulo suggested that persons coming to the Mass should carry a kilo of rice in their left hand and a flower in their right: the rice to support the strikers and the flower for the soldiers.

On the First of May the sight was unforgettable. The morning was radiant. Overhead two big helicopters with machine guns aimed at the people circled at a low altitude the towers of the crowded Cathedral of São Bernardo. The bishop presided at the liturgy. The company of soldiers surrounded the cathedral square, and 200,000 strikers with their families and friends encircled the soldiers. If there had been a panic, a police charge, tear-gas grenades, who knows how many persons would have been trampled in the disorder! The little children walked forward to give their flowers to the soldiers, who were quite embarrassed with this gift. Some stuck them in their rifles, some accepted them awkwardly with their heads hanging down, some hugged the children. The crowd sat down on the ground and called out friendly slogans to the soldiers: "Brother soldier, don't get into it *[não entre nessa]*! You also are exploited!"

These attitudes exercised enormous psychological pressure. Simultaneously the adversary clearly felt the "love" that was being offered them and also a force like a wave, a people's wave in action. Again: force and gentleness. The feelings of the adversary that were reached were their highest ones; the soldiers also had children. Would they fire on a child offering them flowers? That would really be an act of cowardice. Psychologically, this soldier is in a situation of inferiority. If by bad luck he should shoot, a murder of this sort would reverse public opinion and unite it against the oppressor. To move the adversary by touching the noblest and purest part of the person; to conquer the hearts of the millions of humble and poor by an attitude at once courageous, organized, and unarmed: those are the psychological secrets that make nonviolence work. Evidently this type of combat presupposes a high degree both of moral life and of organized intelligence. Much strategy, much ethics! The moral level of this struggle would have had to fall only a little, by provocation or by humiliation of the enemy from hatred in the heart, for the psychological mechanisms to be snapped, which up till then made the people leap and the adversary stumble. Then the war would have fallen back into its traditional patterns: violence and murder.

We need to add that each situation demands a nonviolent response appropriate to it. What worked on May 1, 1980, might not work on May 1, 1981. The factors of society, politics, and repression constantly change. It may happen that the brigade comes ready to kill father, mother, and children together, as is happening today in El Salvador and Guatemala. We need to study very carefully the circumstances where this or that action is to take place. Perhaps we should install movie cameras on the roofs of buildings or in secrecy to film any atrocities. In general, the tactic in the case of a hard war of nonviolent character is to *isolate the incorrigible*. In any shock troops, in any repressive state apparatus, there is bound to be a fascist core ready for anything; but this core is limited. We need to identify the fascist core so as to isolate and condemn it.

Active nonviolence requires a shrewdness that will not be spoon-fed with fairytales. Nonviolence has always had to defend itself against charges of being a naïve sentimentality or a beautiful, irresponsible idealism. "Be as harmless as doves but as wise as serpents," Jesus tells us (Mt. 10:16). If goodness is all one has, one will be plucked like a pear. If one is merely prudent, one will also be cruel. The gospel is an equilibrium of opposites; so Heraclitus makes the universe out to be a "reciprocal harmony, as of the bow and the lyre." To retain these two characteristics, nonviolence must hold itself up to two exacting standards: an intense militancy so as to create a powerful people's force; and exact information about the enemy it will find itself facing. We must set up the Intelligence Service of the poor! Like a good general we must at every instant study the nature of the terrain in order to map out the response best adapted to it, and to analyze the relations of force between friends and enemies.

But now, even though we should take all precautions to avoid being killed, we have to admit that the possibility of sacrifice cannot be totally avoided. Better die than kill! However carefully our action may have been planned, an irreversible event can always occur. But when we think about it, in traditional war many die on both sides. In a nonviolent war, all those who die are on the side of the oppressed, but in much fewer numbers than in a conventional war. The people's cadres who reject violent struggle will survive in much greater numbers; when it takes ten years to train a base community and good militants it is not intelligent to move forward to a massacre. Also the self-sacrifice of the just is a powerful appeal, able to reverse the opinion of many. Later we shall give a Brazilian example. For the meantime we can remember the sacrifice of Jesus. We recall the effect produced by the assassination of Gandhi; of Martin Luther King, Jr.; by the "disappearance" of thousands of Argentinians, which at this writing fuels the resistance of the "crazy women of [the Plaza] de Mayo." (The mothers and grandmothers of the *desaparecidios* of Argentina— who include children and infants—gather every Thursday in front of the palace of the president of the republic in the Plaza de Mayo to demonstrate their indignation. Some have paid for this heroic attitude with their lives. They go on.)

In the episode we are discussing, the body of strikers finally carried off the victory by winning back the stadium. It would take too long to describe all the details of this engagement. Let us just state that the soldiers were given the order to climb back into their personnel carriers, which they did in a hurry, with some making the V sign of victory to the excited crowd. It is also true that afterward the strikers *provisionally* lost their campaign and that repression was unleashed on their leaders. The people cannot expect immediate victory; they must be prepared for a long war.

The Fast at Crateús

In 1981 in the city of Crateús, in the state of Ceará, one of the poorest and driest of the northeast, there was a long drought and much hunger. The peasants flowed into the towns and the shopkeepers were afraid for their stores. The municipality wanted to form a committee to deal with the danger of looting. The bishop, Dom Fragoso, a nonviolent activist, expressed the opinion that it would be better to form a committee to help the hungry and not to expel them. The situation was explosive. A hungry belly has no ears, and the police were ready to shoot. A special diocesan assembly of the base communities was urgently convened. Alfredinho[1] announced his intention to carry out a public fast for eight days, only drinking water. Like Gandhi, Alfredinho invited people to pray with him morning, noon, and night. For only prayer and fasting, he said, can drive out the demons of fear and egotism (Mt. 17:21, in Latin versions). This public fast was carefully organized and publicized throughout the diocese. Alfredinho observed it in a church on the outskirts of the city and many joined him in his times of prayer. At one of them he launched Operation PAF *(Porta Aberta aos Famintos,* "Open Door to the Hungry"). Any family that wanted to open their door to the hungry to offer them what they had—shade against the sun, a glass of water, a plate of rice—would put a placard reading PAF on their front door. The victims would know by that that they would receive a fraternal welcome: no need for fear or shame. Several thousand homes, often very poor, blossomed out in placards; the bishop's house was the first. The city's atmosphere totally changed. What little the people had was shared, the multiplication of loaves was seen again. On the eighth day the fast ended with a downpour of rain! The people organized a great procession of thanksgiving.

The Death of the Just José Silvino Valdevino

All that we set down here comes from the November 9, 1981, report of the regional Coordination for Gospel Nonviolence of the Diocese of João Pessoa in the state of Paraíba.

José was murdered with six bullets in his body on October 7, 1981, at Salamargo near the *fazenda* (plantation) Ana-Cláudia in the municipality of Espírito Santo, Paraíba. He was forty-nine years old and left nine children, five of them under twenty-one. He was murdered by the *capataz* (overseer) of the *fazenda,* Manuel Batista. Ten families besides José's were constantly being threatened with eviction. Together they had been farming 42 hectares where they were living for more than five years. The perpetrator of the crime, following the orders of the proprietor of the *fazenda,* had destroyed José Silvino's hut with a bulldozer a month before. Then, with a group of hired guards, he had begun to move in, forcibly, on the neighbors' fields and plant sugarcane (which is also processed to provide alcohol as motor fuel). The crime

---

1. Alfred Kuntz, a priest of the Sons of Charity, who had been at Crateús for fifteen years, himself a nonviolent activist.

was committed at 6:00 in the morning, the police were notified at 7:30; by noon they had still not arrived on the scene, either to establish the facts or to protect the other farmers, who were also being threatened with death. They had just 20 kilometers to drive.

Here are the facts in order, as determined by the Coordination for Gospel Nonviolence:

Manuel Aureliano, a big *latifundiário* (landed proprietor) tries to evict eleven families living on land which they call their own and which they have been farming for five years. José Silvino has been to the official surveyor's office and has in his possession a certificate that these lands do not belong to Manuel Aureliano. For five years no other person has put in an appearance to claim these lands.

On the fifth of October the eleven families peacefully resist an invasion directed by the *capataz* with four *pistoleiros* (gunmen) and four tractors to destroy the peasants' crops.

On the sixth of October, still being threatened with death, the peasants address a letter to the president of the republic then in office, Aureliano Chaves, as well as to various local officials.

On the seventh of October, at six o'clock in the morning, Manuel Batista arrives at the site where José Silvino is working. He jumps out of his car and says, "You son of a bitch, you have no business being here. Are you setting yourself up as some kind of lawyer?" José Silvino: "No, I am not the lawyer." The *capataz* says, "I'm going to shoot you now." José Silvino: *"Estou aqui com minha vida para viver ou para morrer* [I'm here with my life to live or to die]." Then the *capataz* takes out his revolver and José Silvino falls dead with six bullets in his body.

After the crime, Manuel Batista stayed more than four hours on the scene threatening to kill three other workers. Witnesses testified that the guards, armed with rifles and 38-gauge revolvers, said, "This is to teach you never to encourage people to plant on this land."

The widow of José Silvino, when she came back from her husband's funeral, said, "Now more than ever we will not leave this land."

Seven days after the death of José Silvino, his comrades attended the Mass for him and with him, and spontaneously offered these prayers:

"Let this blood become seed, grow, and give us courage for the struggle."

"Comrade José, your blood is here and gives us courage."

"Another time Jesus was crucified and they said, 'If he is the Son of God, may God let the blood of this just man fall on us.'[2] And so in this

---

2. Note the original exegesis of this popular piety. It has turned "If you are the Son of God" (Mt. 27:40) from derision to faith, and "His blood be on us" (Mt. 27:25) from curse to blessing.

holy Mass we ask that the blood of our brother José Silvino should stay with us as our light and our road so that we can all advance."

"The blood of Jesus spilled on the ground did not stop its work there. From it will grow a tree big enough for the birds of the air to nest in its branches. I ask that all the workers and farmers present here should unite themselves in prayer and in the action of that fighter and struggler, José Silvino our brother, who died for justice."

The Coordination, which prepared this text (which we have summarized above) and sent it out to the communities, ends its report with two questions.

1. What are the elements of violence that we can observe in the attitudes of those in power?

2. In the face of violence, what attitudes, what routes are open to farmers to direct the conflict so that they may resist violence (in themselves, in others, and in their adversaries) and remain on the land?

THE SOCIOPOLITICAL APPROACH

In the second half of the twentieth century, we consider that the nature of social conflict has been totally changed. If it were not shocking to so speak, one might say that it had taken a quantum leap upward! The concentration of wealth and of the means of production in the hands of the ruling class has been accompanied by a parallel concentration of the means of repression in the same circles. Therefore *it is not strategically advantageous for the poor to confront the powerful and rich on the terrain of the latter with* their *weapons.* The example of the Nicaraguan revolution might seem to prove the contrary. But we shall maintain that its circumstances have been quite exceptional. On the principle that "the exception proves the rule," we shall suggest that in other cases, like that of El Salvador, where its exceptional circumstances are not found, the general principle that we propose is valid.

In Nicaragua, the United States during the Carter administration was hesitant about extending full support to the dictator Anastasio Somoza. Later we shall suggest certain reasons. Here we may recall that during this epoch there was an effort at world control of the economy by North America, Japan, and Europe, the Trilateral Commission. From this source came a policy of "opening" in Latin America, orchestrated through the human-rights campaign, to win back a part of public opinion on that continent, to prevent the steam-boilers of many lands there from exploding. But as soon as Ronald Reagan came to the presidency, this policy was reversed. The American people, humiliated by the defeats of President Carter in Iran, for example, but still hesitant (for Reagan was elected by only a minority of the electorate, with many abstentions), brought into power a man determined to repress any desire for independence on the part of countries that might have been contaminated by Cuba: that was the big fear. And so we have come to see what repression undertaken by great powers is capable of when it is unleashed, even if only at second hand.

Until recently a school for torture was maintained in Panama which trained the military of the entire Latin American continent. In El Salvador women and children were decapitated; girls were murdered, with the heads of their fiancés sewn into their bellies. We may have seen the brainwashing of an American Jesuit in Guatemala who, two months after he disappeared, was shown on television confessing his "errors." In Guatemala there have been cases of cannibalism—soldiers eating the brains of children whose heads had been dashed to the ground in front of their mothers. (All this I have verified personally or from the most responsible sources. D.B.) In El Salvador there have been 30,000 deaths in less than three years, and 500,000 refugees; eleven priests and one bishop have been murdered in two years; there have been abominable cases of torture; death squadrons function openly. In short: a terror campaign to destroy support for the guerrillas, in a population of 5 million where fourteen families possess 85 percent of the land. At this writing everybody wants to negotiate except the United States administration.

To repeat, in the form of a question: Is it strategically advantageous for the poor to confront the powerful with *their* weapons?

Everybody knows that the only reason the United States Marines are not already in Cuba, Nicaragua, El Salvador, Guatemala is the pressure exerted both internationally and also within the United States. We have not fully recognized the extent to which the 1970s were marked by an extraordinary proliferation of base groups: not merely the church base communities of Latin America that we have discussed, but also in North America. North American Christianity is in the process of waking up. It is of great importance to link together the networks engaged in nonviolent struggle in Europe, Latin America, and North America; much effort during the last few years has gone into this. Many nations beyond Latin America are opposed to North American intervention out of fear of a major conflict. All this simply goes to show that weapons other than bombs and guns are effective in holding back repression, *on the condition that people become organized*. It is popular pressure that is decisive, and not primarily summit conversations.

The industrialized nations have partially learned one lesson. If for forty years there has been no world war, it is not out of humanitarianism but because the destruction is unthinkable, and victor and vanquished would alike be vanquished. (That is not to say that we should count on the policy of "deterrence" to maintain the peace indefinitely, for the nuclear powers are driven by demonic powers beyond their control, and are constantly taking greater and greater risks for the sake of imagined strategic advantages.) Should it be assumed that the poor are even less motivated by intelligence and prudence than the rich? Why should they take up weapons for their liberation, while the powerful with all their ambivalence take some precautions not to arrive at that point? Gandhi had perceived, intuitively more than rationally, this shift in the nature of conflict, when he confronted England, the greatest industrial power of his time. He must somehow have felt this concentration of the means of repression, which has been made possible by the age of the machine.

It is often said that Gandhi was facing "civilized" people, the British, and further that he settled only the problem of his country's colonial status, not its poverty. People say, "Where are his disciples? Who was there to maintain the continuity of his action after his death? The future of nations must not depend on charismatic leaders; strategies cannot be built on any such unreliable basis." We may say that Gandhi was a forerunner of surpassing genius. He realized that new methods of combat must be systematized and adapted to the industrial age. Just as Lenin brought into reality only a most imperfect sketch of a socialist society in a backward industrial country, so Gandhi only opened the door for a new manner of "living out" conflict in industrial society. The one was an innovator in the realm of social models, the other in that of modes of combat. It is sectarian to put one on a pedestal and disqualify the other. That denies our political culture. All passion blinds the intelligence.

It might be useful to distinguish two types of combat: conventional wars between nations, and people's struggles for liberation. We are concerned here with the second.

The idea proposed here is a very simple one: never to station oneself on the adversary's terrain by making use of weapons that kill; but, rather, to multiply base groups and help people move step by step to massive and organized civil disobedience. There is a whole scheme of escalation in nonviolence: after dialogue, publication of the truth, and popular pressure prove insufficient, the ultimate weapon remains—total paralysis of the country, a general strike. No government, even if armed to the teeth, can for long control a nation against 95 percent of its people. We saw that very well in Iran, where, in the first phase, the people confronted with their bare hands the army of the Shah, one of the most powerful in the world. It cannot be said that the revolution itself in Iran was nonviolent! Its mystique, unfortunately, was quite the reverse. But Islam is capable of quite a different mystique from the "integrist"—really "totalitarian"—one of Khomeini. Still we can say that during that first period, the revolution in Iran was unarmed.

We know further that it is not necessary to organize 95 percent of the population in base communities. All that is needed is an adquate number, perhaps thousands, of small, popular cadres, on the level of the street or the village, coming out of these communities and trained by their "pastorate" or ideology, in order to orient the population-at-large and coordinate its actions. We may give as examples, without making any judgment on their ideology or goals, the French militants of Lip (the watch factory where a strike brought in self-management for a while), the kibbutzim in Israel,

Communist parties in countries that accept or tolerate them, the mullahs in Iran.

For such cadres to come into being presupposes intense militant activity. Cadres with a principled commitment to nonviolence require the most training of all, for it cannot be improvised; it is nothing less than a *spirituality united to an organization.*

Now let us analyze the people's insurrection in Nicaragua. We still do not have adequate information or analysis to draw up a full summation. But it would certainly be at least questionable to claim that, among all the factors working in favor of the insurrection, armed force was the principal one. For a number of years the Frente Sandinista tried without success to get the population to rise up. The first insurrection was a disaster. In fact, what played the decisive role in getting the masses to move was the murder of two innocent journalists: Pedro Chamorro, and the North American reporter Bill Stewart, killed in the middle of the revolution in front of the television cameras of the whole world. Pedro Chamorro was editor of an important liberal newspaper. His summary execution by Somoza brought over into the active opposition a large part of the middle class and intellectuals. Also it must not be forgotten that Somoza had shamefully appropriated for his own benefit the international aid that had poured in after the earthquake that destroyed Managua in 1972: another motive for the people's anger.

Furthermore, the church for some years had been playing an important role: orienting and defending the people; making public protest against the abuses of the government; above all, beginning to create those base communities that are the great force by which the peoples of Latin America are organized. (The base communities of Nicaragua began some time after those in Brazil, and developed especially after the insurrection. The popular revolution in Nicaragua came about with the massive support of Christians—without their having been organized in base communities.) Finally, the second insurrection broke out. When the American journalist died before the eyes of the whole world, indignation exceeded all bounds. Somoza could no longer cover up the savage character of his regime. North American public opinion turned, as one person, from Somoza. The Carter administration, still vacillating, found it impossible to continue its aid to the dictator's regime. *The death of the innocent when seen around the world was a terrible weapon against the dictator.*

In all these facts we can see in cameo the characteristics of a nonviolent action—or, if we prefer, the nonviolent dimensions of every insurrectional struggle, when it is really the poor who move into action. Finally—and we end this brief analysis of the people's revolt in Nicaragua with this very specific feature—there was a real will for nonviolence on the part of the comrades most responsible for the revolution. We should not forget that Miguel d'Escoto and Ernesto Cardenal, two priests who became part of the government, had tried for a number of years to propose a nonviolent alternative to the popular forces and, above all, to the church, which had access to the people and enjoyed their confidence. Their voices were not heard in time, even though the most farsighted bishops had made explicit explorations in this direction a little before the conflict: thus the archbishop of Managua took part in a seminar on nonviolence, held at Bogotá in December 1977, with twenty bishops of the whole continent. There remain evident marks of this concern in the style of living out the conflict. The revolution in Nicaragua was one of the most humane recorded in history. There was a real effort, often heroic, to avoid shedding blood. After the victory the firing-squad was disbanded. There were stunning cases of pardon when yesterday's victims who found themselves face to face with the murderers who had wiped out their families renounced the thought of vengeance.

A revolution continues as it began: "One sows what one reaps" (Gal. 6:8). The Vietnamese revolution was militarized, and the nation continues along the same line. Likewise, each time that Christianity has used force to impose itself, history has taken its vengeance. Saint Augustine used force to bring the Donatists back in, and today the church of Africa no longer exists. We may think of Charlemagne with the Saxons; the Inquisition; the Wars of Religion of the Reformation epoch, which discredited Christianity and perhaps prepared the way for European atheism; the bloody evangelization of Latin America; the United States Civil War, when Christians reading the same Bible fought each other ferociously. This history of violence has left its mark on our collective behavior today.

Nicaragua had the good fortune to expel Somoza without an intervention from the United States. But the possibility of an armed intervention from North America was not eliminated: the contras have been covertly supplied with aid, an economic embargo has been imposed. Here the old law again applies: since the revolution was carried out by force of arms, despite the desire for nonviolence, likewise the resistance to intervention will be in the same manner. A genuinely nonviolent revolution requires more time for preparation (which was not available in Nicaragua); but it will last longer because it cannot be overthrown in the same way by the force of arms.

Perhaps what was lacking in Nicaragua was the availability of a clear option for the mystique and practice of nonviolence, and systematic training of communities for such an action. Perhaps it was the theologians more than the pastors who were to blame. Pastors frequently sense such problems, since they live near the people; but it is the business of thinkers to explain their intuition, develop it, to make it clear enough so that it can be passed on.

Each strategy is all of a piece. An armed, violent combat has advantages and disadvantages. The mystique of "Thou shalt not kill" leads to a specific and different technique of combat: to a different type of mass training, and to a special formation of their leaders.

Finally let us hear what Miguel d'Escoto, priest and minister of foreign affairs, said in an interview with the *Catholic Worker* at Managua in December 1978—that is, before the uprising. He explained that the understanding of the cross had been so distorted in Latin America that there was no hope of making the seed of active nonviolence germinate there. The environment was lacking:

. . . traditionally, in Latin America, we are inclined to look at the cross as a lamentable object, which makes us weep, especially during Lent and Holy Week, as something that should not have happened, instead of contemplating it as the most magnificent act *of life* in existence. . . . *Nonviolence should be considered as a constitutive element in the preaching of the gospel.* This comes down to saying that, in my opinion, we do not preach the gospel today as we should, as long as we do not spread the spirituality and the concept of nonviolence as a means of liberation from oppression. That is essential for evangelization. This is not a devotion left up to each one's free choice. The cross is not something we can take or leave. The cross is not optional. The cross is something central. We should preach the cross, and to preach the cross is to preach nonviolence. Not the nonviolence of submission, but the nonviolence that consists in risking our life for the sake of fraternity. When we do that, we suffer reprisals from those who oppress the others. That is the cross. When we take up the cross, we participate in the birth-pangs of the Christ who suffers violence so as to engender the new humanity.

THE THEOLOGICAL APPROACH

The considerations just reviewed are already theological and are leading us to the third point of view from which we may speak about nonviolence, the theological.

"Love Your Enemies" (Lk. 6:27)

What does this saying of Jesus mean? Above all, it is realistic. It means in the first place we have enemies, including class enemies; conflict exists. But in the second place, it affirms also that these enemies are children of the same God "who makes the sun shine on the evil and good, and rains on the just and unjust" (Mt. 5:45). So the class struggle cannot be deprived of its ethical dimensions. More than that: the enemy, even a class enemy, must be allowed to "feel" this love and this respect, if we do not wish to empty Jesus' word of its content. In any case it cannot be claimed that we love our enemies while at the same time we are unfortunately obliged to kill them! So the question is this: How shall we carry out a "political" and indeed military translation of this commandment of the Lord? How shall we live out the struggle for justice so that it will be at once effective and evangelical? It is evident that our struggle is not neutral; with open eyes it chooses the side of the poor, and at the same time acquires a set of enemies. But this combat must take its inspiration from Jesus' way of conducting himself when he had to deal with his enemies. Jesus, it seems, absolutely rejected two means of combating his enemies: (1) the physical death of the adversary; (2) the contempt that spells the moral death of the adversary when one says to the person, "For me, it is as if you were dead."

Jesus spoke very forceful words, had angry moments, even times of violence, but he never carried out an attack on human life. Even psychologically, for him, his adversary remains "somebody"; the adversary continues to exist. That is the whole point. If God exists, God is the God of all. The words "companion" (one who shares the same bread) and "comrade" (one who shares the same room) are not sufficient by themselves; we must also add "brother" and "sister."

Clarifying an Ambiguity

To say that violence is not according to the gospel does not mean that it is always avoidable. Unfortunately not! But those who are constrained to kill should not say that they have killed out of love! They should say that the weight of evil has been so heavy on them and on the others, that they have been pushed into the corner of using a method that is not evangelical. And let us add this: neither morally nor politically can a nonviolent solution be improvised; if a whole historical process of struggle is traveling toward a violent outcome, a nonviolent outcome cannot suddenly be improvised. It is with nonviolence as with the incarnation of Jesus: it comes at the summit of a gradual ascent of human history marked out by the sacrifice of thousands of saints, known or unknown, through whom humanity has become used to grace. Space had to be created for the incarnation to be possible. Therefore only the appearance of a historical dynamic, at once mystical and political, can make struggles of active nonviolence possible; and that in turn presupposes hard work, an intense and organized militancy, to which the churches are even yet only sparingly dedicated.

The reality of scandal exists: "It is impossible that scandals should not come, but woe to that one by whom they come," Jesus warns us (Lk. 17:1). The evil in the world and in us is so strong that even Christians engaged in living the gospel in a radical manner by their baptism do not always reach the point of living fully the law of love. And thus the order left us by Christ, "love even your enemies," is not obeyed and grace undergoes a serious setback, the kingdom recedes. The responsibility is collective and not solely (or primarily) the act of those who have been backed into violent situations. We can passively allow injustices to be heaped up to such a degree in some corner of the planet that brothers and sisters, even Christians, will be overwhelmed and in practice forced to take up arms. Look at what is going on in El Salvador, Guatemala, perhaps in Poland. The poor, the oppressed, who are thus in effect forced to take up arms, are much closer to be gospel attitude than many other Christians; for their violence, which resists injustice, certainly contains more love than the absence of violence in those who are merely passive in the face of evil. There are three classes: those "without violence," the lukewarm whom God will spew out (Rev. 3:16); the violent, who do something; and the authentic nonviolent, who struggle against evil with the arms of love. Gandhi said in effect: "If you cannot be nonviolent, at least be violent; what you must not be is indifferent, refraining from taking a position in the face of injustice."

When all that has been said, *we must not call evil "good."* Killing is an absolute evil for which we are responsible. This evil could have been avoided if we had worked harder at our individual purification and at the organization of great popular movements, which would then be animated by this spirit and able to withdraw popular support from an unjust social order. The idols stay on their thrones because we do not dare push them off by disobeying them. Active nonviolence will make no ethical concession to the existence of violence. Then we shall have to say that the least bad violence is still bad, and that *the theology of the just war is not a Christian theology.*

The Principal Axis of a Future Theology of Nonviolence

Around us we hear endless analyses of the texts of Scripture and of the practice of the saints to find a loophole for "Christian" violence: Jesus, who expels the moneychangers from the temple, who "kills" the fig tree, who advises his disciples to sell their cloak and buy a sword (Lk. 22:36). (This last verse is a metaphorical saying of Jesus describing the universal hostility surrounding the disciples; at Jn. 18:11 Jesus tells Peter to put his sword back in its sheath, and at Mt. 26:52 he foresees that those who take the sword will perish by the sword.) It is recalled that Saint Bernard preached the Crusades, that Joan of Arc expelled the English from France by force of arms in obedience to her voices, that warrior saints like Martin and George are not rare in Christianity.

It seems to us that our reflection should be differently centered, if we wish not to be lost in details and endless disputes of interpretation. In Christianity as everywhere else there is the subordinate and the essential. What is the profound dynamic of the gospel? As for ourselves, we believe that this dynamic is nonviolent because the axis of the gospel is the resurrection. *It is from the resurrection of Jesus that a nonviolent theology is to be deduced.* Look at it this way.

Christ is risen: What does that mean for our daily lives? Most simply, this: that life is stronger than death, good greater than evil, grace more powerful than *dis*grace. Then any struggle that in its *methodology* includes death inflicted on another as a principle of action distances itself to that precise degree from the axis of the kingdom. For how in fact can one still be included in the sphere of the kingdom, which is life and resurrection, how can one belong to this space of the kingdom that is defined by the triumph of life over death, if one inflicts death on another? The two are incompatible. Scripture says, "Without bloodshed there is no forgiveness" (Heb. 9:22). The whole question is: Whose blood? If it is the blood of one's enemy, one is no longer identified with the Lamb of God that takes way the sins of the world: one takes away the *life* of the adversary, not the sin; one pulls up the good grain along with the tares. If it is one's own blood, then everything changes, and one's sacrifice is proof that one resisted injustice. The masses, as we said, are always moved by the sacrifice of the just one, and they set themselves in turn to reject infamous social structures. They pass from passive nonviolence to active nonviolence.

We have also explained that active nonviolence is not a suicidal attitude: before sacrificing one's life, one needs to learn how to give it for a cause. Hence that intense militancy of which we have spoken. Miguel d'Escoto, in the passage that we have quoted, shows that he has very deeply perceived what must be the authentic methodology of the kingdom: a renewed sense of the cross. Cross and resurrection are indissolubly linked. If we have been snatched out of the empire of darkness to enter into the kingdom of God, that is, into that part of reality where death has been eliminated, the only method of combat remaining to us is the cross and not the revolver. We confront evil and accept in our flesh the blows of the adversary, knowing that such an attitude moves profoundly, on the level of the best that is in them, thousands of persons of goodwill. Only the hardened are unreachable; the sacrifice of the just one liberates the lukewarm from their sins and isolates the evildoers. This is the way in which the Lamb of God continues the redemptive mission today in the person of disciples.

And what about the hardened? one will ask. Are they excluded? That is a mystery. We must not despair of the salvation, the regeneration, of anybody. Not even of Hitler or Somoza. What is sure, on the level of action, is that people of this sort will not change except when forced and constrained by popular pressure. The question is: By what sort of popular pressure? We have explained here the kind that we are thinking of: the pressure of the humble, of the poor who, without magnifying themselves by using the weapons of the powerful, refuse to go on any longer obeying injustice, whatever the consequences, and hold up before the evil the shining face of a pure and humble love that does not blow out the smoking wick, but also does not lower its eyes, any more than Jesus did at his trial.

The resurrection, as the fundamental orienting principle of Christian behavior, can throw fresh light on all kinds of situations in which we or our societies live. How to behave in daily life? How should society be organized to deal with crime? Until the end of time, crimes and punishments will exist. There exist prisons, police commissioners, sentences. Is not prison a violence done to the human person, which the church accepts with a tranquil heart? And the death penalty? For centuries Christian theologians have not felt obliged to say anything in criticism of it. It seems to us that the criterion of the resurrection can help us to see more clearly. Every punishment that comes down to a purely repressive function, for example, by isolating a dangerous person, is on the order of death, and therefore unworthy of the kingdom. But if the punishment is conceived of in such a way that it can genuinely exercise the function of rehabilitation, it reenters the dynamic of the kingdom. Thus it is conceivable for a "nonviolent" criminal-justice system to exist: that is, a system designed to restore life to the one who had lost it. We know that some are taking steps in this direction.

CONCLUSION

Here, as a conclusion, are the "trump cards" of active nonviolence—its strategic advantages over against armed struggle—and the commandments of nonviolence.

The Trump Cards of Active Nonviolence in Brazil

1. The force of the poor is their number, which is always increasing.
2. The force of the poor comes also from the place that they occupy in the economy. They have their fingers on the levers of the machines and they handle the means of production.
3. The weakness of the poor is their disorganization and lack of unity. To unite the poor and organize them is where nonviolence has its most original proposition: it is the *purity* of their combat that most unites the humble. That is a truth ignored by a great number of those who struggle for justice. It is a moral phenomenon. The little ones can be united more durably and in greater numbers, with more firmness and courage, around the just one, persecuted and unarmed, than around a leader in war, even if that leader is reasonably humane and is conducting a "just" war. To achieve this unity requires that there be children of God, "good shepherds," who walk ahead to show the way and to render the combat public and organized.

The Commandments of Active Nonviolence in Brazil

1. Nunca matar.

Do not kill.

2. Jamais ferir com palavras ou atos.

Never wound by word or deed.

3. Estar sempre unidos, atentos, e organizados.

Always be united, alert, and organized.

4. Sair de lutas locais e organizar lutas coletivas.

Start from local struggles and organize collective struggles.

5. Agir com *firmeza permanente*; não renunciar.

Act with *unyielding firmness*; do not draw back.

6. Saber arriscar a vida; dominar o medo da morte; não fugir.

Know how to risk your life; overcome the fear of death; do not run away.

7. Não dissimular.

Do not hide anything. [Nonviolence cannot be clandestine—it would deny itself, for all its strength comes from the truth.]

8. Preservar-se do ódio; orar pelos inimigos.

Stay clear of hatred; pray for your enemies.

9. Purificar-se constantemente.

Purify yourself constantly.

10. Desobedecer às leis e às ordens que pretendem destruir o povo e suas organizações.

Disobey laws and orders that attempt to destroy the people and their organizations.